MORE THAN YOU KNOW

MORE THAN

Finding Financial Wisdom

 Columbia Business School
Publishing

YOU KNOW

in Unconventional Places

Updated and Expanded

Michael J. Mauboussin

Columbia University Press

Publishers Since 1893

New York   Chichester, West Sussex

Copyright © 2008, 2006 Michael J. Mauboussin

Library of Congress Cataloging-in-Publication Data

Mauboussin, Michael J., 1964–

   More than you know : finding financial wisdom in unconventional places /

   Michael J. Mauboussin. — Updated and expanded ed.

      p.   cm.

   Includes index.

   ISBN 978-0-231-14372-1

   1.   Investments.   2.   Investments—Psychological aspects.   3.   Finance, Personal.

   I. Title.

   HG4521.M365   2008

   332.6—dc22   2007030512

⊚

Columbia University Press books are printed on permanent and durable
acid-free paper.

Printed in the United States of America

c 10 9 8 7 6 5 4

A balanced perspective cannot be acquired by studying disciplines in pieces but through pursuit of the consilience among them. Such unification will come hard. But I think it is inevitable. Intellectually it rings true, and it gratifies impulses that rise from the admirable side of human nature. To the extent that the gaps between the great branches of learning can be narrowed, diversity and depth of knowledge will increase.

—Edward O. Wilson, *Consilience*

To my parents

Who always stood behind me but were never too close

CONTENTS

PART 2: Psychology of Investing

ACKNOWLEDGMENTS

I wrote the original versions of these essays while I was at Credit Suisse (formerly Credit Suisse First Boston). In my dozen years at CSFB, management consistently offered me marvelous opportunities for professional development. Allowing me to launch *The Consilient Observer*—the offbeat offering that provided the basis for *More Than You Know*—is a tribute to the firm's open-mindedness and support. In particular, I am indebted to Brady Dougan, Al Jackson, Terry Cuskley, Steve Kraus, and Jim Clark. Credit Suisse was also gracious in granting me the copyrights to these works.

Two names were listed on *The Consilient Observer*'s original masthead. The other belonged to my research associate, Kristen Bartholdson, who made significant contributions in research, editing, number crunching, and producing exhibits. She also helped update material for this edition. Smart and talented, Kristen is also a delightful person to work with.

Dan Callahan, my research associate at Legg Mason Capital Management, picked up where Kristen left off, working tirelessly on all aspects of this book. He was instrumental in updating the material for both editions, getting the exhibits and manuscript in shape, and coordinating all communication. Dan is resourceful, productive, and bright. He's also a great guy, and I'm really pleased he is on my team.

All of my coworkers at Legg Mason Capital Management have been terrific, providing valuable support and cooperation. LMCM also allowed me to use copyrighted material. Thanks to all of you.

Two people have had a major professional influence on me. The first is Al Rappaport, with whom I wrote *Expectations Investing*. I have learned an enormous amount from Al, and he remains a tremendous source of inspiration and constructive feedback.

The other is Bill Miller, whom I now have the honor of calling a colleague. Bill stimulated many of the ideas in these essays, either directly or indirectly. It's one thing to write about how the mental-models approach helps investors, it's quite another to use the approach to generate excess returns. Bill has done both, and for that he deserves all of the admiration he receives.

Both Al and Bill have always been gracious with their time, and have taught me with patience. They are great role models, and I feel privileged to be associated with both of them.

These essays draw from the work of many fabulous scientists, too many to list individually. But a handful of thinkers deserve special mention, including Clayton Christensen, Paul DePodesta, Norman Johnson, Scott Page, Jim Surowiecki, and Duncan Watts. Thanks to each of you for sharing your ideas with me so generously. Steve Waite's suggestions were also of great benefit to me.

I'd like to thank Myles Thompson, my publisher and editor at Columbia University Press, for his boundless enthusiasm and unwavering belief in the power of these ideas. Assistant editor Marina Petrova has also been an immense help in all aspects of the project. Michael Haskell improved the book's flow with his thoughtful edits and supplied the new, comprehensive title. Nancy Fink Huehnergarth was instrumental in shaping the original manuscript, providing both valuable editorial input and a fantastic sense of humor.

I also appreciate Sente Corporation's very talented Jay Smethurst and Bryan Coffman for their artistic contributions. They were with me from the very beginning of the consilient journey. At CSFB, Marian Toy and Ann Funkhouser were great editors to work with: efficient, constructive, and thoughtful. My administrative assistant at CSFB, Melissa Little, also helped in key areas such as exhibit production and distribution.

My wife, Michelle, is a constant source of love, support, and counsel. My mother-in-law, Andrea Maloney Schara, is the rare grandmother who can explain systems theory and throw a football. Finally, I thank my children Andrew, Alex, Madeline, Isabelle, and Patrick for allowing me to see diversity firsthand.

MORE THAN YOU KNOW

INTRODUCTION

More Than You Know's core premise is simple to explain but devilishly difficult to live: you will be a better investor, executive, parent, friend—person—if you approach problems from a multidisciplinary perspective. It's the difference between moving into a fixer-upper home with a full set of power tools versus a simple screwdriver. You are going to be a lot more successful and efficient if you have the proper tool for each job at hand.

The reality is that the majority of us end up with pretty narrow slices of knowledge. Most occupations encourage a degree of specialization, and some vocations, like academia, insist on it. And there are the time constraints. We are all so busy talking on the phone, answering e-mails, and going to meetings that we don't have any time left to read, think, and *play* with ideas.

Following the publication of this book's first edition, a lot of readers contacted me to say they enjoyed the exposure to non-traditional ideas. Most people easily appreciate the value of diverse thinking. But many readers view diversity as something that's nice to have, not something that's essential to success. In contrast, I have come to believe cognitive diversity is crucial to solving complex problems.

The case for cognitive diversity is based on theory and practice. In his book *The Difference*, social scientist Scott Page demonstrates the logic of diversity. He shows, using mathematical models, how and why diversity is necessary to solve certain types of problems. Page deftly nudges the diversity discussion away from metaphor and anecdote toward grounded, timeless theorems.

Notwithstanding Page's theoretical contribution, you might ask whether there's any actual evidence for diversity's value in predicting the outcomes of complex problems. The answer, a resounding yes, is based on psychologist Phil Tetlock's remarkable research summarized in his book *Expert Political Judgment*. Tetlock asked hundreds of experts to make thousands of predictions about economic and political events over a fifteen-year span. He then did something quite rude. He kept track of their results.

Expert forecasters were, on balance, deeply unimpressive. But Tetlock found some were better than others. What separated the forecasters was how they thought. The experts who knew a little about a lot—the diverse thinkers—did better than the experts who knew one big thing.

Two sources in particular have inspired my thinking on diversity. The first is the mental-models approach to investing, tirelessly advocated by Berkshire Hathaway's Charlie Munger. The second is the Santa Fe Institute (SFI), a New Mexico–based research community dedicated to multidisciplinary collaboration in pursuit of themes in the natural and social sciences.

Charlie Munger's long record of success is an extraordinary testament to the multidisciplinary approach. For Munger, a mental model is a tool—a framework that helps you understand the problem you face. He argues for constructing a latticework of models so you can effectively solve as many problems as possible. The idea is to fit a model to the problem and not, in his words, to "torture reality" to fit your model.

Certain character traits encourage the mental-models method to blossom. Fortunately, these are mostly traits you can choose: intellectual curiosity, integrity, patience, and self-criticism. Problem-solving success is not just a matter of IQ. As Munger notes, the great naturalist Charles Darwin's worldview-changing results reflect more his working method than his raw intellect. On the flip side, examples abound of smart people making bad decisions, often showing inflexibility or a failure to appreciate psychology's lessons.

A mental-models approach does not come without a cost, though. You need to spend substantial time and effort learning about various disciplines. Without a doubt, too, your learning may not be useful right away (in fact, it may never be useful). The good news is there are typically only a few big ideas in each discipline that you'll need to master.

I have learned a great deal from Munger's musings over the years, and his influence is clear throughout these pages. Fortunately, Peter Kaufman assembled Munger's background and speeches in *Poor Charlie's Almanack*, a terrific book offering plenty of insight on the mental-models approach.

The Santa Fe Institute sprung from a group of like-minded scientists who decided the world needed a new kind of academic institution. These scientists, each distinguished in his field, recognized that universities often operate in academic isolation; professors spend a lot of time with colleagues in their field but rarely cross disciplinary boundaries. The founders felt strongly that much of the fertile scientific ground was between disciplines, and they were determined to cultivate it. Spend some time at SFI's campus and you are likely to see physicists, biologists, and economists all chiming in with their diverse perspectives on a topic of interest.

The unifying theme at SFI is the study of complex systems. In both the physical and social sciences, lots of systems emerge from the interaction of many heterogeneous parts. Examples include human consciousness, the immune system, and the economy. SFI scientists were early in identifying the salient features of these systems and in considering the similarities and differences across disciplines.

The SFI-inspired idea that has most deeply influenced me is viewing the stock market as a complex adaptive system. Embracing this mental model compelled me to revisit and question almost everything I learned in finance: agent rationality, bell-shaped price-change distributions, and notions of risk and reward. I believe the complex-adaptive-systems framework is not only a much more intuitive way to understand markets but also more consonant with the empirical record.

SFI has sparked my interest in disparate topics—sprinkled throughout the following essays—including ant colonies, power laws, human cognition, and the role of feedback mechanisms. The best way to describe how I feel following an SFI symposium is intellectually intoxicated.

You can read about the Santa Fe Institute's history in Mitchell Waldrop's *Complexity*. While the book came out during the first decade of the institute's existence, it captures much of SFI's spirit.

Finally, a word on how to read this book. Unlike a best-selling thriller, you can read *More Than You Know* from back to front just as easily as from front to back. But I recommend you simply go to the table of contents, find something that interests you, and jump in.

While the essays cover a range of topics, I categorize them into four parts—investment philosophy, psychology of investing, innovation and competitive strategy, and science and complexity theory. Consider these compartments in a toolbox, each addressing a distinct facet of investing. That said, every essay is meant to stand by itself.

This edition has updated tables and charts and new chapters in each part. Fresh topics include thoughts on management assessment, the role of intuition, applications of game theory, and the mechanisms behind the market's mood swings.

More Than You Know leverages the research of many top-flight academics. But given the book's format, there is no way to give those academic ideas their full due. That's why I assembled a detailed reference section, including suggestions for further reading. Hopefully, the references will give you plenty to dig in to should you choose to follow up on an idea or theme.

My sincerest wish is that *More Than You Know* provides readers with some intellectual fun—a new perspective, a cool idea, or a path to self-improvement. I hope you get a fraction of the satisfaction from reading the essays that I got from writing them.

Part 1

Investment Philosophy

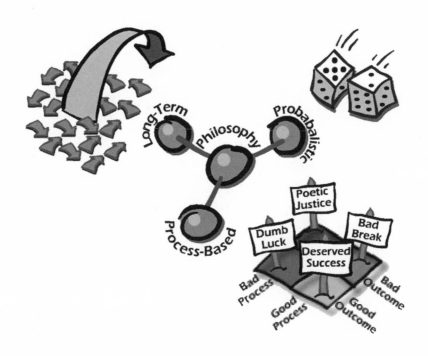

Out of the blue one day, I received a complimentary e-mail from a guy who had read one of my essays. I was appreciative but didn't think much of it until I noticed he had found the piece on a Web site dedicated to *traders*. Given that my focus is almost exclusively on long-term investing, I found it odd that a trader would find use for these ideas.

So I looked to see what else was out there and found something that surprised me even more: one of the essays was highlighted on a gambling Web site. While I study and appreciate gambling methods, I felt—as most self-righteous investors do—that long-term investing is nearly the *opposite* of most forms of gambling. After thinking about it, though, I realized there is a tie that binds all of these worlds: investment philosophy.

Investment philosophy is important because it dictates how you should make decisions. A sloppy philosophy inevitably leads to poor long-term results. But even a good investment philosophy will not help you unless you combine it with discipline and patience. A quality investment philosophy is like a good diet: it only works if it is sensible over the long haul and you stick with it.

Investment philosophy is really about temperament, not raw intelligence. In fact, a proper temperament will beat a high IQ all day. Once you've established a solid philosophical foundation, the rest is learning, hard work, focus, patience, and experience.

Quality investment philosophies tend to have a number of common themes, which the essays in this part reveal. First, in any probabilistic field—investing, handicapping, or gambling—you're better off focusing on the decision-making *process* than on the short-term *outcome*. This emphasis is much easier announced than achieved because outcomes are objective while processes are more subjective. But a quality process, which often includes a large dose of theory, is the surest path to long-term success.

That leads to the second theme, the importance of taking a long-term perspective. You simply cannot judge results in a probabilistic system over the short term because there is way too much randomness. This creates a problem, of course; by the time you can tell an investment process is poor, it is often too late to salvage decent results. So a good process has to rest on solid building blocks.

The final theme is the importance of internalizing a probabilistic approach. Psychology teaches us there are a lot of glitches in the probability module of our mental hardwiring. We see patterns where none exist. We fail to consider the range of possible outcomes. Our probability assessments shift based on how others present information to us. Proper investment philosophy helps patch up some of those glitches, improving the chances of long-term success.

A closing thought: The sad truth is that incentives have diluted the importance of investment philosophy in recent decades. While well intentioned and hard working, corporate executives and money managers too frequently prioritize growing the business over delivering superior results for shareholders. Increasingly, hired managers get paid to play, not to win.

So ask the tough question: Does an intelligent investment philosophy truly guide you or the people running your money? If the answer is yes, great. If not, figure out a thoughtful philosophy and stick with it.

1

Be the House
Process and Outcome in Investing

Individual decisions can be badly thought through, and yet be successful, or exceedingly well thought through, but be unsuccessful, because the recognized possibility of failure in fact occurs. But over time, more thoughtful decision-making will lead to better overall results, and more thoughtful decision-making can be encouraged by evaluating decisions on how well they were made rather than on outcome.

—Robert Rubin, Harvard Commencement Address, 2001

Any time you make a bet with the *best of it*, where the odds are in your favor, you have earned something on that bet, whether you actually win or lose the bet. By the same token, when you make a bet with the *worst of it*, where the odds are not in your favor, you have lost something, whether you actually win or lose the bet.

—David Sklansky, *The Theory of Poker*

Hit Me

Paul DePodesta, a baseball executive and one of the protagonists in Michael Lewis's *Moneyball*, tells about playing blackjack in Las Vegas when a guy to his right, sitting on a seventeen, asks for a hit. Everyone at the table stops, and even the dealer asks if he is sure. The player nods yes, and the dealer, of course, produces a four. What did the dealer say? "Nice hit." Yeah, great hit. That's just the way you want people to bet—if you work for a casino.

This anecdote draws attention to one of the most fundamental concepts in investing: process versus outcome. In too many cases, investors dwell solely on outcomes without appropriate consideration of process. The focus on results is to some degree understandable. Results—the bottom line—are what ultimately matter. And results are typically easier to assess and more objective than evaluating processes.[1]

But investors often make the critical mistake of assuming that good outcomes are the result of a good process and that bad outcomes imply a bad process. In contrast, the best long-term performers in any probabilistic field—such as investing, sports-team management, and pari-mutuel betting—all emphasize process over outcome.

Jay Russo and Paul Schoemaker illustrate the process-versus-outcome message with a simple two-by-two matrix (see exhibit 1.1). Their point is that because of probabilities, good decisions will sometimes lead to bad outcomes, and bad decisions will sometimes lead to good outcomes—as the hit-on-seventeen story illustrates. Over the long haul, however, process dominates outcome. That's why a casino—"the house"—makes money over time.

EXHIBIT 1.1 Process versus Outcome

		Outcome	
		Good	Bad
Process Used to Make the Decision	Good	Deserved Success	Bad Break
	Bad	Dumb Luck	Poetic Justice

Source: Russo and Schoemaker, *Winning Decisions*, 5. Reproduced with permission.

The goal of an investment process is unambiguous: to identify gaps between a company's stock price and its expected value. Expected value, in turn, is the weighted-average value for a distribution of possible outcomes. You calculate it by multiplying the *payoff* (i.e., stock *price*) for a given outcome by the *probability* that the outcome materializes.[2]

Perhaps the single greatest error in the investment business is a failure to distinguish between the knowledge of a company's fundamentals and the expectations implied by the market price. Note the consistency between Michael Steinhardt and Steven Crist, two very successful individuals in two very different fields:

> I defined variant perception as holding a well-founded view that was meaningfully different from market consensus.... Understanding market expectation was at least as important as, and often different from, the fundamental knowledge.[3]

> The issue is not which horse in the race is the most likely winner, but which horse or horses are offering odds that exceed their actual chances of victory.... This may sound elementary, and many players may think that they are following this principle, but few actually do. Under this mindset, everything but the odds fades from view. There is no such thing as "liking" a horse to win a race, only an attractive discrepancy between his chances and his price.[4]

A thoughtful investment process contemplates both probability and payoffs and carefully considers where the consensus—as revealed by a price—may be wrong. Even though there are also some important features that make investing different than, say, a casino or the track, the basic idea is the same: you want the positive expected value on your side.

From Treasury to Treasure

In a series of recent commencement addresses, former Treasury Secretary Robert Rubin offered the graduates four principles for decision making. These principles are especially valuable for the financial community:[5]

1. *The only certainty is that there is no certainty.* This principle is especially true for the investment industry, which deals largely with uncertainty. In contrast, the casino business deals largely with risk. With both uncertainty and risk, outcomes are unknown. But with uncertainty, the underlying distribution of outcomes is undefined, while with risk we know what that distribution looks like. Corporate undulation is uncertain; roulette is risky.[6]

The behavioral issue of overconfidence comes into play here. Research suggests that people are too confident in their own abilities and predictions.[7] As a result, they tend to project outcome ranges that are too narrow. Over the past eighty years alone, the United States has seen a depression, multiple wars, an energy crisis, and a major terrorist attack. None of these outcomes were widely anticipated. Investors need to train themselves to consider a sufficiently wide range of outcomes. One way to do this is to pay attention to the leading indicators of "inevitable surprises."[8]

An appreciation of uncertainty is also very important for money management. Numerous crash-and-burn hedge fund stories boil down to committing too much capital to an investment that the manager overconfidently assessed. When allocating capital, portfolio managers need to consider that unexpected events do occur.[9]

2. *Decisions are a matter of weighing probabilities.* We'll take the liberty of extending Rubin's point to balancing the probability of an outcome (frequency) with the outcome's payoff (magnitude). Probabilities alone are insufficient when payoffs are skewed.

Let's start with another concept from behavioral finance: loss aversion. For good evolutionary reasons, humans are averse to loss when they make choices between risky outcomes. More specifically, a loss has about two and a half times the impact of a gain of the same size. So we like to be right and hence often seek high-probability events.[10]

A focus on probability is sound when outcomes are symmetrical, but completely inappropriate when payoffs are skewed. Consider that roughly 90 percent of option positions lose money. Does that mean that owning options is a bad idea? The answer lies in how much money you make on the 10 percent of options positions that *are* profitable. If you buy ten options each for $1, and 9 of them expire worthless but the tenth rises to $25, you'd have an awful frequency of success but a tidy profit.[11]

So some high-probability propositions are unattractive, and some low-probability propositions are very attractive on an expected-value basis. Say there's a 75 percent probability that a stock priced for perfection makes its earnings number and, hence, rises 1 percent, but there's a 25 percent likelihood that the company misses its forecast and plummets 10 percent. That stock offers a great probability but a negative expected value.[12]

3. *Despite uncertainty, we must act.* Rubin's point is that we must base the vast majority of our decisions on imperfect or incomplete information. But we must still make decisions based on an intelligent appraisal of available information.

Russo and Schoemaker note that we often believe more information provides a clearer picture of the future and improves our decision making. But in reality, additional information often only confuses the decision-making process.

Researchers illustrated this point with a study of horse-race handicappers. They first asked the handicappers to make race predictions with five pieces of information. The researchers then asked the handicappers to make the same predictions with ten, twenty, and forty pieces of information for each horse in the race. Exhibit 1.2 shows the result: even though the handicappers gained little accuracy by using the additional information, their confidence in their predictive ability rose with the supplementary data.[13]

4. *Judge decisions not only on results, but also on how they were made.* A good process is one that carefully considers price against expected value. Investors can improve their process through quality feedback and ongoing learning.

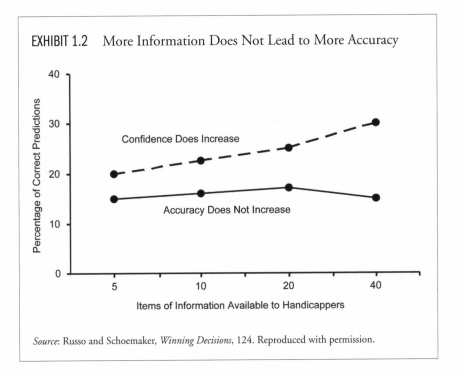

EXHIBIT 1.2   More Information Does Not Lead to More Accuracy

Source: Russo and Schoemaker, *Winning Decisions*, 124. Reproduced with permission.

One of my former students, a very successful hedge fund manager, called to tell me that he is abolishing the use of target prices in his firm for two reasons. First, he wants all of the analysts to express their opinions in expected value terms, an exercise that compels discussion about payoffs and probabilities. Entertaining various outcomes also mitigates the risk of excessive focus on a particular scenario—a behavioral pitfall called "anchoring."

Second, expected-value thinking provides the analysts with psychological cover when they are wrong. Say you're an analyst who recommends purchase of a stock with a target price above today's price. You're likely to succumb to the confirmation trap, where you will seek confirming evidence and dismiss or discount disconfirming evidence.

If, in contrast, your recommendation is based on an expected-value analysis, it will include a downside scenario with an associated probability. You will go into the investment knowing that the outcome will be unfavorable some percentage of the time. This prior acknowledgement, if shared by the organization, allows analysts to be wrong periodically without the stigma of failure.

Prioritizing Process

The investment community, because of incentives and measurement systems, is too focused on outcome and not enough on process. In Rubin's words:

> It's not that results don't matter. They do. But judging solely on results is a serious deterrent to taking risks that may be necessary to making the right decision. Simply put, the way decisions are evaluated affects the way decisions are made.[14]

2

Investing—Profession or Business?
Thoughts on Beating the Market Index

I'm beginning to wonder how to persuade the businessperson who owns a large investment management organization that the first and essential priority is to protect the vital core: the classic disciplines of investing as a *profession.*

—Charles D. Ellis, "Will Business Success Spoil the
Investment Management Profession?"

There seems to be some perverse human characteristic that likes to make easy things difficult. It's likely to continue that way. Ships will sail around the world but the Flat Earth Society will flourish.

—Warren Buffett, "The Superinvestors of
Graham-and-Doddsville"

The Scouting Report

To prepare to win, most sports teams scout their competition. The objective is to create a game plan that exploits the competition's weaknesses and neutralizes its strengths. Teams generally consider intelligent scouting vital to their long-term success.

So what's the competition for a money manager? Investors with particular objectives can typically invest either with active managers or with index funds. For example, an investor seeking exposure to large-capitalization stocks can place money with a large-cap active manager or with an index fund that mirrors the S&P 500.

Accordingly, we can consider an appropriate index's return to be a measure of an investor's opportunity cost—the cost of capital—and that beating the benchmark over time should be an active manager's measure of success.

So how do active managers fare against the competition? Not well. Over a recent five-year period, the indexes outperformed over forty percent of all active managers, and more than half of active funds underperformed the benchmark over ten years. And this type of result has been consistent over time.[1] Given how well the indexes have fared, it might be useful to provide a scouting report on how the indexes compete.

The most widely used benchmark for equity fund performance is the S&P 500. The S&P Index Committee uses five main criteria when looking for index candidates. Here they are—the heart of the strategy that beats the majority of active managers, year in and year out:

1. *Liquidity.* As the committee wants the benchmark to be "investable," it selects stocks with sufficient liquidity (a ratio of monthly trading volume divided by shares outstanding of at least 0.3) and float.

2. *Fundamental analysis.* The profitability criteria are "four quarters of positive net income on an operating basis." That's it.

3. *Market capitalization.* Companies must have market capitalizations in excess of $4 billion. "The guiding principle for inclusion in the S&P 500 is leading companies in leading U.S. industries."

4. *Sector representation.* The committee tries to keep the weight of each sector in line with the sector weightings of the universe (of eligible companies with market cap in excess of $4 billion). It typically does so by adding stocks in underweighted sectors, not by removing stocks in overweighted sectors.

5. *Lack of representation.* S&P defines the lack of representation as follows: "If the index were created today, this company would not be included because it fails to meet one or more of the above criteria." Of the more than 1,000 companies removed from the S&P 500 over the past seventy-five years, the overwhelming majority were the result of mergers and acquisitions.

Our scouting report of the S&P 500 might also note that the committee does no macroeconomic forecasting, invests long-term with low portfolio turnover, and is unconstrained by sector or industry limitations, position weightings, investment-style parameters, or performance pressures. Also critical is that index funds closely track the S&P 500 at a very low cost.

Evaluating the Winners

Some actively managed funds clearly do beat the benchmark, even over longer time periods. To see if we could come to some stylized conclusions about how these successful investors did it, we created a screen of the general equity funds that beat the S&P 500 over the decade that ended with 2006 where the fund had one manager and assets in excess of $1 billion (see exhibit 2.1).[2]

Four attributes generally set this group apart from the majority of active equity mutual fund managers:

- *Portfolio turnover.* As a whole, this group of investors had about 35 percent turnover in 2006, which stands in stark contrast to turnover for all equity funds of 89 percent. The S&P 500 index fund turnover was 7 percent. Stated differently, the successful group had an average holding period of approximately three years, versus roughly one year for the average fund.[3]

- *Portfolio concentration.* The long-term outperformers tend to have higher portfolio concentration than the index. For example, these portfolios have, on average 35 percent of assets in their top ten holdings, versus 20 percent for the S&P 500.

- *Investment style.* The vast majority of the above-market performers espouse an intrinsic-value investment approach; they seek stocks with prices that are less than their value. In his famous "Superinvestors of Graham-and-Doddsville" speech, Warren Buffett argued that this investment approach is common to many successful investors.

- *Geographic location.* Only a small fraction of high-performing investors hail from the East Coast financial centers, New York or Boston. These alpha generators are based in cities like Chicago, Memphis, Omaha, and Baltimore.

EXHIBIT 2.1 A Sample of General Equity Funds That Beat the S&P 500, 1997–2006

Fund Name	Ten-Year Return (%)	Ten-Year After Tax Return (%)	Turnover (%)	Assets in Top Ten Holdings (%)
Calamos Growth A	17.70	15.50	41	26.50
Weitz Partners Value	14.14	12.67	36	48.55
Weitz Value	14.13	12.37	40	50.61
Dodge & Cox Stock	14.05	12.27	12	29.22
Legg Mason Partners Aggressive Growth	13.96	13.11	5	53.83
Hartford Capital Appreciation	13.86	10.70	97	21.94
Third Avenue Value	13.18	11.93	7	37.46
MainStay MAP I	13.14	11.39	100	27.80
Longleaf Partners	12.81	11.02	7	56.04
Gabelli Asset AAA	12.75	11.37	6	16.61
Muhlenkamp	12.68	12.42	6	45.17
American Funds Growth Fund of America	12.45	10.56	22	17.66
Vanguard PRIMECAP	12.08	11.15	10	30.58
DFA U.S. Large Cap Value III	11.99	9.73	7	100.0
Van Kampen Comstock A	11.87	8.47	30	29.00
Legg Mason Value Trust	11.35	10.57	13	44.83
American Century Value Investor	10.87	7.81	134	25.90
American Funds Amcap A	10.87	8.67	20	21.83
Fidelity Contrafund	10.83	9.30	60	21.32
Franklin Rising Dividends A	10.53	8.67	8	40.46

Source: Morningstar, Inc.

Based on the S&P scouting report, these managers seem to follow the index's strategy with regard to turnover and limited time on macro forecasting, and they deviate from the index's strategy with regard to concentration and a sharp focus on price-to-value discrepancies.

I am not suggesting that all investors should or can embrace the approach of this group. A broad ecology of investors constitutes a well-functioning market. The market needs investors with varying time horizons, analytical approaches, and capital resources. And many money managers have seen outstanding results pursuing very different strategies than the ones we describe.

Further, it is worth underscoring that the success of these investors is not the result of their portfolio structure but more likely reflects the quality of their investment processes. I once overheard an investor remark to one of these superior performers, "You can have low turnover because your performance is so good." At once, the manager shot back, "No, our performance is good *because* we have low turnover." It would be futile to try to replicate the portfolio attributes (i.e., low turnover, relatively high concentration) without an appropriate process.

That noted, there is still an obvious question: Why is the profile of an average fund so different from these superinvestors?

The Investment Profession Versus the Investment Business

Part of the answer lies in the tension—and perhaps growing imbalance—between the investment *profession* and the investment *business*. The investment profession is about managing portfolios to maximize long-term returns, while the investment business is about generating (often short-term) earnings as an investment firm. There is nothing wrong with having a vibrant business, of course, and, indeed, a strong business is essential to attracting and retaining top talent.[4] But a focus on the business *at the expense* of the profession is a problem.

A historical perspective on mutual funds suggests a strong swing to the business side. One person uniquely qualified to document the industry's changes is the legendary Jack Bogle, who over the past half century has been an industry advocate, visionary, and gadfly. Here are some of the profound changes Bogle notes:[5]

- The number of common stock funds swelled from 49 in 1945 to over 4,200 in 2006, and they now offer greater specialization as well as geographic scope. The number of new stock funds the industry created (as a percentage of those in existence) reached a record of nearly 600 percent in the 1990s, up from about 175 percent in the 1980s. Notable, too, is that 50 percent of funds failed in the 1990s, and almost 1,000 failed in 2000 through 2004 alone.

- Competition leads to margin compression in most industries. But mutual fund expense ratios, which averaged about 90 basis points in the late 1970s and early 1980s, have *risen* steadily in recent decades, standing at 156 basis points in 2004. We can attribute a good part of the fee increase to asset-gathering costs. And costs matter: from 1945 through 1965, funds generated returns that were 89 percent of the market's. From 1983 through 2003, that ratio was 79 percent.

- Until 1958, the SEC restricted sales of management companies. After the courts struck down the SEC's position, the investment-management industry saw a flurry of initial public offerings and mergers and acquisitions activity. Of the fifty largest fund organizations today, only six are privately held. Eight are public independent companies, U.S. financial conglomerates (twenty-two), foreign financial firms (seven), and major brokerage firms own the rest (six). One mutual remains—Vanguard.

- One nonobvious consequence of active mutual fund marketing, as well as investor proclivity to invest in the latest hot-performing funds, is that the *average* fund performance has no resemblance to *actual* investor returns. The reason is that investors crowd into where the performance has been and inevitably suffer as returns revert to the mean. For example, growth stocks saw their greatest quarter of net inflows ($120 billion) in the first quarter of 2000, coincidental with the Nasdaq's peak, while value funds suffered significant outflows. Bogle calculates that while the market rose 12 percent from 1986 through 2005, the average fund return was less than 10 percent, but the average investor return was only 6.9 percent.

Charley Ellis draws up a list of initiatives an investment firm might pursue to maximize its value as a business. I summarize these in exhibit 2.2. Ellis

EXHIBIT 2.2 Pointers to Make an Investment Firm a Business

- Increase the number and enhance the stature of relationship managers, because whatever the performance, they'll be able to keep clients longer— and retention is the key to profit maximization.
- Charge relationship managers with explicit responsibility for cross-selling more and more asset classes and investment products to each client—to maximize "share of wallet" with each account.
- Expand the number and improve the industrial selling skills of sales professionals.
- Develop your organization's "brand" or market franchise.
- Expand into new markets—at home and abroad.
- If you are strong in retail, expand into institutional. And if strong in institutional, expand into retail.
- Focus on mastering relationships with investment consultants, those powerful intermediaries who are involved in 70% of all institutional manager hiring.
- Extend your firm's product line into new asset classes and into all size variations—to diversify your business risk of dependence on superior investment results.
- Limit the business risk of unexpected short-run investment results by hewing close to the index.

Source: Ellis, "Will Business Success Spoil the Investment Management Profession?" 14. Reproduced with permission.

points out that the crux of the tension between the profession and business is that they operate at different rhythms. Long time horizons, low fees, and contrarian investing are good for the profession. In contrast, short time horizons, higher fees, and selling what's in demand are good for the business.

So what should investment firms do? Ellis says it well:

The optimal balance between the investment profession and the investment business needs always to favor the *profession*, because only in devotion to the disciplines of the profession can an organization have those shared values and cultures that attracts unusually talented individual professionals.[6]

I would argue that many of the performance challenges in the business stem from an unhealthy balance between the profession and the business. Many of the investment managers that do beat the market seem to have the profession at the core.

3

The Babe Ruth Effect
Frequency Versus Magnitude in Expected Value

In the real world there is no "easy way" to assure a financial profit. At least, it is gratifying to rationalize that we would rather lose intelligently than win ignorantly.

—Richard A. Epstein,
The Theory of Gambling and Statistical Logic

Batting with the Babe

Hang around a brokerage office and it will only be a matter of time before you hear one of those great-sounding lines, "Hey, if I can be right 51 percent of the time, I'll come out ahead." If this thought seems sensible to you, read on. You're about to discover one of the most important concepts in investing.

First off, let's acknowledge that the idea that an investor should be right more than wrong is pervasive and certainly comes with intuitive appeal. Here's a portfolio manager's story that illuminates the fallacy of this line of thinking.

This well-known investor explained he was one of roughly twenty portfolio managers a company had hired. The company's treasurer, dismayed with the aggregate performance of his active managers, decided to evaluate each manager's decision process with a goal of weeding out the poor performers. The treasurer figured that even a random process would result in a portfolio of stocks with roughly one-half outperforming the benchmark, so he measured each portfolio based on what *percentage* of its stocks beat the market.

This particular portfolio manager found himself in an unusual spot: while his *total* portfolio performance was among the best in the group, his *percentage* of outperforming stocks was among the worst. The treasurer promptly fired all of the other "poor" performing managers, and called a meeting with the investor to figure out why there was such a large discrepancy between his good results and his bad batting average.

The portfolio manager's answer is a great lesson inherent in any probabilistic exercise: *the frequency of correctness does not matter; it is the magnitude of correctness that matters.* Say that you own four stocks, and that three of the stocks go down a bit but the fourth rises substantially. The portfolio will perform well even as the majority of the stocks decline.

Building a portfolio that can deliver superior performance requires that you evaluate each investment using expected value analysis. What is striking is that the leading thinkers across varied fields—including horse betting, casino gambling, and investing—all emphasize the same point.[1] We call it the Babe Ruth effect: even though Ruth struck out a lot, he was one of baseball's greatest hitters.

The reason that the lesson about expected value is universal is that all probabilistic exercises have similar features. Internalizing this lesson, on the other hand, is difficult because it runs against human nature in a very fundamental way. While it's not hard to show the flaw in the treasurer's logic, it's easy to sympathize with his thinking.

The Downside of Hardwiring

In 1979, Daniel Kahneman and Amos Tversky outlined prospect theory, which identifies economic behaviors that are inconsistent with rational decision making.[2] One of the most significant insights from the theory is that people exhibit significant aversion to losses when making choices between risky outcomes, no matter how small the stakes. In fact, Kahneman and Tversky found that a loss has about *two and a half times* the impact of a gain of the same size. In other words, people feel a lot worse about losses of a given size than they feel good about a gain of a similar magnitude.

This behavioral fact means that people are a lot happier when they are right frequently. What's interesting is that being right frequently is not necessarily consistent with an investment portfolio that outperforms its benchmark (as the story above illustrates). The *percentage* of stocks that go up in a portfolio does not determine its performance; it is the dollar change in the portfolio. A few stocks going up or down dramatically will often have a much greater impact on portfolio performance than the batting average.

Bulls, Bears, and Odds

In his provocative book *Fooled by Randomness*, Nassim Taleb relates an anecdote that beautifully drives home the expected value message.[3] In a meeting with his fellow traders, a colleague asked Taleb about his view of the market. He responded that he thought there was a high probability that the market would go up slightly over the next week. Pressed further, he assigned a 70 percent probability to the up move. Someone in the meeting then noted that Taleb was short a large quantity of S&P 500 futures—a bet that the market would go down—seemingly in contrast to his "bullish" outlook. Taleb then explained his position in expected-value terms. Exhibit 3.1 clarifies his thought.

EXHIBIT 3.1 Frequency Versus Magnitude

Event	Probability	Outcome	Expected value
Market goes up	70 percent	+1 percent	+0.7 percent
Market goes down	30 percent	−10 percent	−3.0 percent
Total	100 percent		−2.3 percent

Source: Author analysis.

In this case, the most *probable* outcome is that the market goes up. But the expected value is negative, because the outcomes are asymmetric.[4] Now think about it in terms of stocks. Stocks are sometimes priced for perfection. Even if the company makes or slightly exceeds its numbers the majority of the time (frequency), the price does not rise much. But if the company misses its numbers, the downside to the shares is dramatic. The satisfactory result has a high frequency, but the expected value is negative.

Now consider the downtrodden stock. The majority of the time it disappoints, nudging the stock somewhat lower. But a positive result leads to a sharp upside move. Here, the probability favors a poor result, but the expected value is favorable.

Investors must constantly look past frequencies and consider expected value. As it turns out, this is how the best performers think in all probabilistic fields. Yet in many ways it is unnatural: investors want their stocks to go up, not down. Indeed, the main practical result of prospect theory is that investors tend to sell their winners too early (satisfying the desire to be right) and hold their losers too long (in the hope that they don't have to take a loss). We now turn to three leading practitioners in separate probabilistic fields: investing, pari-mutuel betting, and blackjack.

From OTC to OTB

Warren Buffett, undoubtedly one of the twentieth century's best investors, says that smarts and talent are like a motor's horsepower, but that the motor's *output* depends on rationality. "A lot of people start out with a 400-horsepower motor but only get 100 horsepower of output," he said. "It's way better to have a 200-horsepower motor and get it all into output."[5] And one of the keys is to consider all investment opportunities in terms of expected value. As Buffett's partner Charlie Munger notes, "one of the advantages of a fellow like Buffett is that he automatically thinks in terms of decision trees."[6] Says Buffett, "Take the probability of loss times the amount of possible loss from the probability of gain times the amount of possible gain. That is what we're trying to do. It's imperfect, but that's what it's all about."[7]

Naturally, coming up with likely outcomes and appropriate probabilities is not an easy task. But the discipline of the process compels an investor to think through how various changes in expectations for value triggers—sales, costs, and investments—affect shareholder value, as well as the likelihood of various outcomes. Such an exercise also helps overcome the loss-aversion pitfall.[8]

The expected-value mindset is by no means limited to investing. The book, *Bet with the Best*, offers various strategies for pari-mutuel bettors. Steven Crist, CEO, editor, and publisher of the *Daily Racing Form*, shows the return on investment, including the track's take, of a hypothetical race with four horses. To summarize the lesson, he writes, "The point of this exercise is to illustrate that even a horse with a very high likelihood of winning can be either a very good or a very bad bet, and that the difference between the two is determined by only one thing: the odds." So a horse with a 50 percent probability of winning can be either a good or bad bet based on the payoff, and the same holds true of a 10-to-1 shot. He is saying, in plain words, it is not the frequency of winning that matters, but the frequency times the magnitude of the payoff.[9]

Crist also solicits a confession from his readers: "Now ask yourself: Do you really think this way when you're handicapping? Or do you find horses you 'like' and hope for the best on price? Most honest players admit they follow the latter path." Replace the word "handicapping" with "investing" and "horses" with "stocks," and Crist could be talking about the stock market.

Yet another domain where expected-value thinking is pertinent is blackjack, as Ed Thorp's best-selling book, *Beat the Dealer*, shows. In blackjack, the payoffs are set, and the player's principal task is to assess the probability of drawing a favorable hand. Thorp showed how to count cards in order to identify when the probabilities of a winning hand tilt in a player's favor. When the odds favor the player, the ideal strategy is to increase the bet (effectively increasing the payout). Thorp notes that even under ideal circumstances, favorable situations only arise 9.8 percent of the time; the house has the advantage the other 90.2 percent.[10]

So we see that the leading thinkers in these three domains—all probabilistic exercises—converge on the same approach. We also know that in these activities, the vast majority of the participants don't think through expected value as explicitly as they should. That we are loss averse and avoid losses compounds the challenge for stock investors because we shun situations where the probability of upside may be low but the expected value is attractive.

A Useful Analogy

Long-term success in any of these probabilistic exercises shares some common features. I summarize four of them:

- *Focus*. Professional gamblers do not play a multitude of games—they don't stroll into a casino and play a little blackjack, a little craps, spend a little time on the slot machine. They focus on a specific game and learn the ins and outs. Similarly, most investors must define a circle of competence—areas of relative expertise. Seeking a competitive edge across a spectrum of industries and companies is a challenge, to say the least. Most great investors stick to their circle of competence.

- *Lots of situations.* Players of probabilistic games must examine lots of situations because the market price is usually pretty accurate. Investors, too, must evaluate lots of situations and gather lots of information. For example, the very successful president and CEO of Geico's capital operations, Lou Simpson, tries to read five to eight hours a day and trades very infrequently.

- *Limited opportunities.* As Thorp notes in *Beat the Dealer,* even when you know what you're doing and play under ideal circumstances, the odds still favor you less than 10 percent of the time. And rarely does anyone play under ideal circumstances. The message for investors is that even when you are competent, favorable situations—where you have a clear-cut variant perception vis-à-vis the market—don't appear very often.

- *Ante.* In the casino, you must bet every time to play. Ideally, you can bet a small amount when the odds are poor and a large sum when the odds are favorable, but you must ante to play the game. In investing, on the other hand, you need not participate when you perceive the expected value as unattractive, and you can bet aggressively when a situation appears attractive (within the constraints of an investment policy, naturally). In this way, investing is much more favorable than other games of probability.

Constantly thinking in expected-value terms requires discipline and is somewhat unnatural. But the leading thinkers and practitioners from somewhat varied fields have converged on the same formula: focus not on the frequency of correctness but on the magnitude of correctness.

4

Sound Theory for the Attribute Weary
The Importance of Circumstance-Based Categorization

One reason why platitudes and fads in management come and go with such predictability is they typically are not grounded in a robust categorization scheme. They are espoused as one-size-fits-all statements of cause and effect. Hence, managers try the fad out because it sounds good, and then discard it when they encounter circumstances in which the recommended actions do not yield the predicted results. Their conclusion most often is, "It doesn't work"—when the reality often is that it works well in some (as yet undefined) circumstances, but not others.

—Clayton M. Christensen, Paul Carlile, and David Sundahl,
"The Process of Theory-Building"

Circumstance Over Attributes

You'd probably guess it isn't too hard to categorize slime mold, the somewhat yucky stuff you see on walks through cool, damp parts of the forest. But you'd be wrong. As it turns out, slime mold has some strange behavior—so strange, in fact, that it stumped scientists for centuries.

When food is abundant, slime mold cells operate as independent single-celled units. They move around, eat bacteria, and divide to reproduce. When food is in short supply, however, the slime-mold cells converge and form a cluster of tens of thousands of cells. The cells literally stop acting as individuals and start acting like a collective. That's why slime mold is so hard to categorize: it is an "it" or a "they" depending on the circumstances.[1]

Investment approaches based solely on attributes, without considering the circumstances, also don't make sense. Sometimes a stock that looks expensive is cheap, and what looks cheap is expensive. It's context dependent.

Yet investment consultants encourage, nay, compel most investment professionals to articulate an attribute-based investment approach and stick with it. The game is pretty straightforward. Growth investors strive to beat the market by filling their portfolios with companies that are rapidly increasing sales and earnings, without too much concern about valuation. Value investors load up on cheap stocks with a decent yield and consider corporate growth gravy.

Organization or external constraints aside, most money managers actually believe their attribute-based investment style—combined with their skill—will generate market-beating results.[2] These various investment approaches are grounded in theory: a belief that investor actions will lead to satisfactory outcomes.

The word "theory," however, makes most investors and corporate managers leery because they associate theory with *theoretical*, which implies *impractical*. But if you define theory as a contingent explanation of cause and effect, it is eminently practical. A sound theory helps predict how actions or events lead to specific outcomes across a broad range of circumstances.[3]

The main message is that much of investment theory is unsound because it is based on poor categorization. We can say the same about much of management theory.[4] More specifically, investors generally dwell on attribute-based categorizations (like low multiples) versus circumstance-based categorizations. A shift from attribute- to circumstance-based thinking can be of great help to investors and managers. Take a lesson from the slime mold.

The Three Steps of Theory Building

In a thought-provoking paper, Clayton Christensen, Paul Carlile, and David Sundahl break the process of theory building into three stages (see exhibit 4.1). I discuss each of these stages and provide some perspective on how this general theory-building process applies specifically to investing:

1. *Describe what you want to understand in words and numbers.* In this stage, the goal is to carefully observe, describe, and measure a phenomenon to be sure that subsequent researchers can agree on the subject.

Stock market performance is an example of a phenomenon that requires good theory. Today we largely take for granted this descriptive phase for the market, but the first comprehensive study of the performance of all stocks wasn't published until 1964. In that paper, University of Chicago professors Lawrence Fisher and James Lorie documented that stocks delivered about a 9 percent return from 1926 to 1960. Peter Bernstein notes that the article was a "bomb-shell" that "astonished" academics and practitioners alike. The description itself caused a stir in the finance and investing worlds.[5]

2. *Classify the phenomena into categories based on similarities.* Categorization simplifies and organizes the world so as to clarify differences between phenom-ena. An example of categorization in physics is solids, liquids, and gases. In innovation research—Christensen's specialty—the categories are sustaining and disruptive innovations.

Investing has many variations of categorization, including value versus growth stocks, high risk versus low risk, and large- versus small-capitalization stocks. These categories are deeply ingrained in the investment world, and many investment firms and their products rely on these categories.

3. *Build a theory that explains the behavior of the phenomena.* A robust theory based on sound categorization explains cause and effect, why the cause and effect works, and most critically *under what circumstances* the cause and effect operates. Importantly, a theory must be falsifiable.

The investment world is filled with theories about investment returns. Pro-ponents of the efficient-market theory argue that no strategy exists to gener-ate superior risk-adjusted investment returns. Active money managers pursue myriad strategies—many along specific style boxes—based on the theory that their approach *will* lead to excess returns.

How does a theory improve? Once researchers develop a theory, they can then use it to predict what they will see under various circumstances.

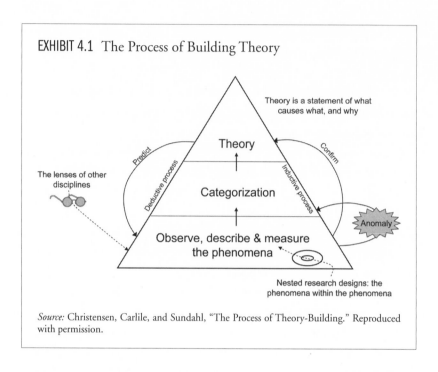

EXHIBIT 4.1 The Process of Building Theory

Theory is a statement of what causes what, and why

Theory

The lenses of other disciplines

Categorization

Observe, describe & measure the phenomena

Anomaly

Nested research designs: the phenomena within the phenomena

Source: Christensen, Carlile, and Sundahl, "The Process of Theory-Building." Reproduced with permission.

In so doing, they often find anomalies, or results that are inconsistent with the theory (see the right side of exhibit 4.1). Anomalies force researchers to revisit the description and categorization stages. The goal is to be able to explain the phenomenon in question more accurately and thoroughly than in the prior theory. Proper theory building requires researchers to cycle through the stages in search of greater and greater predictive power.

That a theory must be falsifiable is a challenge for economists because a number of economic constructs assume an answer in their definitions. One example is utility maximization, which asserts that individuals act so as to maximize utility. But since we can define utility in any way that is consistent with the outcome, we can't falsify the construct.

An example from finance is the capital asset pricing model. Economists use the CAPM to test market efficiency, while the CAPM assumes market efficiency. In the words of noted financial economist Richard Roll, any test of CAPM is "really a joint test of CAPM and market efficiency."[6] Christensen et al. suggest that a number of central concepts in economics should be properly labeled as "constructs" rather than "theories" precisely because they cannot be directly falsified.

To be sure, not all researchers are committed to improving theory. Many are satisfied to develop a theory and demonstrate *that it is not false*. Much of the advice that management consultants dole out fits this description. For instance, the consultants may argue that "outsourcing is good" and find a few examples to "confirm" the theory. Since researchers have not refined the theory by iterating it through the description/categorization/improved-theory process, the theory may not be at all robust. The theory looks good on paper but fails upon implementation.[7]

When, Not What

Perhaps the single most important message from Christensen et al. is that proper categorization is essential to good theory. More specifically, theories evolve from attribute-based categories to circumstance-based categories as they improve. Theories that rest on circumstance-based categories tell practitioners what to do in different situations. In contrast, attribute-based categories prescribe action based on the traits of the phenomena.

This message is critical for investors, who often rely heavily on attribute-based categories. One example is low-price-earnings-multiple investing, often a central plank in the value investor's theory. An investor would have fared poorly using P/E as a tool to time moves in (when the ratio is low) and out (high ratio) of the market over the past 125 years.[8] This doesn't mean that low P/Es are bad but does mean that buying the market when the P/E is low is not a valid theory for generating superior long-term returns.

Indeed, onlookers often describe the investment strategy of successful investors as eclectic. Perhaps it is more accurate to describe their approach as circumstance-based, not attribute-based. Legg Mason Value Trust's Bill Miller, the only fund manager in the past four decades to beat the S&P 500 fifteen years in a row, is a good case in point. Miller's approach is decidedly circumstance based, yet he is routinely criticized for straying from an attribute-based mindset:

> Legg Mason Value's portfolio has hardly reflected the stocks with low price-to-book and price-to-earnings ratios you would expect to find in a value fund. According to Morningstar, at the end of 1999 its price-to-book ratio was 178 percent higher

than the value category average, and its price-to-earnings ratio was 45 percent higher than average.[9]

All investors use theory, either wittingly or unwittingly. The lesson from the process of theory building is that sound theories reflect context. Too many investors cling to attribute-based approaches and wring their hands when the market doesn't conform to what *they* think it should do.

5

Risky Business
Risk, Uncertainty, and Prediction in Investing

> The practical difference between . . . risk and uncertainty . . . is that in the former the distribution of the outcome in a group of instances is known . . . while in the case of uncertainty, this is not true . . . because the situation dealt with is in high degree unique.
>
> —Frank H. Knight, *Risk, Uncertainty, and Profit*

> Our knowledge of the way things work, in society or in nature, comes trailing clouds of vagueness. Vast ills have followed a belief in certainty.
>
> —Kenneth Arrow, " 'I Know a Hawk from a Handsaw' "

Rocket Science

Cognitive scientist Gerd Gigerenzer noted something unusual when he took a guided tour through Daimler-Benz Aerospace, maker of the Ariane rocket. A poster tracking the performance of all ninety-four launches of Ariane 4 and 5 showed eight accidents, including launches sixty-three, seventy, and eighty-eight. Curious, Gigerenzer asked his guide what the risk of accident was. The guide replied that the security factor was around 99.6 percent.

When Gigerenzer asked how eight accidents in ninety-four launches could translate into 99.6 percent certainty, the guide noted that they didn't consider human error in the computation. Rather, DASA calculated the security factor based on the design features of the individual rocket parts.[1]

This DASA story smacks of the probabilities surrounding the 2003 space shuttle catastrophe. NASA engineers estimated the rate of failure for the shuttle at 1-in-145 (0.7 percent), but the program suffered two complete losses in its first 113 launches.[2] The DASA and NASA calculations call into question how we relate uncertainty and risk to probability.

So how should we think about risk and uncertainty? A logical starting place is Frank Knight's distinction: Risk has an unknown outcome, but we know what the underlying outcome distribution looks like. Uncertainty also implies an unknown outcome, but we don't know what the underlying distribution looks like. So games of chance like roulette or blackjack are risky, while the outcome of a war is uncertain. Knight said that objective probability is the basis for risk, while subjective probability underlies uncertainty.

To see another distinction between risk and uncertainty, we consult the dictionary: Risk is "the possibility of suffering harm or loss." Uncertainty is "the condition of being uncertain," and uncertain is "not known or established." So risk always includes the notion of loss, while something can be uncertain but might not include the chance of loss.

Why should investors care about the distinctions between risk and uncertainty? The main reason is that investing is fundamentally an exercise in probability. Every day, investors must translate investment opportunities into probabilities—indeed, this is an essential skill. So we need to think carefully about *how* we come up with probabilities for various situations and *where* the potential pitfalls lie.

From Uncertainty to Probability

In his book *Calculated Risks*, Gigerenzer provides three ways to get to a probability. These classifications follow a progression from least to most concrete and can help investors classify probability statements:[3]

- *Degrees of belief.* Degrees of belief are subjective probabilities and are the most liberal means to translate uncertainty into a probability. The point here is that investors can translate even onetime events into probabilities provided they satisfy the laws of probability—the exhaustive and exclusive set of alternatives adds up to one. Also, investors can frequently update probabilities based on degrees of belief when new, relevant information becomes available.

- *Propensities.* Propensity-based probabilities reflect the properties of the object or system. For example, if a die is symmetrical and balanced, then you have a one-in-six probability of rolling any particular side. The risk assessment in the DASA and NASA cases appears to be propensity-based. This method of probability assessment does not always consider all the factors that may shape an outcome (such as human error in the rocket launchings).

- *Frequencies.* Here the probability is based on a large number of observations in an appropriate reference class. Without an appropriate reference class, there can be no frequency-based probability assessment. So frequency users would not care what someone believes the outcome of a die roll will be, nor would they care about the design of the die. They would focus only on the yield of repeated die rolls.

What about long-term stock market returns? Much of the ink spilled on market prognostications is based on degrees of belief, with the resulting probabilities heavily colored by recent experience. Degrees of belief have a substantial emotional component.

We can also approach the stock market from a propensity perspective. According to Jeremy Siegel's *Stocks for the Long Run*, U.S. stocks have generated annual real returns just under 7 percent over the past 200 years, including many subperiods within that time.[4] The question is whether there are properties that underlie the economy and profit growth that support this very consistent return result.

We can also view the market from a frequency perspective. For example, we can observe the market's annual returns from 1926 through 2006. This distribution of returns has an arithmetic average of 12.0 percent, with a standard deviation of 20.1 percent (provided that the statistics of normal distributions apply). If we assume that distribution of future annual returns will be similar to that of the past (i.e., the last eighty years is a legitimate reference class), we can make statements about the probabilities of future annual returns.[5]

Of the three ways to come up with probabilities, the academic finance community is largely in the last camp. Most of the models in finance assume that price changes follow a normal distribution. One example is the Black-Scholes options-pricing model, where one of the key inputs is volatility—or the standard deviation of future price changes.

But stock price changes are not normally distributed, which has implications for our notions of risk and uncertainty, market timing, and money management. More specifically, stock price change distributions show high kurtosis—the mean is higher, and the tails fatter, than a normal distribution. (We may still say that a distribution exists that characterizes the market; it's just not a normal distribution.) These return outliers are of particular interest in understanding the characteristics of stock market returns over time.

To demonstrate this point, I looked at daily S&P 500 Index price changes from January 3, 1978, to March 30, 2007. The index's annual return (excluding dividends) in that period was 9.5 percent. I then knocked out the fifty worst days, and then the fifty best days, from the sample (over 7,000 days). Had you been able to avoid the worst fifty days, your annual return would have been 18.2 percent, versus the realized ten percent. Without the fifty best days, the return was just 0.6 percent.

This analysis may be attention grabbing, but it lacks a point of reference. To provide better context, I calculated a mean and standard deviation based on the actual underlying data and used those statistics to generate a random sample of the same size and characteristics. When I knocked out the fifty worst

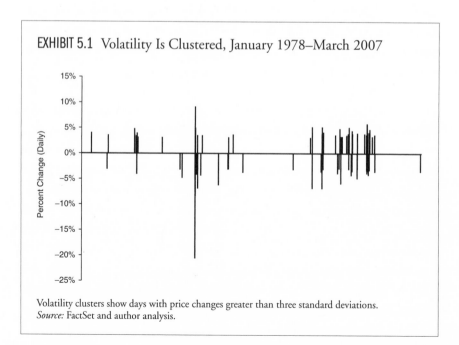

EXHIBIT 5.1 Volatility Is Clustered, January 1978–March 2007

Volatility clusters show days with price changes greater than three standard deviations.
Source: FactSet and author analysis.

days from the sample I created, the returns were just 15.2 percent (versus 18.2 percent for the real data). Likewise, when I knocked out the fifty best days, the return was 3.5 percent, significantly higher than that for the real data.

In plain words, this analysis shows that extreme-return days play a much more significant role in shaping the market's total returns than a normal distribution suggests. It also makes a strong case against market timing, unless an investor has a systematic way to anticipate extreme-return days.

A final thought on extreme-return days is that they do not appear randomly throughout the time series but rather tend to cluster (see exhibit 5.1). So our exercise of knocking out high and low return days is not very realistic because in the real data these extreme days (up and down) come in bunches.

How Predictions Change Future Payoffs

A lot of issues surround prediction, but in this discussion of risk and uncertainty, I focus on how, in markets, acting on a prediction can change the prediction's outcome.

One way to think about it is to contrast a roulette wheel with a pari-mutuel betting system. If you play a fair game of roulette, whatever prediction you make will not affect the outcome. The prediction's outcome is independent of the prediction itself. Contrast that with a prediction at the racetrack. If you believe a particular horse is likely to do better than the odds suggest, you will bet on the horse. But your bet will help shape the odds. For instance, if all bettors predict a particular horse will win, the odds will reflect that prediction, and the return on investment will be poor.

The analogy carries into the stock market. If you believe a stock is undervalued and start to buy it, you will help raise the price, thus driving down prospective returns. This point underscores the importance of expected value, a central concept in any probabilistic exercise. Expected value formalizes the idea that your return on an investment is the product of the probabilities of various outcomes and the payoff from each outcome.[6]

Peter Bernstein once said, "The fundamental law of investing is the uncertainty of the future." As investors, our challenge is to translate those uncertainties into probabilities and payoffs in the search for attractive securities. An ability to classify probability statements can be very useful in this endeavor.

6

Are You an Expert?
Experts and Markets

Overall, the evidence suggests there is little benefit to expertise. . . . Surprisingly, I could find no studies that showed an important advantage for expertise.

—J. Scott Armstrong, "The Seer-Sucker Theory: The Value of Experts in Forecasting"[1]

Man Versus Machine

If you enter a hospital with chest pains, doctors will quickly administer an electrocardiogram (EKG) test. The EKG measures electrical impulses in your heart and translates them into squiggles on graph paper. Based in part on the readout, the doctor determines whether or not you're having a heart attack. Sometimes the readouts are clear. But often they're equivocal, which means you are relying on the doctor's expertise to come to a proper diagnosis.

So how good are doctors at reading EKGs? In a 1996 showdown, Lund University researcher Lars Edenbrandt pitted his computer against Dr. Hans Ohlin, a leading Swedish cardiologist. An artificial intelligence expert, Edenbrandt had trained his machine by feeding it thousands of EKGs and indicating which readouts were indeed heart attacks. The fifty-year-old Ohlin routinely read as many as 10,000 EKGs a year as part of his practice.

Edenbrandt chose a sample of over 10,000 EKGs, exactly half of which showed confirmed heart attacks, and gave them to machine and man. Ohlin took his time evaluating the charts, spending a week carefully separating the stack into heart-attack and no-heart-attack piles. The battle was reminiscent of Garry Kasparov versus Deep Blue, and Ohlin was fully aware of the stakes.

As Edenbrandt tallied the results, a clear-cut winner emerged: the computer correctly identified the heart attacks in 66 percent of the cases, Ohlin only in 55 percent. The computer proved 20 percent more accurate than a leading cardiologist in a routine task that can mean the difference between life and death.[2]

Our society tends to hold experts in high esteem. Patients routinely surrender their care to doctors, investors listen to financial advisors, and receptive TV viewers tune in to pundits of all stripes. But what is the basis for this unquestioning faith in experts?

Where Do Experts Do Well?

In some domains, experts clearly and consistently outperform the average person: just imagine playing chess against a grandmaster, trading volleys on Wimbledon's center court, or performing brain surgery. Yet in other domains experts add very little value, and their opinions are routinely inferior to collective judgments. Further, experts in some fields tend to agree most of the time (e.g., weather forecasters), while in other fields they often stand at complete odds with one another. What's going on?

Let's narrow our discussion to cognitive tasks. One way to look at expert effectiveness is based on the nature of the problem they address. We can consider problem types on a continuum.[3] One side captures straightforward problems inherent to static, linear, and discrete systems. The opposite side reflects dynamic, non-linear, and continuous problems. Exhibit 6.1 offers additional adjectives for each of the two extremes.

While tens of thousands of hours of deliberate practice allows experts to internalize many of their domain's features, this practice can also lead to reduced cognitive flexibility. Reduced flexibility leads to deteriorating expert performance as problems go from the simple to the complex.

Two concepts are useful here. The first is what psychologists call *functional fixedness*, the idea that when we use or think about something in a particular way we have great difficulty in thinking about it in new ways. We have a tendency to stick to our established perspective and are very slow to consider alternative perspectives.

EXHIBIT 6.1 Edges of the Problem Continuum

Discrete	Continuous
Static	Dynamic
Sequential	Simultaneous
Mechanical	Organic
Separable	Interactive
Universal	Conditional
Homogenous	Heterogeneous
Regular	Irregular
Linear	Nonlinear
Superficial	Deep
Single	Multiple
Stationary	Nonstationary

Source: Paul J. Feltovich, Rand J. Spiro, and Richard L. Coulsen, "Issues of Expert Flexibility in Contexts Characterized by Complexity and Change," in *Expertise in Context: Human and Machine,* ed. Paul J. Feltovich, Kenneth M. Ford, and Robert R. Hoffman (Menlo Park, Cal.: AAAI Press and Cambridge, Mass.: MIT Press, 1997), 128–9 and author.

The second idea, *reductive bias*, says that we tend to treat non-linear, complex systems (the right-hand side of the continuum) as if they are linear, simple systems. A common resulting error is evaluating a system based on attributes versus considering the circumstances. For example, some investors focus solely on statistically cheap stocks (attribute) and fail to consider whether or not the valuation indicates value (circumstance).

Reductive bias also presents a central challenge for economists, who attempt to model and predict complex systems using tools and metaphors from simpler equilibrium systems. The bias demonstrates a number of conceptual challenges, including the failure to consider novel approaches, novelty clues, and system change.

None of this is to say that experts are inflexible automatons. Experts act with demonstrably more flexibility than novices in a particular domain. Psychologists specify two types of expert flexibility. In the first type, the expert internalizes many of the domain's salient features and hence sees and reacts to most of the domain's contexts and their effects. This flexibility operates effectively in relatively stable domains.

The second type of flexibility is more difficult to exercise. This flexibility requires experts to recognize when their cognitively accessible models are unlikely to work, forcing the experts to go outside their routines and their familiar frameworks to solve problems. This flexibility is crucial to success in nonlinear, complex systems.

So how do experts ensure they incorporate both types of flexibility? Advocates of cognitive flexibility theory suggest the major determinant in whether or not an expert will have more expansive flexibility is the amount of reductive bias during deliberate practice.[4] More reductive bias may improve efficiency but will reduce flexibility. To mitigate reductive bias, the theory prescribes exploring abstractions across diverse cases to capture the significance of context dependence. Experts must also look at actual case studies and see when rules do and don't work.

Exhibit 6.2 consolidates these ideas and offers a quick guide to expert performance in various types of cognitive domains. Consistent with Exhibit 6.1, we show a range of domains from the most simple on the left to the most complex on the right. The exhibit shows that expert performance is largely a function of the type of problem the expert addresses.

For rules-based systems with limited degrees of freedom, computers consistently outperform individual humans.[5] Humans perform well, but the computers are better and often cheaper. Computer algorithms beat people for reasons psychologists have documented: humans are easily influenced by

EXHIBIT 6.2 Expert Performance Depends on the Problem Type

Domain Description	Rules based: Limited Degrees of Freedom	Rules based: High Degrees of Freedom	Probabilistic: Limited Degrees of Freedom	Probabilistic: High Degrees of Freedom
Expert Performance	Worse than computers	Generally better than computers	Equal to or worse than collectives	Collectives outperform experts
Expert Agreement	High (70–90%)	Moderate (50–60%)	Moderate/Low (30–40%)	Low (<20%)
Examples	• Credit scoring • Simple medical diagnosis	• Chess • Go	• Admissions officers • Poker	• Stock market • Economy

Source: Beth Azar, "Why Experts Often Disagree," *APA Monitor Online* 30, no. 5 (May 1999) and author.

suggestion, recent experience, and how information is presented. Humans also do a poor job of weighing variables.[6] Because most decisions in these systems are rules based, experts tend to agree. The EKG-reading story illustrates this point.

The next column shows rules-based systems with high degrees of freedom. Experts tend to add the most value here. For example, while Deep Blue narrowly beat chess master Garry Kasparov, no computer is even close to beating a top player in Go, a game with simple rules but a larger 19-by-19 board.[7] Improving computing power, however, will eventually challenge the expert edge in this domain type. Agreement among experts in this domain remains reasonably high.

A move to the right reveals a probabilistic domain with limited degrees of freedom. The value of experts declines because outcomes are probabilistic, but experts still hold their own versus computers and collectives. Expert agreement dips again in these domains. Statistics can improve expert decision making with these problems, a point Michael Lewis develops fully for professional baseball player selection in his bestseller *Moneyball*.

The right-most column shows the most difficult environment: a probabilistic domain with high degrees of freedom. Here the evidence clearly shows that collectives outperform experts.[8] The stock market provides an obvious case in point, and it comes as no surprise that the vast majority of investors add no value. In this domain, experts can, and often do, hold diametrically opposite views on the same issue.[9]

We often rely on experts. But how good are their predictions, really? Psychologist Phil Tetlock asked nearly three hundred experts to make literally tens of thousands of predictions over nearly two decades. These were difficult predictions related to political and economic outcomes—similar to the types of problems investors tackle.

The results were unimpressive. Expert forecasters improved little, if at all, on simple statistical models. Further, when Tetlock confronted the experts with their poor predicting acuity, they went about justifying their views just like everyone else does. Tetlock doesn't describe in detail what happens when the expert opinions are aggregated, but his research certainly shows that ability, defined as expertise, does not lead to good predictions when the problems are hard.

Decomposing the data, Tetlock found that while expert predictions were poor overall, some were better than others. What mattered in predictive ability was not who the people were or what they believed, but rather *how* they thought. Using a metaphor from Archilochus (via Isaiah Berlin), Tetlock segregated the experts into hedgehogs and foxes. Hedgehogs know one big thing and extend the explanatory reach of that thing to everything they encounter. Foxes, in contrast, tend to know a little about a lot and are not wedded to a single explanation for complex problems.

Two of Tetlock's discoveries are particularly relevant. The first is a correlation between media contact and poor predictions. Tetlock notes that "better-known forecasters—those more likely to be fêted by the media—were less calibrated than their lower-profile colleagues."[10] The research provides yet another reason to be wary of the radio and television talking heads.

Second, Tetlock found foxes tend to be better predictors than hedgehogs. He writes:

High scorers look like foxes: thinkers who know many small things (tricks of their trade), are skeptical of grand schemes, see explanation and prediction not as deductive exercises but rather exercises in flexible "ad hocery" that require stitching together diverse sources of information, and are rather diffident about their own forecasting prowess.[11]

We can say that hedgehogs have one power tool while foxes have many tools in their toolbox. Of course, hedgehogs solve certain problems brilliantly—they certainly get their fifteen minutes of fame—but don't predict as well over time as the foxes do, especially as conditions change. Tetlock's research provides scholarly evidence of diversity's power.

7

The Hot Hand in Investing
What Streaks Tell Us About Perception,
Probability, and Skill

Long streaks are, and must be, a matter of extraordinary luck
imposed on great skill.

—Stephen Jay Gould, "The Streak of Streaks"

Anyone can theoretically roll 12 sevens in a row.

—Bill Gross, *Barron's*

Finding the Hot Shot

Humans are natural pattern seekers. One well-known example is the hot
hand in basketball. A player who makes a few baskets in a row is considered
to have a hot hand, which implies that he has a higher-than-normal chance
of sinking his next shot. Research shows that sports fans, and the athletes
themselves, believe in the hot hand phenomenon.

There's only one problem: The hot hand does not exist. Scientists studied
a season's worth of shooting statistics of the Philadelphia 76ers and free-throw
records of the Boston Celtics and found no evidence for the hot hand. Players
did make successive shots, of course, but those streaks were completely consistent with probabilities. Streaks and slumps lie within the domain of chance.[1]

We see patterns where none exist because we're wired to expect that
the characteristics of chance show up not just in a total sequence but also
in small parts of the sequence. Psychologists Amos Tversky and Daniel
Kahneman call this "belief in the law of small numbers."

For example, if you show someone a short section of a long coin-toss
series, he will expect to see a fifty/fifty mix between heads and tails even
though a short section will generally deviate systematically from chance.

Even a short sequence of repeated heads is enough to convince most people (falsely) that the longer sequence is not random. That's the reason we believe in hot hands.[2]

The main point here, though, is not that humans are poor at relating probabilities to sequences of outcomes. The more important issue is that streaks inform us about probabilities. In human endeavors, unlike a fair coin toss, the probabilities of success or failure are not the same for each individual. Long success streaks happen to the most skillful in a field precisely because their general chance of success is higher than average.

Streaks and Skill

Here's an illustration of the link between streaks and skill. Let's say you have two basketball players, Sally Swish and Allen Airball. Sally, the more skilled of the two, makes 60 percent of her shot attempts. Allen only makes 30 percent of his. What are the probabilities of each player making five shots in a row? For Sally, the likelihood is $(0.6)^5$, or 7.8 percent. That means that Sally will get five in a row about every thirteen sequences. Allen's chances are only $(0.3)^5$, or 0.24 percent. So Allen's only going to hit five straight once every 412 sequences. Without violating any probability principle, Sally is going have a lot more streaks than Allen.[3]

Consistent with this thesis, Wilt Chamberlin drained eighteen consecutive shots on February 24, 1967, to earn the NBA record for the longest field-goal streak in a game. Chamberlin made 54 percent of his field-goal attempts over his career, placing him among the game's top twenty in shooting accuracy.

Baseball hitting streaks are another good way to test the notion that we should associate long streaks with skill (as well as luck). In Major League Baseball history, forty-two players have staked hitting streaks of thirty or more games. The average lifetime batting average of these players is .311. To put that in perspective, a .311 lifetime average would place a hitter among the top one hundred in the history of the game.

In addition, the five players with the most twenty-game hitting streaks in history—Pete Rose, Ty Cobb, Tris Speaker, Heinie Manush, and Chuck

Klein—have a combined lifetime batting average of .333. Over time, the batting average in baseball has hovered around .260.[4]

The one streak in sports that defies the probabilities is Joe DiMaggio's fifty-six-game hitting streak in 1941. (The longest streak after DiMaggio's is 44 games, 80 percent of DiMaggio's record, achieved by both Pete Rose and Wee Willie Keeler.) Ed Purcell, a Nobel laureate in physics, combed baseball's streak and slump records and concluded that everything that has happened in baseball was within the realm of probability—except DiMaggio's streak.[5]

Granted, DiMaggio was a great hitter—his lifetime batting average is the twenty-seventh best in baseball history—but the likelihood of his streak was less than a one in a million, even for him.[6] For this reason, most statistically oriented baseball fans believe that DiMaggio's streak is the record least likely to be broken.[7]

Toss Out the Coin Toss

Most finance professionals attribute money manager streaks (consecutive years of benchmark outperformance) to luck. For example, finance teachers enthusiastically invoke a coin-tossing metaphor to demonstrate market efficiency.[8] The basic idea is that if you start with a sufficiently large sample of money managers, the probabilities tell you a priori that some will have a streak of outperformance. Start with a group of, say, 1,000 funds, assume a fifty/fifty chance of beating the market, and roughly thirty funds will outperform five years in a row: $(0.5)^5 \times 1,000$.

There is nothing wrong with this logic as far as it goes. The problem is that not all fund managers are of equal skill—the money-management industry has its versions of Sally Swish and Allen Airball. So attributing *any* fund streak to chance misses the point that skilled participants are the most likely to post a streak.

The streak that has garnered the most attention in the mutual fund world is that of Legg Mason's Bill Miller, whose Value Trust fund managed to outperform the S&P 500 for fifteen consecutive years through 2005. No other fund has ever outperformed the market for that long in the last forty years. What are the odds of that?

Some pundits are perfectly satisfied to chalk up Miller's record to chance. For example, Gregory Baer and Gary Gensler write: "While we are happy for Legg Mason and its manager, Bill Miller, we view that outcome as roughly in line with random chance and as an indictment of active management."[9] More incredible is the comment (quoted at top) by well-regarded bond manager Bill Gross. In 2003, when the streak was at twelve years, Gross "snarled" that Miller's performance is equivalent to rolling twelve sevens in a row with a pair of dice. We can only hope that Gross, who has a great investment track record and familiarity with gambling, was misquoted: The odds of rolling twelve sevens in a row are approximately 1 in 2.2 billion.

We can look at Miller's streak two ways. The first assumes that a constant percentage of funds outperform the market each year. We can then select a percentage and calculate the probability of one fund outperforming each and every year (see exhibit 7.1). For example, if you assume that mutual fund performance is essentially a coin toss—half of all funds beat the market and half underperform—the odds of one fund beating the market for

EXHIBIT 7.1 Probability That One Fund Will Outperform Each Year

Percent of Funds That Outperform the Market

Years		30%	40%	50%	60%
1	1 in	3	3	2	2
2	1 in	11	6	4	3
3	1 in	37	16	8	5
4	1 in	123	39	16	8
5	1 in	412	98	32	13
6	1 in	1,372	244	64	21
7	1 in	4,572	610	128	36
8	1 in	15,242	1,526	256	60
9	1 in	50,805	3,815	512	99
10	1 in	169,351	9,537	1,024	165
11	1 in	564,503	23,842	2,048	276
12	1 in	1,881,676	59,605	4,096	459
13	1 in	6,272,255	149,012	8,192	766
14	1 in	20,907,516	372,529	16,384	1,276
15	1 in	69,691,719	931,323	32,768	2,127
16	1 in	232,305,731	2,328,306	65,536	3,545

Source: Author analysis.

fifteen consecutive years is 1 in 32,768. Given that there were only 900 comparable mutual funds at the beginning of Miller's streak, his performance looks impressive.

The problem with this analysis, though, is that outperforming the market is not a fifty/fifty proposition for the average mutual fund. In fact, the average percentage of outperformance over the past fifteen years was 44 percent. If we assume a 44 percent ratio, the probability of one fund outperforming for fifteen years is roughly 1 in 223,000.[10]

The second way of looking at Miller's streak is to look at the actual percentages of funds that beat the market in each year (see exhibit 7.2). This allows us to determine the cumulative probability given what actually happened. This calculation shows that the probability of beating the market fifteen years in a row (ended 2005) was about 1 in 2.3 million. A quick glance at the numbers shows why the odds are so low. Two years, 1995 and 1997, create the camel-through-the-needle's-eye probability, as only about 10 percent of all funds beat the market in those two years.

EXHIBIT 7.2 Percentage of Funds That Beat the S&P 500, 1991–2006

Year	Funds	Percent that Beat S&P 500
1991	889	47.7
1992	1,018	50.9
1993	1,289	72.0
1994	1,733	24.0
1995	2,325	12.6
1996	2,894	20.7
1997	3,761	7.9
1998	4,831	26.1
1999	5,873	51.4
2000	6,966	62.2
2001	8,460	49.7
2002	9,749	58.7
2003	10,780	56.7
2004	11,466	54.9
2005	11,329	67.1
2006	12,500	38.3

Source: Lipper Analytical Services and author analysis.

Streaks and Luck

In money management, the magnitude of market outperformance (adjusted for risk) is the true bottom line. But streaks are intriguing because they are without exception—they allow no bad years. Further, as the streak lengthens, the tension and pressure mount.

Was Miller lucky along the way? Without a doubt. But as Stephen Jay Gould says, long streaks are extraordinary luck imposed on great skill.[11] The central message is that across domains, long streaks typically *indicate* skill. And since humans have a hard time relating to all but the easiest probabilities, we often fail to see the significance of streaks.

8

Time Is on My Side
Myopic Loss Aversion and Portfolio Turnover

The attractiveness of the risky asset depends on the time horizon of the investor. An investor who is prepared to wait a long time before evaluating the outcome of the investment as a gain or a loss will find the risky asset more attractive than another investor who expects to evaluate the outcome soon.

—Richard H. Thaler, Amos Tversky, Daniel Kahneman, and
Alan Schwartz, "The Effect of Myopia and Loss Aversion on
Risk Taking: An Experimental Test"

Loss aversion . . . can be considered a fact of life. In contrast, the frequency of evaluations is a policy choice that presumably could be altered, at least in principle.

—Shlomo Benartzi and Richard H. Thaler,
"Myopic Loss Aversion and the Equity Premium Puzzle"

One or One Hundred

In the early 1960s, economist Paul Samuelson offered his lunch colleagues a bet where he would pay $200 for a correct call of a fair coin toss and he would collect $100 for an incorrect call. But his partners didn't bite. One distinguished scholar replied, "I won't bet because *I would feel the $100 loss more than the $200 gain*. But I'll take you on if you promise to let me make 100 such bets" (emphasis added).

This response prompted Samuelson to prove a theorem showing that "no sequence is acceptable if each of its single plays is not acceptable." According to economic theory, his learned colleague's answer was irrational.[1]

Even though the lunch bet has a positive expected value, Samuelson's proof doesn't feel quite right to most people. The concept of loss aversion explains why. One of prospect theory's main findings, loss aversion says that given a choice between risky outcomes we are about two times as averse to losses than to comparable gains.[2]

So Samuelson's theoretical proof notwithstanding, most people intuitively agree with his lunch partner: The prospective regret of losing $100 on a single toss exceeds the pleasure of winning $200. An opportunity to take the bet repeatedly, on the other hand, seems sensible because there are lower odds of suffering regret.

One significant difference between expected-utility theory (the basis for Samuelson's proof) and prospect theory is the decision frame. Expected-utility theory considers gains and losses in the context of the investor's *total wealth* (broad frame). In contrast, prospect theory considers gains and losses versus *isolated components of wealth*, like changes in a specific stock or a portfolio price (narrow frame). Experimental studies show that investors use price, or changes in price, as a reference point when evaluating financial transactions. Said differently, investors pay attention to the narrow frame.[3]

If prospect theory does indeed explain investor behavior, the probabilities of a stock (or portfolio) rising and the investment-evaluation period become paramount. I want to shine a light on the policies regarding these two variables.

Explaining the Equity-Risk Premium

One of finance's big puzzles is why equity returns have been so much higher than fixed-income returns over time, given the respective risk of each asset class. From 1900 through 2006, stocks in the United States have earned a 5.7 percent annual premium over treasury bills (geometric returns). Other developed countries around the world have seen similar results.[4]

In a trailblazing 1995 paper, Shlomo Benartzi and Richard Thaler suggested a solution to the equity risk premium puzzle based on what they called "myopic loss aversion." Their argument rests on two conceptual pillars:[5]

1. *Loss aversion.* We regret losses two to two and a half times more than similar-sized gains. Since the stock price is generally the frame of reference, the

probability of loss or gain is important. Naturally, the longer the holding period in a financial market the higher the probability of a positive return. (Financial markets must have a positive expected return to lure capital, since investors must forgo current consumption.)

2. *Myopia.* The more frequently we evaluate our portfolios, the more likely we are to see losses and hence suffer from loss aversion. Inversely, the less frequently investors evaluate their portfolios, the more likely they are to see gains.

Exhibit 8.1 provides some numbers to illustrate these concepts.[6] The basis for this analysis is an annual geometric mean return of 10 percent and a standard deviation of 20.5 percent (nearly identical to the actual mean and standard deviation from 1926 through 2006).[7] The table also assumes that stock prices follow a random walk (an imperfect but workable assumption) and a loss-aversion factor of 2. (Utility = Probability of a price increase − probability of a decline × 2.)

EXHIBIT 8.1 Time, Returns, and Utility

Time Horizon	Return	Standard Deviation	Positive Return Probability	Utility
1 Hour	0.01%	0.48%	50.40%	−0.488
1 Day	0.04	1.27	51.20	−0.464
1 Week	0.18	2.84	53.19	−0.404
1 Month	0.80	5.92	56.36	−0.309
1 Year	10.0	20.5	72.6	0.177
10 Years	159.4	64.8	99.9	0.997
100 Years	1,377,961	205.0	100.0	1.000

Source: Author analysis.

A glance at the exhibit shows that the probability of a gain or a loss in the very short term is close to fifty/fifty. Further, positive utility—essentially the avoidance of loss aversion—requires a holding period of nearly one year.

If Benartzi and Thaler are right, the implication is critical: Long-term investors (individuals who evaluate their portfolios infrequently) are willing to pay more for an identical risky asset than short-term investors (frequent evaluation). *Valuation depends on your time horizon.*

This may be why many long-term investors say they don't care about volatility. Immune to short-term squiggles, these investors hold stocks long enough to get an attractive probability of a return and, hence, a positive utility.

Benartzi and Thaler, using a number of simulation approaches, estimate that the evaluation period consistent with the realized equity-risk premium is about one year. It is important to note that the evaluation period is *not* the same as the investor's planning horizon. An investor may be saving for retirement thirty years from now, but if she evaluates her portfolio (or more accurately, experiences the utility of the gains and losses) annually or quarterly, she is acting as if she has a short-term planning horizon.[8]

I will now make a leap (and hopefully it's not too far) and suggest that for most funds, portfolio turnover is a reasonable proxy for the evaluation period. High turnover would be consistent with seeking gains in a relatively short time, and low turnover suggests a willingness to wait to assess gains and losses. For many successful funds (and companies), the evaluation period is a policy choice. And as Warren Buffett says, you eventually get the shareholders you deserve.

The Value of Inactivity

We now turn to the empirical data on the relationship between portfolio turnover and performance. We separate mutual funds into four types based on portfolio-turnover rate. The data consistently show that the low-turnover funds (which imply two-year-plus investor holding periods) perform best over three-, five-, ten-, and fifteen-year time frames (see exhibit 8.2).

We may be able to attribute this performance difference to lower costs—a reason in and of itself to reduce turnover for many portfolios—but we would note that transaction costs tend to represent only about one-third of total costs for the average mutual fund.

Despite consistent evidence supporting the performance benefits of a buy-and-hold strategy, the average actively managed mutual fund has annual turnover nearly 90 percent. What gives? First off, an efficient stock market *requires* investor diversity—across styles and time horizons. Not everyone can, or should, be a long-term investor. This fallacy of composition is the flaw behind the "Dow 36,000" theory, which argues that if all

EXHIBIT 8.2 Portfolio Turnover and Long-Term Performance

Turnover (%)	Three-Year Annual Return (%)	Five-Year Annual Return (%)	Ten-Year Annual Return (%)	Fifteen-Year Annual Return (%)
≤20	9.8	8.7	9.5	11.2
20–50	10.3	9.1	9.3	11.3
50–100	10.1	8.4	8.1	10.0
≥100	9.2	7.6	6.6	8.8

Note: Data through 12/31/06.
Source: Author analysis, Morningstar, Inc.

EXHIBIT 8.3 Aggregate Return and Standard Deviation

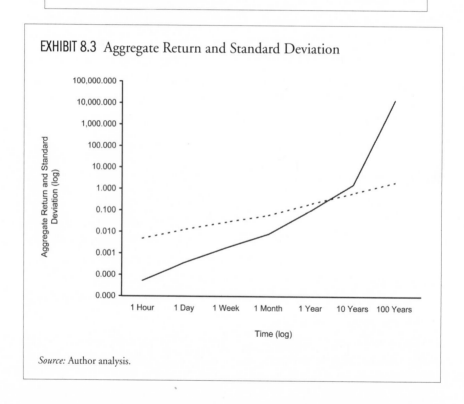

Source: Author analysis.

investors adopt a long-term horizon, the equity-risk premium will dissipate and the market will enjoy a onetime rise.[9] Changing the nature of the investors changes the nature of the market. If *all* investors were long-term oriented, the market would suffer a diversity breakdown and hence be *less* efficient than today's market.

A second and much more profound reason for high turnover is agency costs. Studies show that a portfolio of stocks trading below expected value will outperform the market (adjusted for risk) *over time*. But because there is such a focus on outcome versus process, most institutional investors have time horizons that are substantially shorter than what an investment strategy requires to pay off.

Portfolio managers who underperform the market risk losing assets, and ultimately their jobs.[10] So their natural reaction is to minimize tracking error versus a benchmark. Many portfolio managers won't buy a controversial stock that they think will be attractive over a three-year horizon because they have no idea whether or not the stock will perform well over a three-month horizon. This may explain some of the overreaction we see in markets and shows why myopic loss aversion may be an important source of inefficiency.

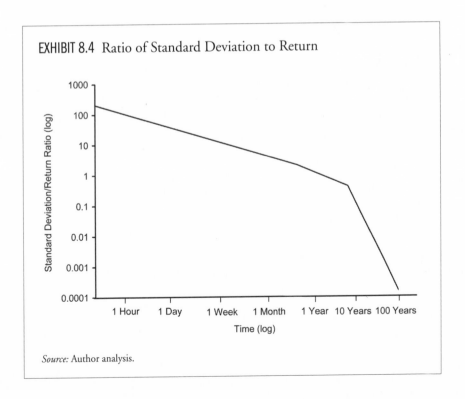

EXHIBIT 8.4 Ratio of Standard Deviation to Return

Source: Author analysis.

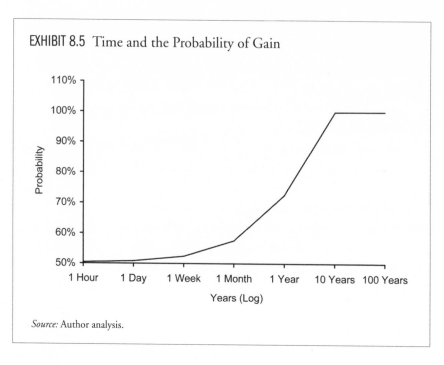

EXHIBIT 8.5 Time and the Probability of Gain

Probability

110%
100%
90%
80%
70%
60%
50%

1 Hour   1 Day   1 Week   1 Month   1 Year   10 Years   100 Years

Years (Log)

Source: Author analysis.

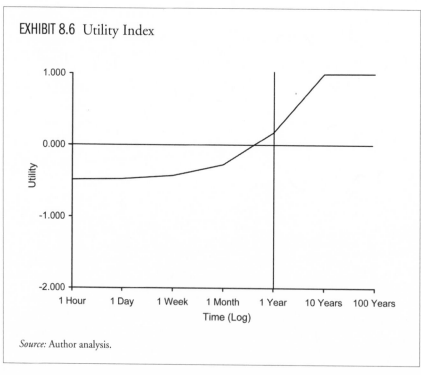

EXHIBIT 8.6 Utility Index

Utility

1.000

0.000

-1.000

-2.000

1 Hour   1 Day   1 Week   1 Month   1 Year   10 Years   100 Years

Time (Log)

Source: Author analysis.

Pictures Worth a Thousand Words

Exhibits 8.3 through 8.6 recreate some of investment sage William Bernstein's pictures to help quantify the key ideas behind myopic loss aversion.[11]

Exhibit 8.3 shows the relationship between risk and reward. Because risk (measured as standard deviation) increases as a function of the square root of time but reward (measured as return) compounds with time, there is a sharp inflection point in the risk and reward trade-off. Note that the axes are on a log scale.

Another way to look at the same picture is to show a plot of the ratio of risk to reward—that is, standard deviation divided by return (exhibit 8.4).

We can now look at the probability of a positive outcome. Given the assumed underlying statistical properties, exhibit 8.5 shows how the probability that the investment will be up increases with time. If investors use gains and losses versus a purchase price as their frame of reference, this picture reveals the relationship between time and regret.

Based on the probabilities in exhibit 8.5, and assuming that losses have twice the impact of comparable gains, we can plot a simple utility function (exhibit 8.6). The scale ranges from -2.0 (a 100 percent chance of a loss $\times$ 2) to 1.0 (a 100 percent chance of a gain).

9

The Low Down on the Top Brass
Management Evaluation and the
Investment Process

At our annual meetings, someone usually asks "What happens to this place if you get hit by a truck?" I'm glad they are still asking the question in this form. It won't be too long before the query becomes: "What happens to this place if you don't get hit by a truck?"

—Warren E. Buffett, Berkshire Hathaway Annual Letter to Shareholders, 1993[1]

Level 5 leaders channel their ego needs away from themselves and into the larger goal of building a great company. It's not that Level 5 leaders have no ego or self-interest. Indeed, they are incredibly ambitious—but their ambition is first and foremost for the institution, not themselves.

—Jim Collins, *Good to Great*[2]

Management Counts

"Is assessing management important in the investment process?" is one of the most frequent questions I get from clients and students.

The answer is a qualified, but emphatic, yes. I suggest three areas for careful consideration: management's leadership, incentives, and capital allocation skills. I do not purport that this discussion is all encompassing—indeed, dedicated scholars have written countless articles and books on each of these topics. My more modest goal is to stimulate thought in this vital, yet often overlooked, area.

When is management assessment unnecessary? Understanding management's motivation is not particularly important for investors—perhaps more accurately, speculators—who intend to have a short holding period. In the short term, stock prices are sensitive to specific events and the vagaries of the market. In the long term, management actions are much more likely to leave a lasting imprint on a company's performance, and hence its stock price.

Make no mistake. Chief executive officers (CEOs) do not have an easy job, especially in the current environment. According to recent studies, forced turnover of CEOs was up sharply in 2006 versus a decade ago. And this trend is not limited to just the United States—the researchers found similar, if not more pronounced, trends in Europe and Asia.[3]

So what makes for a shareholder-friendly management team? I discuss some thoughts in the following sections.

Leadership

Leadership is tricky to define, let alone assess. But I look for three qualities in a senior manager that, taken together, seem like a reasonable means to judge leadership. These qualities are *learning, teaching,* and *self-awareness.*

A consistent thirst to *learn* marks a great leader. On one level, this is about intellectual curiosity—a constant desire to build mental models that can help in decision making. A quality manager can absorb and weigh contradictory ideas and information as well as think probabilistically. I add hesitantly that this aspect of learning is borderline academic. I like CEOs who read and think.[4]

Another critical facet of learning is a true desire to understand what's going on in the organization and to confront facts with brutal honesty. The only way to understand what's going on is to get out there, visit employees and customers, and *ask* questions and *listen* to responses. In almost all organizations, there is much more information at the edge of the network—the employees in the trenches dealing with the day-to-day issues—than in the middle of the network, where the CEO sits. CEOs who surround themselves with managers seeking to please, rather than prod, are unlikely to make great decisions.

A final dimension of learning is creating an environment where everyone in the organization feels they can voice their thoughts and opinions without the risk of being rebuffed, ignored, or humiliated. The idea here is not that management should entertain all half-baked ideas but rather that management should encourage and reward intellectual risk taking.[5]

Robert Rubin embodies this leadership dimension:

> Our Treasury meetings were characterized by searching, questioning and debate, all for the sake of the fullest possible exploration of alternatives. This was a discussion, rather unusual for Washington, in which rank hardly mattered. A thirty-four-year-old deputy assistant secretary and the Treasury Secretary both felt fully entitled to express their views. That informality reflected my experience both on Wall Street and inside the White House about what kinds of discussions tended to be the most illuminating and productive. So if someone, particularly someone junior, who was often closest to an issue, seemed to be holding back, I tried to draw out his or her view. What mattered to me was the merit of the argument, not the title of the person who made it.[6]

Next is *teaching* or the ability to communicate a simple, clear vision to the organization. Teaching requires a balance between the need to repeat a message over and over (great CEOs find themselves repeating core messages literally hundreds of times to myriad constituencies) and the need to adapt to the environment as business circumstances change. Executives with this skill include Jack Welch and Bill Gates.

Teaching tends to come easier for executives who are passionate. I love to see leaders who have a passion for the business and, as a result, love to come to work. Success often follows passion.

This final aspect of leadership assessment, *self-awareness*, requires a balance between self-confidence and humility. Self-confidence means that given a set of facts, an executive can draw on his or her knowledge, experience, and inputs from others to make a good decision. Humility is recognition that none of us has it all—we all have weak spots that we need to fortify. A self-aware executive understands his or her flaws and offsets those flaws with the talents of truly excellent people.

Self-awareness also implies a measure of emotional intelligence—an ability to engage others and the organization on an emotional level. This skill requires not only an ability to read individuals on a one-to-one basis but also an ability to judge the organizational culture and mood.

Incentives

While supporting its share of critics, economics has made a great contribution to our understanding of the link between incentives and behavior. Long-term investors must go beyond typical managerial platitudes and understand what *truly* motivates management. The proxy statement may be the least read, and most important, public filing.

Consider that many investors and pundits have nodded approval at the recent compensation trend away from employee stock options toward restricted stock. I don't necessarily share this enthusiasm, because the form of remuneration doesn't answer the basic question, "Are the incentives motivating the managerial behavior that long-term shareholders desire?"

Take employee stock options. A strong argument can be made that typical option programs do *not* provide employees with appropriate incentives. Specifically, in bull markets, all option holders stand to benefit, and in bear markets, all suffer, without any clear distinction between companies that deliver superior performance and those that don't. Throw in option repricing (heads I win, tails you lose) and muddled thinking about option accounting, and it's not hard to see why options never satisfied the incentive question.

Restricted stock also fails to answer the incentive question clearly. What is the basis for the *magnitude* of the stock grant? If grants are not clearly tied to economic performance, and grant recipients are not in a position to influence the stock price (the majority of employees), then how are stock grants acting as an appropriate incentive?

I believe that incentives—if they are truly to have an impact on day-to-day behavior—must link directly to a facet of the business that an employee can control. This means aligning incentives at all levels of the firm with the appropriate value drivers is central in getting the execution managers and owners demand.[7]

Managers often trumpet an "ownership culture" and seek to distribute equity widely throughout the organization. While employees are pleased to be shareholders, I suspect that most think about their stake using "mental accounting." They consider the stock in a mental account that is separate from their cash income, don't count on the stock for day-to-day budgeting, and don't consider it when they do their jobs.

Another critical judgment is whether managers are paid to deliver accounting or economic performance. In the cases where there is a large owner-manager, this potentially huge agency cost rarely arises. But for managers who are paid to deliver earnings per share (EPS) growth, or for those who perceive EPS growth to be the be-all and end-all (still too large a group), the risk of significant agency costs is immense. To be more concrete, you want managers who, when facing a choice between adding to accounting earnings or economic value, always opt for value.

Consider the following from Enron's in-house risk-management manual as the antithesis of this ideal:

> Reported earnings follow the principles of accounting. The results do not always create measures consistent with underlying economics. However, corporate management's performance is generally measured by accounting income, not underlying economics. Therefore, risk management strategies are directed to accounting, rather than economic, performance.[8]

Incentive is defined as what motivates effort. Long-term shareholders should look for proper incentives. And in reality, these are rare.

Capital Allocation

All roads in managerial evaluation lead to capital allocation. I define capital allocation as apportioning the firm's resources so as to generate long-term returns in excess of the cost of capital. As money managers know all too well, capital allocation is the name of the game.

How do you assess capital allocation skills? The first step is to carefully study past capital allocation choices. How and where has management invested the firm's capital? Have the investments earned sufficient returns? If so, why? If not, why not? Past capital allocation often provides a good indication of the business's capital appetite and often reveals management's focus and preferences.

Mergers and acquisitions (M&A) deserve special mention. Innumerable M&A studies come to the same conclusion: most acquisitions destroy value for the acquirer and those that create value add very little. This is not to say that M&A does not create value in the aggregate—of course, selling shareholders tend to do well. The problem is that acquirers often offer a control premium that exceeds the present value of the synergies.

Reversion to the mean is the microeconomic equivalent of the grim reaper: all high-return companies succumb to it sooner or later (great managers make it later). Significant M&A activity almost always suggests a company's returns are gravitating to the cost of capital.[9]

The second step in assessing capital allocation skills is interviewing managers to understand their capital allocation framework. How do they think about their investments? Do they have a realistic understanding of potential shifts in the industry? Do they understand competitive strategy?

Consider the observation of Warren Buffett, one of the great capital allocators in American business history:

[T]he heads of many companies are not skilled in capital allocation. Their inadequacy is not surprising. Most bosses rise to the top because they have excelled in an area such as marketing, production, engineering, administration or, sometimes, institutional politics.

Once they become CEOs, they face new responsibilities. They now must make capital allocation decisions, a critical job that they may have never tackled and that is not easily mastered. To stretch the point, it's as if the final step for a highly-talented musician was not to perform at Carnegie Hall but, instead, to be named Chairman of the Federal Reserve.

The lack of skill that many CEOs have at capital allocation is no small matter: After ten years on the job, a CEO whose company annually retains earnings equal to 10% of net worth will have been responsible for the deployment of more than 60% of all the capital at work in the business. CEOs who recognize their lack of capital-allocation skills (which not all do) will often try to compensate by turning to their staffs, management consultants, or investment bankers. Charlie and

I have frequently observed the consequences of such "help." On balance, we feel it is more likely to accentuate the capital-allocation problem than to solve it.

In the end, plenty of unintelligent capital allocation takes place in corporate America. (That's why you hear so much about "restructuring.")[10]

Finally, a word on people. Does management understand how to put the right people into the right jobs? Too often companies seek to promote executives with the "right stuff"—good communication skills, smarts, and success in a specific context—without full consideration of their actual work skills and experience. As a result, these companies misallocate human capital, with poor results for both the business and the executive.

The Bottom Line

Assessing management's leadership, incentives, and capital allocation discipline is essential for long-term shareholders. Despite a heightened focus on corporate governance, few boards are sufficiently proactive to appropriately address these areas. I've attempted to give some guidelines in thinking through some of the issues.

Part 2

Psychology of Investing

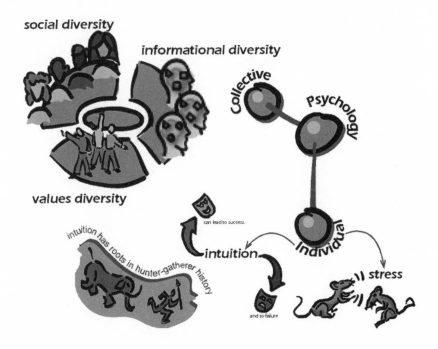

Cigar-chomping Puggy Pearson was a gambling legend. Born dirt poor and with only an eighth-grade education ("that's about equivalent to a third grade education today," he quipped), Pearson amassed an impressive record: he won the World Series of Poker in 1973, was once one of the top ten pool players in the world, and managed to take a golf pro for $7,000—on the links.

How did he do it? Puggy explained, "Ain't only three things to gambling: Knowin' the 60–40 end of a proposition, money management, and knowin' yourself." For good measure, he added, "Any donkey knows that."[1]

The first two of Pearson's prescriptions are in the realm of investment philosophy, last part's topic. But the third, "knowin' yourself," falls squarely in the psychological domain.

Psychology may be the most underappreciated, undertaught, and under-contemplated facet of investing. It is critical because it helps explain what errors you are likely to make under various circumstances, offers insight into how others will influence your decisions, and provides perspective on how you should behave. In most cases, a traditional business school education won't help you much in these crucial areas.

In the last few decades, behavioral finance has considerably narrowed the gap between finance theory and psychology. For example, Daniel Kahneman and Amos Tversky developed a theory that concretely demonstrates how humans operate suboptimally versus what standard economic theory suggests. But even today, behavioral finance falls short of providing investors a cohesive approach to markets. The goal of this section's essays is to provoke you to evaluate your decision-making process.

When people mention psychology, they are almost always referring to how individuals behave. But there's an important and often-overlooked distinction between *individual* and *collective* decisions. Both are relevant, but collective decision making is really the key when dealing with markets.

Make no mistake, improving individual decision making is valuable, as Pearson's admonishment to "know yourself" suggests. On that level, this section delves into topics like how stress affects decision making, the tricks people use to convince you to do something, and intuition's double-edged sword.

Why are collective decisions central to markets? The main reason is that individual errors often cancel out: if you and I are both overconfident but you say buy when I say sell, our independent mistakes may still result in an accurate, or efficient, price. In fact, diversity of opinion looks like one of the necessary conditions of a well-functioning market.

So for the most part, a true picture emerges from lots of investors erring independently. Since each individual is a small part of a greater whole, asking an individual to explain the whole is folly. Once you recognize that point, you'll realize the talking heads on television satisfy a human *need* for an expert, without providing the *value* of an expert.

So individual independence is good, but it doesn't always prevail. The reason is that humans—like many other animals—are inherently social. While being social has lots of pluses, it also has some minuses. Take, for example, imitation. Imitation is incredibly useful in life, especially when someone has valuable information that you don't have. But like other things in life, too much of a good thing is bad. Mindless imitation can lead to consequences from the inane (the pet rock fad) to the disastrous (market crash of 1987).

So when you're dealing in markets, it's not enough to have your own view, *you have to consider what other people think.* Neoclassical economics likes to treat humans as deductive processing machines; we can go from general premises to specific conclusions. The trouble is, in all but the simplest situations (think tic-tac-toe), we simply don't have the computational ability to operate deductively. Indeed, humans tend to be superb pattern recognizers—so good, in fact, that we see patterns where none exist. Toss out rational decision making, and things start to get complicated.

Investing is interactive, probabilistic, and noisy. As a result, successful decision making requires an investor to have a good grasp of psychology. Unfortunately, there's no one source with all of the answers, and improvement requires constant effort. But there's no way to avoid it. As Puggy Pearson once said, "Everything's mental in life."[2]

10

Good Morning, Let the Stress Begin
Linking Stress to Suboptimal Portfolio Management

It has become evident time and again that when events become too complex and move too rapidly as appears to be the case today, human beings become demonstrably less able to cope.

—Alan Greenspan,
"The Structure of the International Financial System"

Why Zebras Don't Get Ulcers

What would be tops on a zebra's list of things that cause stress? Well, a zebra certainly worries about physical stressors. A lion has just attacked you, you've succeeded in escaping, but the lion is still after you with lunch on its mind. Evolution has assured that zebras, like most animals including humans, respond very effectively to these types of emergencies.

Now draw up the list of things *you* find stressful. There probably isn't much overlap with the zebra's list. For the most part, the kinds of things we worry about are not physical, but mental—work deadlines, the performance of the stock you put in the portfolio last week, personal relationships. Humans deal largely with stressors that are psychological and social.

In his delightful book *Why Zebras Don't Get Ulcers*, renowned brain researcher and stress expert Robert Sapolsky highlights a crucial point: the body's physiological responses are well adapted for dealing with short-term physical threats. Those are the kinds of threats that we humans have faced for most of our existence. The problem is the *psychological* stress that we experience today triggers the same physiological responses. The source of our stress is different, but the reaction is the same. Psychological stress, if chronic, can lead to severe health and performance problems because it throws our bodies out of balance.[1]

What kinds of things do we do in response to stress? Sapolsky notes that our reactions are "generally short-sighted, inefficient, and penny-wise and dollar-foolish." The body mobilizes to deal with the immediate threat. This stress response is effective in a crisis but can be very costly if you experience *every day* as an emergency.[2]

Why Money Managers *Do* Get Ulcers

The research shows that stress stems from a loss of *predictability* and a loss of *control*, where the common element is novelty. I believe that secular trends in the economy and in the money management industry are contributing mightily to the sensation of less predictability and control.

The loss of predictability, for instance, reflects the accelerating rate of innovation in the global economy. For example, the average life of a company in the S&P 500 Index has gone from roughly twenty-five to thirty-five years in the 1950s to about ten to fifteen years today (see exhibit 10.1).[3]

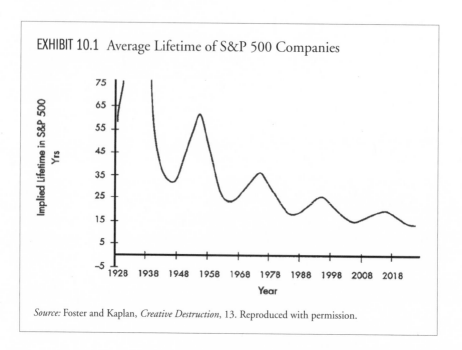

EXHIBIT 10.1 Average Lifetime of S&P 500 Companies

Source: Foster and Kaplan, *Creative Destruction*, 13. Reproduced with permission.

The spectacular rise and fall of companies in recent years certainly adds to the feeling that business is less predictable than ever before.

We also see the lack of predictability in the volatility data. While market-level volatility has been stable, firm-specific risk has been steadily rising since the 1970s. Although the volatility of a market portfolio has not changed much in the last few generations, money managers today have a higher risk than ever of being in the wrong stocks.[4]

The loss of control not only reflects actions *within* the portfolio but also evaluation *of* the portfolio by the owners. Shareholders and mutual fund rating companies judge money managers at least every ninety days, and in order to keep their assets, many money managers try to minimize tracking error versus their benchmark. Managing tracking error often requires mirroring the market and generally entails short-term trading.[5] In a sense, reducing tracking error is rational for money managers because there's no use worrying about how the portfolio will perform over the next three years if you're out of a job along the way. But closet indexing is not ideal for shareholders.

The concern about a flightier investor base is well founded. In the 1950s, the average holding period for a mutual fund was over fifteen years. By 2006 the holding period had shrunk to about four years.[6] Pension fund administrators, too, are becoming more active in hiring and firing fund managers. For example, in 2001 the state of Florida sacked Alliance Capital in part because of losses in Enron and despite Alliance's good long-term performance.[7]

I believe the perceived loss of predictability and control is causing many money managers chronic stress. And the predictable reaction to stress can lead to suboptimal portfolio-management decisions.

Shortening Horizons

What are the physical responses to stress? In effect, we get primed to take care of business in the here and now. Our blood pressure rises, our body mobilizes energy to the tissues that need it most, our short-term memory improves, and we set aside long-term projects like immune systems and reproduction. With a physical stressor, focusing on the short term versus the long term can be the difference between life and death. When the stress passes, we can return to a more balanced state. But *chronic* stress keeps us on high alert, suppressing our natural balance.

Of particular importance for money managers, stress encourages a short-term focus.[8] Recent research shows that people (like other animals) often prefer small, immediate rewards to larger rewards in the future. For example, people prefer one apple today over two apples tomorrow. But if the trade-off is far enough in the future—for example, one apple in a year versus two apples in a year and a day—people are prepared to wait for the higher reward. Seeking short-term gains at the expense of more attractive long-term rewards is suboptimal for long-term investors.[9]

How do we know that money managers are increasingly short-term oriented? We see it in the portfolio turnover data. Average portfolio turnover has surged in recent decades, going from roughly 20 percent in the 1950s to well nearly 100 percent today (see exhibit 10.2). In 2006 alone, one out of fourteen equity funds turned its portfolio over at an annual rate of 200 percent or more; three in ten funds in excess of a 100 percent rate; and only one in four turned less than 30 percent.[10]

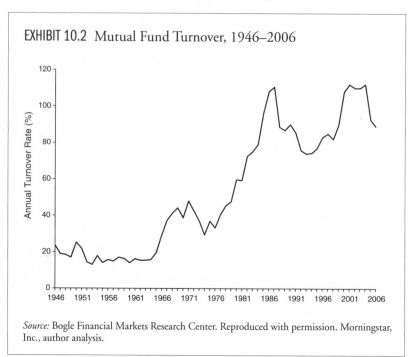

EXHIBIT 10.2 Mutual Fund Turnover, 1946–2006

Source: Bogle Financial Markets Research Center. Reproduced with permission. Morningstar, Inc., author analysis.

The turnover rise in the "passive" S&P 500 Index and lower commission costs suggest that a reasonable turnover level today is certainly higher than it was thirty or forty years ago. But most money managers are turning their portfolios too rapidly, resulting in substantial transaction and market impact costs, as well as an unnecessary tax burden. Short-termism is eating portfolio performance.

In the highly competitive money-management business, costs often play a prime role in separating the best- from the worst-performing funds. So we would expect to see a correlation between high turnover and low relative return. The data bear this out. In 1997, Morningstar did a comprehensive study of turnover and performance for U.S. equity funds. It showed that low-turnover funds outperformed high-turnover funds over various time horizons (see exhibit 10.3).[11] The study also suggested that turnover did enhance performance for riskier funds, a finding that the academic research also supports.[12]

When updated through year-end 2006, these data show a similar result. Analysis confirms that the second-lowest turnover group (20 to 50 percent) delivered the best returns over the past one-, three-, and five-year periods. Based on this analysis, we believe that the appropriate turnover for an active fund is somewhere in the 20 to 100 percent range. The low end, with an eighteen-month to five-year implied average holding period, appears appropriate for value funds and the upper end's twelve to eighteen months

EXHIBIT 10.3 Portfolio Turnover and Long-Term Performance

Turnover %	One-Year Annual Return %	Three-Year Annual Return %	Five-Year Annual Return %	Ten-Year Annual Return %
<20	27.0	23.9	17.2	12.9
20–50	23.1	21.9	16.6	12.5
50–100	21.8	21.8	17.0	12.6
>100	17.6	19.8	15.0	11.3

Note: Data through 6/30/97.
Source: Morningstar, Inc.

look reasonable for growth funds. These guidelines are subject to numerous caveats.[13]

Imitating Ulysses

Go to your doctor with the symptoms of stress, and you'll get a standard list of recommendations: seek support from social networks, exercise sufficiently, and make sure you have a healthy diet. How do you deal with the repercussions of stress in money management? The prescription is to work hard on maintaining an appropriate long-term focus.

Ulysses had the crew bind him to the mast of his ship to protect him from the call of the Sirens. Money managers, especially when feeling a loss of predictability and control, are drawn to short-term activity. Like Ulysses, money managers should take the steps necessary to focus on the long term if they are to optimize long-term fund performance. If the source of stress is largely psychological, so too is the means to cope with it.

11

All I Really Need to Know I Learned at a Tupperware Party
What Tupperware Parties Teach You About Investing and Life

Anybody familiar with the workings of a Tupperware party will recognize the use of various weapons of influence.

—Robert Cialdini, *Influence: The Psychology of Persuasion*

Tupperware . . . developed what I believe to be a corrupt system of psychological manipulation. But the practice . . . worked and had legs. Tupperware parties sold billions of dollars of merchandise for decades.

—Charlie Munger, in Whitney Tilson, "Charlie Munger Speaks—Part 2"

A Tip from Shining Shoes

Nearby my old office building, the window of a shoe store advertised the generous offer of a free shoe shine. I walked by this store dozens of times and thought nothing of it. One day, though, with my shoes looking a little scuffed and some time on my hands, I decided to avail myself of this small bounty.

After my shine, I offered the shoeshine man a tip. He refused. Free was free, he said. I climbed down from the chair feeling distinctly indebted. "How could this guy shine my shoes," I thought, "and expect *nothing?*"

So I did what I suspect most people who take the offer do—I looked around for something to buy. I had to even the score, somehow. Since I didn't need shoes, I found myself mindlessly perusing shoe trees, laces, and polish. Finally, I slinked out of the store empty-handed and uneasy. Even though I had managed to escape without pulling out my wallet, I was sure many others weren't so fortunate.

A topic that is fascinating in investing—and in life—is why humans act the way they do. A few months after my sweat-on-the-brow-inducing shine, I read Robert Cialdini's *Influence: The Psychology of Persuasion*, a book that provides many of the answers to this question.

Cialdini's work over the past three decades has concentrated on what induces a specific form of behavior change: compliance with a request. Cialdini argues that six tendencies of human behavior spur a positive response to a request.[1] All these tendencies are important to understand for life, and a few of them are particularly important for investors.

As I read Cialdini I realized that the shoe store was preying on an essential rule of human conduct—the code of reciprocity. If someone gives you something, you feel that you must give something in return. If you want to use this innate tendency to your advantage, you give something small and ask for something large in return. A two-dollar shoeshine for two-hundred-dollar wing tips is a good trade.

I take a brief look at each of the tendencies, discuss how party sellers use them, and highlight the three tendencies most important for investors.

You *Can* Fool Mother Nature

Here are the six tendencies—reciprocation, consistency, social validation, liking, authority, and scarcity—along with brief descriptions. While Cialdini does not strongly stress the point, I believe these tendencies are deeply rooted in evolutionary psychology. Each behavior likely contributed to the reproductive success of our forebears.

- *Reciprocation.* Research shows that there is no human society that does not feel the obligation to reciprocate.[2] Companies make ample use of this tendency, from charitable organizations sending free address labels to real estate firms offering free house appraisals.
- *Commitment and consistency.* Once we have made a decision, and especially if we've validated that decision through public affirmation, we're loath to change our view. Cialdini offers two deep-seated reasons for this. First, consistency allows us to stop thinking about the issue—it gives us a mental break. And

second, consistency allows us to avoid the consequence of reason—namely, that we have to change. The first allows us to avoid thinking; the second allows us to avoid acting.

- *Social validation.* One of the main ways we make decisions is by observing the decisions of others.[3] In a famous illustration of this point, psychologist Solomon Asch put a group of eight subjects in a room and showed them a series of slides with vertical lines of various lengths. He asked the group to identify which line on the right matched the length of the one on the left (see exhibit 11.1). The answer was obvious, but Asch instructed every member of the group, save one, to give the same, wrong answer.

The subjects, bright college students, were clearly confused, and one-third of them went with the majority view even though it was obviously incorrect. While extreme, Asch's experiment shows how we all rely to some degree on what others do.[4]

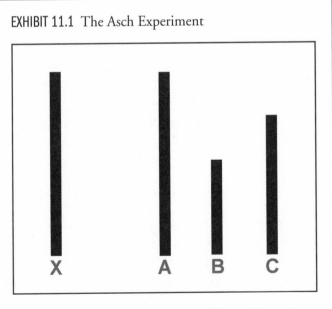

EXHIBIT 11.1 The Asch Experiment

Source: Illustration by author, based on Asch, "Effects of Group Pressure Upon the Modification and Distortion of Judgment."

- *Liking.* We all prefer to say yes to people we like. We tend to like people who are similar to us, who compliment us, cooperate with us, and who are attractive.

- *Authority.* In one of the most enlightening and unsettling human experiments ever, social psychologist Stanley Milgram (of "six degrees of separation" fame) had subjects come in and play the role of "teacher" for a "learner." The subjects asked the learner questions, and were told by a stern, lab-coated supervisor to administer progressively stronger electric shocks in return for incorrect answers. The learners would scream in pain and beg for mercy to avoid the increasingly painful shocks. Even though they were never forced to do anything, nor were they subject to reprisal, many of the subjects ended up doling out lethal shocks.

  The learners in this experiment were actors and the shocks fake, but Milgram's findings were real and chilling: People obey authority figures against their better judgment. Here again, the behavior generally makes sense—authorities often know more than others about their field—but such obedience can lead to inappropriate responses.[5]

- *Scarcity.* Evidence shows humans find items and information more attractive if they are either scarce or perceived to be scarce. Companies routinely leverage this tendency by offering products or services for a limited time only.

These tendencies are singularly powerful. But when they are invoked in combinations, they are even more potent and create what Charlie Munger calls lollapalooza effects (yes, lollapalooza is in the dictionary).

All I Really Need to Know . . .

The seemingly innocuous Tupperware party, which according to *The New York Times* is "back with a vengeance" in the affluent suburbs of New York City, captures such lollapalooza effects.[6]

The Tupperware party takes advantage of four of the six tendencies. This is big business: Tupperware generates annual sales of about $1 billion from its in-home "consultants."

First is reciprocity. Early in the party, there is a quiz game that allows participants to win play money that they can "spend" on giveaway items.

Each participant is also encouraged to share with the group the uses of products she has already purchased—evidence of commitment. Once the buying starts, each transaction demonstrates that others want the product, providing social validation.

But perhaps the single most important facet of the Tupperware formula is the tendency to say yes to people you like. The purchase request comes not from a stranger, but rather a friend. Indeed, the Tupperware handbook counsels the salespeople to use the "feel, felt, found" method, effectively encouraging similarity through empathy while still highlighting product features.

Combine these effects, and it's not hard to see why many people try to avoid going to Tupperware parties in the first place: they know that once they are there, they will buy something. For example, the *Times* reported that one attendee spent "far more than she had planned," no doubt swept up by the lollapalooza effect.

The Psychology of Investing

Investors need to pay a great deal of attention to what influences their behavior. Three of Cialdini's six tendencies are particularly relevant for investors: consistency and commitment, social validation, and scarcity.

Psychologists discovered that after bettors at a racetrack put down their money, they are more confident in the prospects of their horses winning than immediately before they placed their bets.[7] After making a decision, we feel both internal and external pressure to remain consistent to that view, even if subsequent evidence questions the validity of the initial decision.

So an investor who has taken a position in a particular stock, recommended it publicly, or encouraged colleagues to participate, will feel the need to stick with the call. Related to this tendency is the confirmation trap: postdecision openness to confirming data coupled with disavowal or denial of disconfirming data. One useful technique to mitigate consistency is to think about the world in ranges of values with associated probabilities instead of as a series of single points. Acknowledging multiple scenarios provides psychological shelter to change views when appropriate.

There is a large body of work about the role of social validation in investing. Investing is an inherently social activity, and investors periodically act in concert. Awareness of breakdowns in the diversity of opinion and respect for extreme valuations can help offset the deleterious impact of social validation.

Finally, scarcity has an important role in investing (and certainly plays a large role in the minds of corporate executives). Investors in particular seek informational scarcity. The challenge is to distinguish between what is truly scarce information and what is not. One means to do this is to reverse-engineer market expectations—in other words, figure out what the market already thinks.

12

All Systems Go
Emotion and Intuition in Decision Making

People base their judgments of an activity or a technology not only on what they *think* about it but also on what they *feel* about it. If they like an activity, they are moved toward judging the risks as low and the benefits as high; if they dislike it, they tend to judge the opposite—high risk and low benefit. Under this model, affect comes prior to, and directs, judgments of risk and benefit.

—Slovic, Finucane, Peters, and MacGregor,
"Risk as Analysis and Risk as Feelings"

We sometimes delude ourselves that we proceed in a rational manner and weight all of the pros and cons of various alternatives. But this is seldom the actual case. Quite often "I decided in favor of X" is no more than "I liked X." . . . We buy the cars we "like," choose the jobs and houses we find "attractive," and then justify these choices by various reasons.

—Robert B. Zajonc, "Feeling and Thinking:
Preferences Need No Inferences"

The strategies of human reason probably did not develop, in either evolution or any single individual, without the guiding force of the mechanisms of biological regulation, of which emotion and feeling are notable expressions. Moreover, even after reasoning strategies become established in the formative years, their effective deployment probably depends, to a considerable extent, on the continued ability to experience feelings.

—Antonio Damasio,
Descartes' Error: Emotion, Reason, and the Human Brain

Emotions and Decisions

Neuroscientist Antonio Damasio describes how early in his career he realized that traditional views on rationality had to be wrong. He saw a patient with all the faculties for rational behavior intact—attention, memory, logic. But brain damage had eviscerated the man's ability to experience feelings, and this had robbed him of the ability to make successful decisions day to day. Damasio saw the link: impaired feelings and flawed decisions go hand in hand.[1]

Damasio's later work confirmed his observation. In one experiment, he harnessed subjects to a skin-conductance-response machine and asked them to flip over cards from one of four decks; two of the decks generated gains (in play money) and the other two were losers. As the subjects turned cards, Damasio asked them what they thought was going on. After about ten turns, the subjects started showing physical reactions when they reached for a losing deck. About fifty cards into the experiment, the subjects articulated a hunch that two of the four decks were riskier. And it took another thirty cards for the subjects to explain why their hunch was right.[2]

This experiment provided two remarkable decision-making lessons. First, the unconscious knew what was going on before the conscious did. Second, even the subjects who never articulated what was going on had unconscious physical reactions that guided their decisions.

When Damasio replicated the experiment on brain-damaged patients, he saw none of the typical reactions. The skin-conductance response and verbal descriptions confirmed that the patients had no idea what was going on—either unconsciously or consciously.[3]

Two Follows One

In his Nobel Prize lecture, Daniel Kahneman describes two systems of decision making.[4] System 1, the experiential system, is "fast, automatic, effortless, associative, and difficult to control or modify." System 2 is analytical and "slower, serial, effortful, and deliberately controlled." Exhibit 12.1 compares these systems.

EXHIBIT 12.1 Comparison of the Experiential and Analytical Systems

Experiential System	Analytical System
1. Holistic	1. Analytic
2. Affective: Pleasure/pain oriented (what feels good)	2. Logical: Reason oriented (what is sensible)
3. Associationistic connections	3. Logical connections
4. Behavior mediated by "vibes" from past experiences	4. Behavior mediated by conscious appraisal of events
5. Encodes reality in concrete images, metaphors, and narratives	5. Encodes reality in abstract symbols, words, and numbers
6. More rapid processing: Oriented toward immediate action	6. Slower processing: Oriented toward delayed action
7. Slower to change: Changes with repetitive or intense experience	7. Changes more rapidly: Changes with speed of thought
8. More crudely differentiated: Broad generalization gradient; stereotypical thinking	8. More highly differentiated
9. More crudely integrated: Dissociative, emotional	9. More highly integrated: Cross-context processing
10. Experienced passively and preconsciously: We are seized by our emotions	10. Experienced actively and consciously: We are in control of our thoughts
11. Self-evidently valid: "Experiencing is believing"	11. Requires justification via logic and evidence

Source: Epstein, "Cognitive-Experiential Self-Theory." Adapted by permission.

In Kahneman's model, system 1 uses perception and intuition to generate *impressions* of objects. These impressions are involuntary, and an individual may not be able to verbalize them. He argues that system 2 is involved in all *judgments*, whether or not the individual is making decisions overtly. Intuition is a judgment that reflects an impression. Kahneman's work (along with that of his collaborator, Amos Tversky) shows how impressions can lead to judgments that are suboptimal according to classical economic theory.

So the evidence suggests that you can't separate emotions (system 1) from decisions (system 2). In fact, as Damasio showed, system 1 needs to operate normally in order for you to make good judgments. From an investor's standpoint, two questions become central: What influences our impressions, and how do these impressions shape perceptions of risk and reward?

The Affect Heuristic

One of the main shapers of our impressions is what psychiatrists call "affect."[5] Affect is the "goodness" or "badness" we feel based on a stimulus. For example, a word like "treasure" generates positive affect, while a word like "hate" is negative.

Affect operates in the realm of system 1 and hence is rapid and automatic. And affect often directs our impressions in a reasonable way: most things you feel good about *are* good. But affect, like other heuristics (or rules of thumb), has biases. Investors need to heed the biases that emanate from affect.

Affect is a noteworthy extension to prospect theory—which shows that investors are risk averse when facing gains and risk seeking when facing losses. Experiments show that affect—how we feel about a financial opportunity—can *amplify* the suboptimal biases that arise from prospect theory (see exhibit 12.2).

Let's get more concrete. The goal of an investor is to buy an asset below its expected value. Expected value is the weighted-average value for a distribution of possible outcomes. You calculate expected value by multiplying the payoff for a given outcome by the probability that the outcome will occur.

Research on affect demonstrates two central principles related to expected value. First, when the outcomes of an opportunity don't have strong affective meaning, we tend to overweight the probabilities. Second, when the outcome does have strong affective meaning, we tend to overweight the outcome.

Paul Slovic tested the first principle, probability dominance, with a simple experiment. He asked subjects to rate one of sixteen gambles by crossing various probabilities (7/36, 14/36, 21/36, and 28/36) and various payoffs ($3, $6, $9, and $12). He found that even though the subjects wanted to weight the probability and payoffs equally (and thought they had done so), the actual weighting for probability was five to sixteen times higher than for payoff.[6]

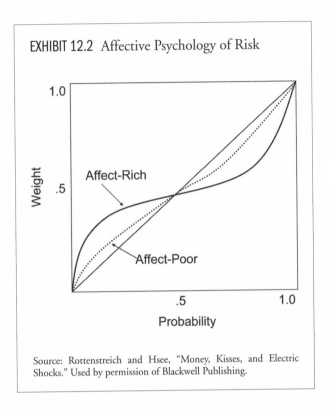

EXHIBIT 12.2 Affective Psychology of Risk

Source: Rottenstreich and Hsee, "Money, Kisses, and Electric Shocks." Used by permission of Blackwell Publishing.

The researchers posit that the subjects leaned on probabilities because there was no way for them to judge the attractiveness of the payoffs—the payoffs lacked affective meaning. Scientists see examples of this probability dominance in other fields as well, including studies of life-saving interventions.

In contrast, when payoffs are vivid—that is, when they carry substantial affective meaning—subjects tend to place too little emphasis on probabilities and too much emphasis on outcomes. For example, researchers find that lottery players tend to have the same feelings about playing the lottery whether the probability of winning is one-in-ten million or one-in-ten thousand because the payoff is so affective. This feature of the theory also offers an explanation as to why handicappers consistently overestimate the odds of a long shot at the racetrack and why people fear flying.

The bottom line is that when investors feel good about an investment idea, they deem the risks low and the returns high irrespective of more objective probabilities.[7] And when they dislike an idea, the inverse is true—risk is high and reward is low. Great investors aren't too swayed by affect. Perhaps this is a result of how their system 1s are wired.

When the Experiential Fails

Our experiential systems function well by and large. When do they fail?

Our experiential system can fail us when outside forces manipulate it. One example is advertising. Advertisers often try to appeal to your affect by providing you with a vivid perception. So whenever you face a probability-and-outcome decision, be very aware of how you feel (or are being made to feel) about the outcomes, and try not to let that feeling cloud the objective probabilities.

Experiential systems also fail in nonlinear or nonstationary systems. In nonlinear systems, cause and effect are not neatly linked. As a result, outcomes can be very counterintuitive. In nonstationary systems, the underlying statistical properties of the system change over time, which means that the past may not be a good predictor of the future. The stock market exhibits both nonlinearity and nonstationarity. Accordingly, investors must take a very methodical and self-aware approach to judging expected values.

Affect: Individual Versus the Collective

One should be careful about extrapolating the implications of affect to suggest that markets are inefficient. We all have our individual hard wiring and experiences; hence we are all going to feel affect in different ways. As markets are an aggregation of individual views, they can be efficient (or near efficient) provided that affect-driven biases are uncorrelated.

A dominant idea in Western society is that we should separate emotion and rationality. Advances in science show that such a separation is not only impossible but also undesirable. Yet successful investing requires a clear sense of probabilities and payoffs. Investors who are aware of affect are likely to make better decisions over time.

13

Guppy Love
The Role of Imitation in Markets

> When people are free to do as they please, they usually imitate each other.

> —Eric Hoffer, *The True Believer*

Guppy See, Guppy Do

At first blush, biologist Lee Dugatkin appears to be a guy with way too much time on his hands. The focus of his research is the apparently esoteric question of how female guppies select mates. As it turns out, female guppies have a genetic preference for bright-orange males. But when Dugatkin arranged for some females to observe other females choosing dull-colored males, the observing females also selected the dull males. Surprisingly, in many instances female observers overruled their instincts and chose instead to imitate other females.[1]

Why should anyone care about how female guppies pick their partners? The answer gets to the core of a lively debate about whether animal behavior is shaped solely by genetic factors or if culture plays a part. Dugatkin's work demonstrates that imitation—a form of cultural transmission—is clearly evident in the animal kingdom and plays a central role in species development.[2]

Certainly, too, imitation is a vital force with humans. Fashions, fads, and traditions are all the result of imitation. And since investing is inherently a social activity, there is every reason to believe that imitation plays a prime part in markets as well.

Most investors and businesspeople have fundamental philosophies that are supposed to define their behavior—much like genetics shape guppy mate selection. But we know that for money managers and guppies alike, imitation sometimes has a substantial influence on decision making. So is imitation good or bad for investors?

Feedback—Negative and Positive

Well-functioning financial markets, like other decentralized systems, rely on a healthy balance between negative and positive feedback. Negative feedback is a stabilizing factor, while positive feedback promotes change. Too much of either type of feedback can leave a system out of balance.[3]

The classic example of negative feedback in markets is arbitrage. Indeed, arbitrage is a central plank in the case for efficient markets. For example, if the price of a security diverges from its warranted value, arbitrageurs buy or sell the appropriate securities in order to close the price/value gap. Negative feedback resists change by pushing in the opposite direction.[4]

Positive feedback, on the other hand, reinforces an initial change in the same direction. The snowball effect, cascades, and amplification are all examples of positive feedback. While investors often view positive feedback as undesirable, especially when it leads to a runaway process, it isn't always bad.

When is positive feedback good? Well, it can help promote a smart decision. For instance, early investors in a promising new industry may encourage others to invest, sparking the industry's growth. Positive feedback can also get a system out of a bad situation. In nature, a "follow-your-neighbor" strategy may allow a flock of birds to elude a predator. Analogously, it can help investors flee a bad investment.[5]

Follow the Ant in Front of You

Imitation is one of the prime mechanisms for positive feedback. Momentum investing, for example, assumes that a stock that is rising will continue to rise. If enough investors follow a momentum strategy, the prophecy of a high price becomes self-fulfilling.

Most investors view pure imitation with some misgiving, belying their often-imitative actions. But imitation often has a rational basis. Consider the following cases, for example:[6]

> *Asymmetric information.* Imitation can be very valuable when other investors know more about a particular investment than you do. We all routinely use imitation in our day-to-day decision making, allowing us to leverage the specialized knowledge of others.
>
> *Agency costs.* Many money-management firms must make trade-offs between maximizing the performance of the investment portfolio (long-term absolute returns) and maximizing the value of the money-management business (by collecting assets and fees). Companies that choose to maximize the value of the business have an incentive to do what everybody else is doing. This imitation minimizes tracking error versus a benchmark.
>
> *Preference for conformity.* As Keynes said, "Worldly wisdom teaches that it is better for reputation to fail conventionally than to succeed unconventionally." Humans like being part of a crowd, as the group often bestows safety and reassurance.

So positive feedback is desirable under some circumstances and investor imitation can make sense. But positive feedback can also lead to excesses.

Financial economists describe herding as when a large group of investors make the same choice based on the observations of others, independent of their own knowledge.[7] In effect, herding occurs when positive feedback gets the upper hand. Given that markets need a balance between positive and negative feedback, such an imbalance leads to market inefficiency. This is in contrast to the classical view that investors trade solely on the basis of fundamental information.

Determining exactly how much positive feedback is too much may be an impossible task. Extensive scientific studies of innovation and idea diffusion reveal that there is typically a critical threshold, a tipping point, beyond which positive feedback takes over and the trend dominates the system. The relative frequency of bubbles and crashes strongly suggests that there are consistent discrepancies between price and value.[8]

The market is not the only decentralized system that exhibits suboptimal imitation. For example, there is the fascinating case of army ants. A group

EXHIBIT 13.1 A Circular Mill of Army Ants

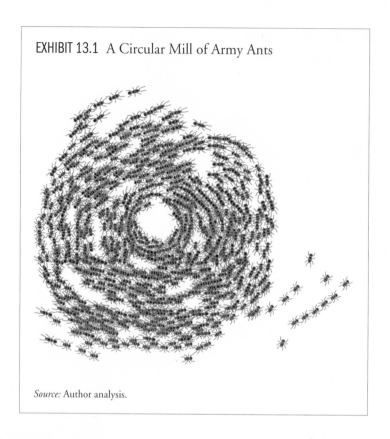

Source: Author analysis.

of worker ants, which are essentially blind, sometimes separates from the colony. Since no individual ant has any idea how to relocate the rest of the colony, all of the ants rely on a simple decision rule: follow the ant in front of you. If enough individuals follow the strategy (i.e., they reach the tipping point), they develop a circular mill, where ants follow each other around in circles until death. One such mill persisted for two days, had a 1,200-foot circumference, and a circuit time of two and a half hours (see exhibit 13.1). Eventually, a few workers created the requisite diversity by breaking away from the trail, and the mill dissipated.[9]

Of course, for the ants imitation is hard-wired genetic behavior, not cultural. Investors, in contrast, have the ability to think independently. However, Charles MacKay's famous words from over 150 years ago remind us that avoiding the imitation trap is an age-old problem: "Men, it has been well said, think in herds; it will be seen that they go mad in herds, while they recover their senses slowly, and one by one."[10]

Herding from the Grapevine

George Soros is the most prominent investor to explicitly cite the role of positive feedback in his investment philosophy. Soros's theory of reflexivity argues that there is positive feedback between a company's stock price and its fundamentals, and that this feedback can lead to booms and crashes. Soros's strategy was to take advantage of these trends by either buying or shorting stocks.

The finance literature also reveals a number of examples of herding among investors:

- *Mutual funds.* Russ Wermers found evidence of herding among mutual funds, especially in small-capitalization stocks and growth-oriented funds. He found that the stocks the herd buys outperformed the stocks the herd sells by 4 percent during the subsequent six months.[11]
- *Analysts.* Ivo Welch shows that a buy or sell recommendation of a sell-side analyst has a significantly positive influence on the recommendations of the next two analysts. Analysts often look to the left and to the right before they make their recommendations.[12]
- *Fat tails.* Econophysicists, using simple herding models, have replicated the fat-tail price distributions that we empirically observe in markets. These models provide a much more convincing picture of market reality than those that assume investor rationality.[13]

In markets, a symbiotic relationship between positive and negative feedback generally prevails. If all speculators destabilized prices, they would buy high and sell low, on average. The market would quickly eliminate such speculators. Further, arbitrage—speculation that stabilizes prices—unquestionably plays a prime role in markets. But the evidence shows that positive feedback can dominate prices, if only for a short time.[14] Imitation can cause investors to deviate from their stated fundamental investment approach and likely provides important clues into our understanding of risk. Next time you buy or sell a stock, think of the guppies.

14

Beware of Behavioral Finance
Misuse of Behavioral Finance Can Lead to Bad Thinking

Optimization by individual agents, often used to derive competitive equilibria, are unnecessary for an actual economy to approximately attain such equilibria. From the failure of humans to optimize in complex tasks, one need not conclude that the equilibria derived from the competitive model are descriptively irrelevant. We show that even in complex economic systems, such equilibria can be attained under a range of surprisingly weak assumptions about agent behavior.

—Antoni Bosch-Domènech and Shyam Sunder,
"Tracking the Invisible Hand"

How could economics not be behavioral? If it isn't behavioral, what the hell is it?

—Charlie Munger, *Psychology of Misjudgment*

Sorry Syllogism

Classical economic theory assumes that all people have the same preferences, perfect knowledge of all alternatives, and an understanding of the consequences of their decisions. In short, people behave rationally. No one really believes that this idyllic state exists. In fact, ample empirical research and anecdotal evidence show that people are not perfectly rational. This gap between theory and practice has spawned the relatively new field of behavioral finance.[1] Behavioral-finance researchers seek to bridge the gap between classical economics and psychology to explain how and why people, and markets, do what they do.

Behavioral finance raises a couple of important issues for investors. The first is whether it is possible to systematically exploit irrational market behavior when it occurs. Another issue is how to avoid making suboptimal decisions as an investor. The goal is to close the gap between how we actually make decisions and how we should make decisions.[2]

Behavioral finance is undoubtedly important for an intelligent investor. But poor thinking sometimes sneaks under the behavioral finance umbrella—even by the field's experts. Misusing behavioral-finance concepts can be as problematic as failing to acknowledge the role of psychology in investing.

What's the issue? We can express the essence of the poor-thinking problem with the following syllogism:

Humans are irrational
Markets are made up of humans
Markets are irrational

This logic stream appears to generate one of behavioral finance's main conclusions. Hersh Shefrin, a leading behavioral-finance researcher, writes: "Behavioral finance assumes that heuristic-driven bias and framing effects cause market prices to deviate from fundamental values."[3] The simple (and somewhat intuitive) message is that the aggregation of irrational individuals must lead to an irrational market.

To see the weakness in this case, we have to consider investor behavior on two levels: collective and individual. Collective behavior addresses the potentially irrational actions of groups. Individual behavior dwells on the fact that we all consistently fall into psychological traps, including overconfidence, anchoring and adjustment, improper framing, irrational commitment escalation, and the confirmation trap.

Here's my main point: *markets can still be rational when investors are individually irrational.*[4] Sufficient investor *diversity* is the essential feature in efficient price formation. Provided the decision rules of investors are diverse—even if they are suboptimal—errors tend to cancel out and markets arrive at appropriate prices. Similarly, if these decision rules lose diversity, markets become fragile and susceptible to inefficiency.

So the issue is not whether individuals are irrational (they are) but whether they are irrational in *the same way at the same time.* So while understanding individual behavioral pitfalls may improve your own decision making, appreciation of the dynamics of the collective is key to outperforming the market. Behavioral-finance enthusiasts often fail to distinguish between the individual and the collective.

Mug's Game?

Behavioral-finance experts understand the role of diversity in price formation. As Andrei Shleifer writes in his excellent book *Inefficient Markets: An Introduction to Behavioral Finance*:

> The efficient market hypothesis does not live or die by investor rationality. In many scenarios where some investors are not fully rational, markets are still predicted to be efficient. In one commonly discussed case, the irrational investors in the market trade randomly. When there are a large number of such investors, and when their trading strategies are uncorrelated, their trades are likely to cancel each other out. In such a market . . . prices are close to fundamental values.

The issue is that the field views this investor diversity as a special case, not the rule. Shleifer continues: "This argument relies crucially on the lack of correlation in strategies of the irrational investors, and, for that reason, is quite limited."[5]

Finally, Shleifer argues that arbitrage—another means to bring prices in line with value—is risky and hence restrained in the real world. To sum up the case: Since investors are irrational and their strategies are rarely uncorrelated, markets are inefficient. Further, arbitrage is insufficient to bring markets back to efficiency. So inefficiency is the rule, and efficiency is the exception. Active portfolio management in a fundamentally inefficient market is a mug's game.

We suspect that most professionals have the sense that efficiency is the rule and inefficiency is the exception. Indeed, we see diverse individuals generate efficient outcomes in many complex systems. In case after case, the collective outperforms the average individual. A full ecology of investors is generally sufficient to assure that there is no systematic way to beat the market. Diversity is the default assumption, and diversity breakdowns are the notable (and potentially profitable) exceptions.

Bombs Away

An unusual search procedure provides an interesting example of the power of the collective. On January 17, 1966, a B-52 bomber and a refueling airplane collided in midair while crossing the Spanish coastline. The bomber carried four nuclear bombs, three of which landed on shore and were immediately found. The fourth bomb, however, was lost in the Mediterranean, and its rapid recovery was essential to U.S. national security.

Assistant Secretary of Defense Jack Howard called a young naval officer, John Craven, to find the bomb. Craven assembled a diverse group of experts and asked them to place Las Vegas–style bets on where the bomb landed. Craven ran their approaches and scenarios through the bet-generated probabilities and found the bomb shortly thereafter. No individual expert had the answer, but the combination of all the experts did.[6]

Diversity is also a fundamental feature in the problem-solving capabilities of social insects such as ants and bees, including how they acquire food and find new nests. A number of simple illustrations prove the point for human systems as well, including Jack Treynor's famous jellybean jar experiment. Treynor fills a jar with jellybeans and asks his finance students to guess the total in the jar. He consistently finds that the average guess is both a good estimate of the actual number and better than almost all individual guesses.[7]

Given what we know about suboptimal human behavior, the critical question is whether investors are sufficiently diverse to generate efficiency. If you think across multiple dimensions, including information sources, investment approach (technical versus fundamental), investment style (value versus growth), and time horizon (short versus long term), you can see why diversity is generally sufficient for the stock market to function well.

Money See, Money Do

Just as diversity tends to yield an efficient market, a diversity breakdown makes markets susceptible to inefficiency. More directly, the collective level is the right place to search for investment opportunities within behavioral finance.[8]

Herding is a good example. Herding is when many investors make the same choice based on the observations of others, independent of their own knowledge.[9] Markets do tend to have phases when one sentiment becomes dominant. These diversity breakdowns are consistent with booms (everyone acts bullish) and busts (everyone acts bearish).

To the best of my knowledge, there is no one barometer that accurately and consistently measures investor diversity. An objective assessment of public (media) and private opinion probably gives some good clues. The key to successful contrarian investing is to focus on the folly of the many, not the few.

15

Raising Keynes
Long-Term Expectations, the El Farol Bar, and Kidding Yourself

> The social object of skilled investment should be to defeat the dark forces of time and ignorance which envelop our future. The actual, private object of the most skilled investment today is "to beat the gun", as Americans so well express it, to outwit the crowd, and to pass the bad, or depreciating, half-crown to the other fellow.
>
> —John Maynard Keynes, *The General Theory of Employment*

What Do You Expect?

Mark Twain defined a classic as something everyone wants to have read and nobody wants to read. One classic that deserves the attention of all investors is John Maynard Keynes's *General Theory of Employment*, and more specifically chapter 12, "The State of Long-Term Expectation." Expectations are embedded in all the decisions we make, especially investment decisions, but we rarely step back and consider how and why we form our expectations. Keynes guides this reflection.

Let's take a deeper look at two facets of expectations. The first distinguishes expectations built on deductive processes from those based on inductive processes: deductive processes move from general premises to specific conclusions; inductive processes go from specific facts to general principles.

Deductive rationality, a building block of neoclassical economics, breaks down in the real world because human logical reasoning can't handle situations that are too complicated (i.e., we have bounded rationality), and any action that deviates from rationality in human interactions ignites speculation about how others will behave.[1] In other words, if no one else is rational, it doesn't pay for you to be.

The second facet of expectations is that after an event occurs, humans tend to overestimate their pre-event knowledge of the outcome. This hindsight bias erodes the quality of the feedback we need to sharpen our analytical skills.

Speculation and Enterprise

Keynes divides the basis for expectations of future returns (he uses the word "yield") into two parts: facts that are more or less certain, and events that you can forecast with varying degrees of confidence. These latter, uncertain events include the magnitude and type of investment, as well as demand fluctuations. He calls the psychological expectations for these events the "state of long-term expectation."

In forming forecasts, most people fall back on what Keynes calls a "convention"—they start with the current situation and modify it when they have definite reasons to expect a change.[2] He notes that the magnitude of the modification reflects "the state of confidence," a combination of actual market observations and business psychology. But there is no way to anticipate what the state of confidence will be because it relies on feedback. Markets affect psychology and psychology affects markets.[3]

Keynes argues that conventions are inherently precarious for a host of reasons. The most famous of these is that many investors focus not on "enterprise"—forecasting long-term return on investments—but rather on "speculation"—forecasting the market's psychology. Here, he invokes his most famous metaphor: markets as a beauty contest. The goal is not to identify the person you find the most beautiful, or even the person you think the average beholder finds most beautiful. You soon find yourself trying to decipher what the average opinion thinks the average opinion is. Through the beauty contest metaphor, Keynes describes the limitations of a deductive approach to economics and markets.

This is not to say, though, that Keynes perceives markets to run solely on emotion. In his words,

> The state of long-term expectation is often steady, and, even when it is not, the
> other factors exert their compensating effects. We are merely reminding ourselves

that human decisions affecting the future, whether personal or political or economic, cannot depend on strict mathematical expectation, since the basis for making such calculations does not exist.[4]

In what is a timeless observation, Keynes adds, "Speculators may do no harm as bubbles on a steady stream of enterprise. But the position is serious when enterprise becomes the bubble on a whirlpool of speculation."[5]

Are today's institutional investors more focused on enterprise or speculation? This is a difficult question to answer, and markets certainly need an ecology of investors to remain robust. But the aggregate statistics on equity portfolio turnover give any intelligent investor pause. Annual turnover has shot from roughly 30 to 40 percent in the early 1970s to about 90 percent today. This means the average holding period for a stock is now just over one year. Not only is this turnover costly, it has also attended a disquieting decline in corporate governance.[6]

Visiting El Farol

Economist Brian Arthur has made important contributions to our understanding of inductive versus deductive approaches to problem solving (including stock picking). Arthur notes that you can solve only the easiest problems deductively: you can do it for tic-tac-toe but not for chess. Indeed, experiments show that humans aren't that good at deductive logic. But humans are superb at recognizing and matching patterns. We're inductive machines.

Arthur offers a model of inductive reasoning, effectively picking up where Lord Keynes left off. The model is based on the El Farol bar in Santa Fe, New Mexico, which played Irish music on Thursday nights.[7] Attending the El Farol when it isn't too crowded is fun; you can enjoy your pint and the band without being disturbed. But the bar is a turn-off when it is packed—the jostling crowd spills your beer and the loud voices drown out the band. So how do you decide whether or not you should go to El Farol?

To make the problem more concrete, Arthur suggests that the bar has a hundred-person capacity and that with sixty people or fewer it is not crowded and with more than sixty it is. So an individual expecting that less than sixty people will be there will go, while one expecting more than sixty will stay home. The decision to go is independent of past choices, the patrons don't talk or coordinate, and the only basis for making a decision is past attendance.

This problem has two notable features. First, the problem is too complicated for a deductive solution. As individuals can only look at past attendance, there are a large number of legitimate expectational models. The potential bar goers must use an inductive approach. Second, common expectations backfire. If all believe most will go, nobody will go. And if all believe nobody will go, all will go. Like Keynes's beauty contest, the issue is not just what you believe but rather what you believe others to believe.

Researchers have constructed models of the El Farol problem by assigning individuals evolving decision rules. With sufficient rule diversity and enough iterations, the mean attendance for the bar approximates the overcrowding threshold of sixty. One study assumed 20,000 iterations, which is about 385 years worth of Thursday nights.[8] This means that even inductive approaches may generate results similar to deductive methods, provided there is sufficient strategy diversity.

Keynes and Arthur both draw out a fundamental truth about markets: many investment choices are not, and cannot be, based on mathematical, deductive methods. I would add that, on the whole, a full ecology of strategies is sufficient to generate efficient markets. But when diversity is jeopardized—which it frequently is—markets depart significantly from the underlying fundamentals.

Kidding Yourself

A discussion of expectation is not complete without noting an odd human feature: once an event has passed, we tend to believe that we had better knowledge of the outcome *before* the fact than we really did. Known as hindsight bias, or more commonly the Monday-morning-quarterback syndrome, this research shows that people are not very good at recalling the way an uncertain situation appeared to them before finding out the results.[9]

Finance professor Hersh Shefrin illustrates the point by analyzing the comments of a former Orange County treasurer, Robert Citron.[10] In his annual report dated September 1993, Citron wrote, "We will have level if not lower interest rates through this decade. Certainly, there's nothing in the horizon that would indicate that we will have rising interest rates for a minimum of three years." In February 1994, the Federal Reserve Board raised rates. Citron's response: "The recent increase in rates was not a surprise to us; we expected it and were prepared for it." Now, there is a chance that Citron changed his view prior to the rate hike. But the much more plausible view is that he suffered from hindsight bias.

Hindsight bias stands in the way of quality feedback—understanding how and why we made a particular decision. One antidote to this bias is to keep notes of why you make decisions as you make them. Those notes become a valuable source of objective feedback and can help sharpen future decision making.

16

Right from the Gut
Investing with Naturalistic Decision Making

People who make decisions for a living are coming to realize that in complex or chaotic situations—a battlefield, a trading floor, or today's brutally competitive business environment—intuition usually beats rational analysis. And as science looks closer, it is coming to see that intuition is not a gift but a skill.

—Thomas A. Stewart, "How to Think with Your Gut"[1]

Guns and Better (Decisions)

As part of his Marine Corps training, retired lieutenant general Paul Van Riper learned classical decision making: frame the problem, formulate alternatives, and evaluate the options. Not surprisingly, he also taught the classical rational approach as the head of the Marine leadership and combat development program in the 1990s. But Van Riper realized that in combat simulations, the rational decision-making approach didn't work the way it was supposed to.

Van Riper turned to cognitive psychologist Gary Klein, who had studied how firefighters really make decisions in complex settings. Klein's research found that firefighters don't weigh options at all—they use the first satisfactory idea that comes along, and then look for the next one, and so on. Firefighters don't make decisions based on anything that resembles classical theory.

It occurred to Van Riper that the New York Mercantile Exchange trading pits had a lot in common with combat war rooms. So in 1995, he brought a group of Marines to New York and pitted them against the floor pros on a trading simulator. The traders trounced the Marines—to no one's shock.

But about a month later, the traders went to Quantico, Virginia to play war games against the Marines. The traders again trounced the Marines—to everyone's shock.[2]

The study of decision making has a long history. The classical model of decision making that Daniel Bernoulli launched over two hundred fifty years ago is still the prescriptive model of choice in much of economics.[3] But the model is not realistic. In the 1950s, economist Herb Simon fashioned an important case against the classical theory by noting that the theory's informational requirements vastly exceed human cognitive capacity. Human rationality is bounded. As a result, people don't make decisions based on optimal outcomes; they make choices based on what's good enough. Simon argued that people don't maximize; they "satisfice."

In recent years, a new approach, naturalistic decision making, has emerged to explain how experts make decisions in real-world contexts that are meaningful and familiar to them.[4] Evidence suggests that the key attributes and principles of naturalistic decision making apply to experienced investors. An understanding of naturalistic decision making may help investors better appreciate their own approach and has important implications for training.[5]

Chopping Down the Decision Tree

In a recent paper, Robert Olsen lists five conditions that are present in naturalistic tasks and relates them to investors:[6]

1. *Ill-structured and complex problems.* In these cases, no obvious best procedure exists to solve the problem. Determining a fair value for a security, for instance, is an ill-structured and complex task.

2. *Information is incomplete, ambiguous, and changing.* That stock picking relies on expectations about future financial performance means that there is no way to contemplate all information.

3. *Ill-defined, shifting, and competing goals.* Even though investing may seem to have clear-cut goals for the long term, goals can change significantly over shorter horizons. For example, a portfolio manager may take a defensive posture to preserve performance or a more aggressive stance to make up a performance shortfall.

4. *Stress because of time constraints, high stakes, or both.* Stress is clearly a feature of investing.

5. *Decisions may involve multiple participants.* This means that the decision maker may be working with various partners who may impose decision-making constraints.

How *do* naturalistic decision makers decide? Olsen identifies three primary behaviors. The first is an ability to rely heavily on mental imagery and simulation in order to assess a situation and possible alternatives.[7]

The second behavior is the ability to recognize problems based on pattern matching. Experts are able to connect a known pattern to a specific situation. Gary Klein and his colleagues studied the average move quality of chess masters and class B players under regulation (135 seconds per move) and blitz (6 seconds per move) conditions. They found that while the average move quality improved markedly for the class B players under regulation conditions, the quality of the moves under either set of conditions was relatively unchanged for the masters (see exhibit 16.1). Chess masters can

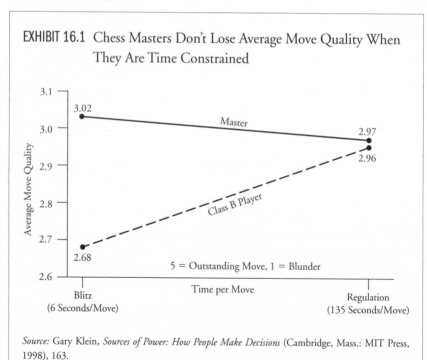

EXHIBIT 16.1 Chess Masters Don't Lose Average Move Quality When They Are Time Constrained

Source: Gary Klein, *Sources of Power: How People Make Decisions* (Cambridge, Mass.: MIT Press, 1998), 163.

glance at a board and quickly see a pattern, allowing them to make relatively good moves in a short time.[8]

The third behavior of naturalistic decision makers is that they reason through analogy. Experts have the ability to see similarities in situations that may appear dissimilar on the surface.

One intriguing facet of naturalistic decision making is how experts make decisions with very little conscious awareness. In one experiment, neuroscientist Antonio Damasio gave subjects four decks of cards, two rigged to produce gains (in play money) and two rigged to lose. He asked the subjects to flip cards, picking from any deck. Damasio hooked the subjects up to measure skin conductance responses (SCRs), the same measure as lie-detector tests, and asked periodically what they thought was going on in the game. By the time they'd turned roughly ten cards, the subjects started showing physical reactions when they reached for a losing deck. But they couldn't articulate their hunch that two of the four decks were riskier until they had turned over about four dozen cards. And only after they turned over an additional thirty cards could the participants explain why their hunch was right. Even those subjects who could never put their hunches into words had physical reactions.[9]

Researcher Ray Christian sheds some light on the possible role of the unconscious in decision making. He notes that what we perceive at any given moment—our conscious bandwidth—is an extremely small subset of the information stream flowing to the sense organs. Specifically, he estimates that the capacity of our sensory system is 11 *mega*bits per second while our conscious bandwidth is just 16 bits per second.[10]

Investing au Naturel

Olsen tested whether or not naturalistic decision making explains how real investors work. Since naturalistic decision theory relates to experts in a given domain, he studied investors who had earned the Chartered Financial Analyst (CFA®) designation. Of his 250-plus sample, over 90 percent had six or more years of investment experience and over 50 percent had been in the industry fifteen or more years. Olsen posed eight questions in order to understand their investment behavior.

Exhibit 16.2 shows the results. As Olsen summarizes, the response to the first question supports the idea that expert investors make heavy use of mental imagery. Over 90 percent of the respondents say that creating a story based on facts is important to their investment decisions.

The answers to questions two to four suggest that the decision process of the investment pros is context dependent. Investors change their approaches as the circumstances dictate.

EXHIBIT 16.2 Behavior Responses of CFA Charterholders

Question 1. The ability to construct a coherent and complete "story" with the facts of a situation is the most important task when making a decision or recommendation.

| Agree 93% | Disagree 7% |

Question 2. As a forecasting/recommendation task becomes more complex and difficult, I tend to rely more on judgment and less on formal, quantitative analysis.

Agree 64%   Disagree 36%

Question 3. Quantitative valuation models are less useful in analyzing securities of new or more volatile companies.

Agree 89%   Disagree 11%

Question 4. When a high level of outcome accuracy is difficult or costly to achieve, I tend to use procedures that are less costly even though they are less accurate.

Agree 80%   Disagree 20%

Question 5. I make decisions manageable by ignoring unlikely outcomes.

Agree 62%   Disagree 38%

Question 6. I make decisions manageable by ignoring outcome states that are not grossly different from others.

Agree 82%   Disagree 18%

Question 7. I make decisions manageable by associating outcomes with a probability range instead of a point estimate.

Agree 75%   Disagree 25%

Question 8. As I become more uncertain about my ability to predict outcomes, I give greater weight to negative information about alternatives.

Agree 86%   Disagree 14%

Source: Robert A. Olsen, "Professional Investors as Naturalistic Decision Makers: Evidence and Market Implications," *The Journal of Psychology and Financial Markets* 3, no. 3 (2002): Table 2, 163.

Responses to the final three questions are consistent with the idea that investors use "satisficing" behavior. Investors don't optimize in the classical sense; they ignore outcomes or collapse categories to make their decision process more tractable.

Olsen's study strongly suggests that expert investors are naturalistic decision makers. This conclusion is not too earth shattering for anyone who's watched a great investor up close. One important implication is that investor training might emphasize the equivalent to a flight simulator—simulations and scenario analysis complete with timely and clear feedback.

The Fine Print

Naturalistic decision making is clearly relevant for investors and the investment process. But in thinking about the importance of the theory, there are a few points worth bearing in mind.

To start, naturalistic decision making is most relevant in complex environments. When a problem is covered by rules or is simply complicated, classical frameworks are often very effective. Different decision-making approaches are relevant under different environmental circumstances.

A related point is that a collective of diverse individuals often solves complex problems better than the average individual. The stock market is a great example. Even "expert" investors struggle to beat the market over time. Successful experts seem to be those who can mentally represent a complex situation in their heads. Naturalistic decision making is not synonymous with beating the market.

This leads to the final point. The skill sets of the best naturalistic decision makers may not be transferable. The finest investors appear to combine innate ability (hardwiring) with hard work (diverse information input). While all investors can undoubtedly improve their decision making (even naturalistic decision making), we speculate that only a handful of investors have the combination of hardwiring and work ethic to consistently beat the market.

17

Weighted Watcher
What Did You Learn from the Last Survey?

The art of drawing conclusions from experiments and observations consists in evaluating probabilities and in estimating whether they are sufficiently great or numerous enough to constitute proofs. This kind of calculation is more complicated and more difficult than it is commonly thought to be.

—Antoine Lavoisier[1]

There are three kinds of lies: lies, damn lies, and statistics.

—Leonard H. Courtney[2]

I Do—Do You?

Not all bits of information are created equal. Saying "I do" wearing a tuxedo in front of clergy and congregation carries greater significance than replying "I do" when your host asks if you take milk with your coffee. An ability to properly weight information is very useful in life and especially important for investors.

An investment process requires gathering and analyzing information. Investors have historically emphasized either the gathering or the analyzing piece as their source of competitive advantage. But gaining an informational edge has become much more difficult in recent years as the direct result of technological advances and regulation.

For example, the ubiquity of networked personal computers has made information dissemination extremely rapid and nearly costless. Today, an online day trader has at her fingertips information and access that leading institutions could only dream about twenty-five years ago. And Regulation FD (fair disclosure) seeks to assure that *all* investors—from the largest fund manager to the smallest individual—receive material information at the same time.

Yet analysts have not given up their search for proprietary information. In recent years, we have seen a blossoming in the number of surveys and channel checks, as well as other less savory information-gathering attempts. While there is clearly nothing wrong with pursuing better information—and some firms do it very well—I question the investment value of much of today's "proprietary" research.

There are three sources of skepticism. The first is whether or not investors can properly weight information. The second is sampling problems, or the degree to which the sampling techniques analysts use actually reflect the underlying population. The final issue is whether or not today's proprietary research leads to superior investment performance.

Sifting Weights

In the mid-1990s, Bill Gates carried with him a list of Microsoft's business priorities. The Internet, which was starting to take off, was fifth or sixth on his list. But once Gates realized the significance of the Internet to Microsoft's future, he moved it to the top priority.[3] Gates substantially reweighted already-known information, and hence added a lot of value for shareholders. Likewise, how we weight information has a significant impact on how we view the world and how we value assets.

Our degree of belief in a particular hypothesis typically integrates two kinds of evidence: the *strength*, or extremeness, of the evidence and the *weight*, or predictive validity.[4] For instance, say you want to test the hypothesis that a coin is biased in favor of heads. The proportion of heads in the sample reflects the strength, while the sample size determines the weight.

Probability theory prescribes rules for how to combine strength and weight correctly. But substantial experimental data show that people do not follow the theory. Specifically, the strength of evidence tends to dominate the weight of evidence in people's minds.

This bias leads to a distinctive pattern of over- and underconfidence. When the strength of evidence is high and the weight is low—which accurately describes the outcome of many Wall Street-sponsored surveys—people tend to be overconfident. In contrast, when the strength is low and the evidence is high, people tend to be underconfident.

Exhibit 17.1 shows strength and weight combinations. When both are high, the conclusion is likely to be obvious. When both are low, the finding is unlikely to be relevant. In the two remaining boxes, however, we run the risk of misjudging the evidence.

The winner's curse is another concrete example of the risk of weighting information incorrectly.[5] The winner's curse says that in a competitive auction, the highest bidder will typically overpay for the asset. Hence the bidder "wins" the auction but is "cursed" by the overpayment. When appraising an asset's worth, investors often dwell on the average value that various bidders are likely to pay. But the only value that ultimately matters is what the highest bidder is willing to pay.[6]

Information weighting underscores that not all information is of equal value and relevance. Investors must be constantly diligent to avoid pitfalls related to improper information weighting.

EXHIBIT 17.1 Strength and Weight of Hypothesis Test

		Strength (Extremeness)	
		Low	High
Weight (Predictive Validity)	Low	Not yet relevant	Overconfidence
	High	Underconfidence	Obvious

Source: Dale Griffin and Amos Tversky, "The Weighing of Evidence and the Determinants of Confidence," and author analysis.

Misleading by Sample

Understanding what's going on—what value-added resellers are saying, how employees feel about their company, or the purchase intentions of chief information officers (CIOs)—can be very useful to an investor. But getting an accurate view of the group is often not easy.

Statistics provide some guidelines for how large a population sample you need to create a reasonably accurate picture of the group. But in many cases, the underlying population is normally distributed. An appropriate sample of the height of adult women, for example, would provide a good sense of the average and distribution of female heights.

Many populations are not normally distributed, however, and here is where some problems arise. For instance, CIO surveys of expected technology spending often target Fortune 1000 companies. Assuming that technology spending as a percentage of sales is randomly distributed, which CIOs are included in the survey can make a huge difference to the outcome.

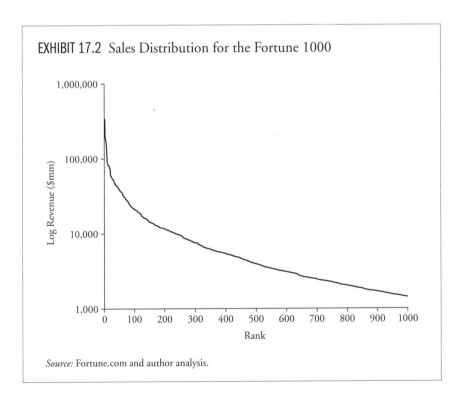

EXHIBIT 17.2 Sales Distribution for the Fortune 1000

Source: Fortune.com and author analysis.

To illustrate, the top 10 percent of the companies generate over 50 percent of Fortune 1000 aggregate sales, while the bottom 10 percent produce less than 2 percent. Weighting the responses of all CIOs equally could distort the underlying picture meaningfully unless the sample is properly stratified. Exhibit 17.2 shows the distribution of sales for the Fortune 1000.

The overconfidence that comes from strong evidence, yet weak predictive validity, seems very prominent in today's markets. Investors appear satisfied using two or three data points to guide the next trade. This is a very difficult way to make a living.[7] This leads to my final point.

Tell Me Something the Market Doesn't Know

The most basic test of the value of survey-based research is whether or not it leads to superior stock selection. The answer is ambiguous at best, in our view.

The first reason relates to how quickly the market assimilates new information.[8] The evidence shows that the market does adjust to new information rapidly. If so, then generating excess returns from that data is unlikely. Gaining an informational edge is difficult: Sell-side-sponsored surveys and channel checks must be disseminated uniformly, of course, and incremental information that a large buy-side firm encounters is often reflected in share prices in short order. Information about what is going on now, or what is likely to happen in the near future, is most likely to be efficiently priced into stocks. In contrast, some evidence suggests that the market is short sighted with regard to long-term information.[9]

The second issue is that there is a substantial difference between understanding the fundamentals (or changes in fundamentals) of an industry or company and a grasp of the expectations built into the current stock price.[10] Prices reflect collective expectations and generally incorporate more information than any one individual can claim. So the central question is whether or not information that is new to you is also new to the market.

Finally, at risk of exposing my own overconfidence, I tested the correlation between one well-known CIO survey and excess returns in the stock market (see exhibit 17.3).[11] The evidence in favor of a link between the two is not persuasive.

Some investors don't use results for assessing the sector directly surveyed but rather look for the derivative call—which other industries are affected

EXHIBIT 17.3 Correlation Between CIO Survey Data and Stock Price Performance

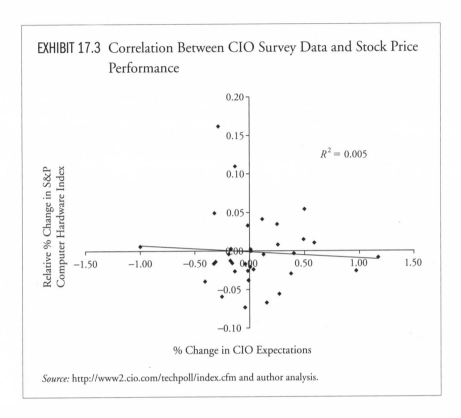

$R^2 = 0.005$

Relative % Change in S&P Computer Hardware Index

% Change in CIO Expectations

Source: http://www2.cio.com/techpoll/index.cfm and author analysis.

by perceived trends. This analysis can run into the problem of contingent probability. Say that you judge the probability of a company's orders being below expectations at 70 percent based on some new survey results. And say that there's a 70 percent chance that a specific supplier will suffer as well. The chance that the supplier misses its number is less than 50 percent $(0.70 \times 0.70 = 0.49)$.

Researchers have shown that people tend to overestimate the likelihood of two events occurring. This error is called the conjunction fallacy and occurs because we tend to lump thoughts into categories. Investors working off derivative calls must be very alert to avoid the conjunction fallacy.[12]

Seeking new information is a worthy goal for an investor.[13] My fear is that much of what passes as incremental information adds little or no value, because investors don't properly weight information, rely on unsound samples, and fail to recognize what the market already knows. In contrast, I find that thoughtful discussions about a firm's or an industry's medium- to long-term competitive outlook are extremely rare.

Part 3

Innovation and Competitive Strategy

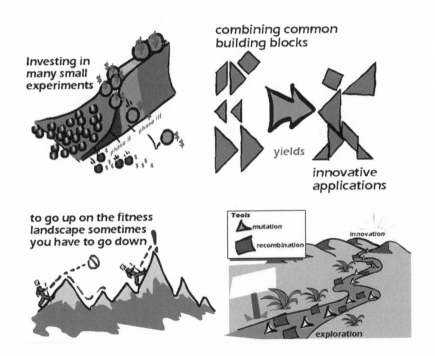

Investing in many small experiments

combining common building blocks

yields

innovative applications

to go up on the fitness landscape sometimes you have to go down

Tools

mutation

recombination

Innovation

exploration

Just to give you some sense of how much change we've seen in the past hundred years or so, take a gander at the first list of industrial stocks Charles Dow assembled in May 1896:

American Cotton Oil	Laclede Gas
American Tobacco	North American
Chicago Gas	Tennessee Coal & Iron
Distilling and Cattle Feeding	U.S. Leather
General Electric	U.S. Rubber

The only company that's still around is General Electric, and today it's a lot more general than electric. These were the blue chip companies of their day and reflected the commodity-based economy in which they competed. It's hard to imagine that Distilling and Cattle Feeding and American Cotton Oil were hot stuff, but future generations might get similar chuckles from Microsoft and Merck.

Do the changes of the past century give us any inkling about the next century? Well, we know a couple of things for sure. First, any predictions about the distant future are likely to be wildly off the mark. And second, the only thing we can pretty much count on going forward is *innovation*. How to think about and cope with innovation is the theme of this section.

Investors need to understand innovation because it's the primary mechanism shaping which companies will win and lose. But here's the problem: Even though most investors acknowledge that tomorrow's successful companies will be very different from today's leaders, the changes driving the overhaul are generally small and incremental. So unless you think carefully about innovation's *cumulative* effects, the small changes will escape your detection and you'll end up with yesterday's favorites.

One of this section's main ideas is that innovation is inevitable. Innovation is the result of recombining existing idea building blocks. So the more ideas that exist and the quicker we can manipulate them, the more rapidly we can come up with useful solutions—innovations. Indeed, there's a good case for an *accelerating* pace of innovation. Naturally, innovation implies winners and losers. Evidence shows that today's winners are likely targets for competition and that once companies go from good to bad, they rarely recover.

Another key principle is that humans are terrible at dealing with change. As investors, we tend to extrapolate. The expectations embedded in valuations frequently assume more of the same: good companies will continue to thrive and poor performers will remain in the doghouse. Corporate executives, too, settle into comfortable routines, sowing the seeds for future competitive failure.

A final theme is how to deal with change. When new industries emerge, sorting good from bad strategies is nearly impossible. So the pattern we often see is that the industry tries many different strategies and lets the marketplace dictate which ones are good (there's a fascinating parallel here with brain development). The result is a set of attractive strategies, but at the significant cost of many failures. Rather than view these failures as undesirable, we might consider them as a vital part of business-model search.

A firm grasp of innovation's underlying principles may not help you anticipate what stocks your grandchildren will hold, but it will aid immensely in your ability to anticipate expectations changes for your portfolio.

18

The Wright Stuff
Why Innovation Is Inevitable

All innovations represent some break from the past—the light-bulb replaced the gas lamp, the automobile replaced the horse and cart, the steamship replaced the sailing ship. By the same token, however, all innovations are built from pieces of the past—Edison's system drew its organizing principles from the gas industry, the early automobiles were built by cart makers, and the first steamships added steam engines to existing sailing ships.

—Andrew Hargadon, *How Breakthroughs Happen*

We must see to it that our industry shall be able to produce annually up to 50,000,000 tons of pig iron, up to 60,000,000 tons of steel, up to 500,000,000 tons of coal, and up to 60,000,000 tons of oil. Only when we succeed in doing that can we be sure that our Motherland will be insured against all contingencies.

—Josef Stalin, Speech, 1946

The empires of the future are the empires of the mind.

—Winston Churchill, Speech at Harvard University, 1943

Take Off with Recombination

On December 17, 1903, Orville Wright made history when he controlled his engine-powered plane for a sustained flight, covering 120 feet in twelve seconds (see exhibit 18.1). With that, the Wright brothers launched multiple industries and forever altered the nature of long-distance travel.

How did the Wright brothers achieve their world-changing feat? They neither relied on divine inspiration nor started with a clean slate. You could best describe the first plane as a recombination of known ideas and technologies.[1] As management professor Andrew Hargadon says, all innovations represent some break from the past, built from pieces of the past. The Wrights's genius was the insight that combining a light gasoline engine, some cables, a propeller, and Bernoulli's principle would result in a flying contraption.

Investors need to appreciate the innovation process for a couple of reasons. First, our overall level of material well-being relies heavily on innovation. Second, innovation lies at the root of creative destruction—the process by which new technologies and businesses supersede others. More rapid innovation means more success and failure for companies.

EXHIBIT 18.1 The Wright Brothers First Flight *Source:* Corbis Corporation.

How Does Wealth Happen?

Economist Paul Romer often starts with a very simple question, How is it that we are wealthier today than we were 100 or 1,000 years ago? After all, the underlying quantity of the world's raw materials—in the extreme, the earth's total physical mass—hasn't changed, and we have to divide this mass among a much larger human population. Yet worldwide per capita GDP is roughly thirty times what it was a millennium ago, with much of the increase occurring in the past 150 years (see exhibit 18.2).[2]

Romer's rather straightforward explanation is that we have progressively learned how to rearrange raw materials to make them more and more valuable. Whereas control over physical resources was the primary source of wealth one hundred years ago (in 1896, ten of the twelve companies in the Dow were in commodity businesses), today the ideas and formulas to manipulate raw materials form the engine of wealth creation.

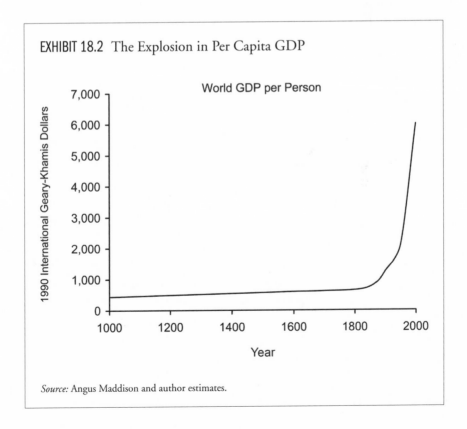

EXHIBIT 18.2 The Explosion in Per Capita GDP

Source: Angus Maddison and author estimates.

As Churchill correctly noted sixty years ago, the empires of the future are empires of the mind.[3]

To make his point more concrete, Romer distinguishes between two parts of the value-creation process: the discovery of new instructions, ideas, or formulas and the carrying out of those instructions. New instructions are of no value unless someone can effectively execute them.

Romer suggests that a contrast between U.S. Steel in 1900 and Merck in 2000 represents the shift in our economy at large. Had you studied U.S. Steel a century ago, you would have seen many employees following instructions—transporting ore, feeding furnaces, shaping steel—and only a handful working on identifying new instructions. The evolution of instructions was important, of course; it was just much less visible.

Take a tour of a pharmaceutical company like Merck today, and the emphasis is flipped. Most employees are trying to find new instructions. No doubt there are workers carrying out instructions, but they are a small part of the picture. You can use these terms to recast the ongoing debate about job outsourcing: Is it all right to outsource the jobs that execute instructions provided you encourage opportunities for those who create instructions?

That instructions to shape the world are central to wealth creation (an element that, ironically, classical economic growth models consider exogenous) comes with some important implications.

The first is the difference between what economists call rival and non-rival goods. With a rival good, one individual's consumption reduces the quantity available to others. A car, a pen, and a shirt are examples. In contrast, many people can use a nonrival good—a set of instructions—at once. Software is the prototype. A company can distribute software widely. And since the additional use of this knowledge does not rely on scarce resources, wider sharing may lead to more growth.[4]

A second implication is that since innovation is about recombining the building blocks of ideas, the more building blocks that exist, the more opportunities there are to solve problems. A simple mathematical example illustrates this principle. Say you had four building blocks to create potential solutions. The number of possible combinations is $4 \times 3 \times 2 \times 1$, or 24. Now increase the number of building blocks to six. The potential combinations—$6 \times 5 \times 4 \times 3 \times 2 \times 1$, or 720—is thirty times larger. As Romer likes to point out, you can sequence twenty steps in roughly 10^{19} ways, a number larger than the total number of seconds that have elapsed since the Big Bang created the universe.

This leads to the final implication: more idea building blocks lead to more innovation, which ultimately leads to faster aggregate growth. For companies that largely rely on physical resources, the costs associated with scarcity lead to diseconomies of scale and hence limit size and growth. Companies that primarily create knowledge don't face the same barriers (although they may face other challenges).

We can see how this theme of size begetting growth plays out on a national level. The per capita GDP growth of the United States (which we measure in roughly forty-year increments) has actually been *accelerating* over the past two hundred years in spite of the economy's increasing size (see exhibit 18.3). In a world of ideas, size per se may not be a governor of growth. In fact, the opposite may be true.

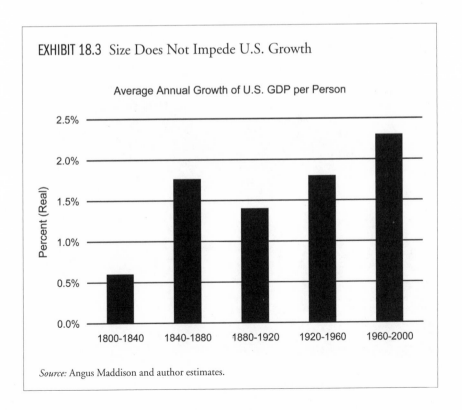

EXHIBIT 18.3 Size Does Not Impede U.S. Growth

Average Annual Growth of U.S. GDP per Person

Source: Angus Maddison and author estimates.

Sic Itur ad Astra (This Is the Way to the Stars)

We should expect three interrelated drivers—scientific advances, information storage capacity, and gains in computing power driven by Moore's Law[5]—to continue to spur innovation at an accelerating rate. Here I focus on one aspect of innovation: changes in information transmission.

In his provocative book *As the Future Catches You*, Juan Enriquez traces the evolution of human symbolic communication.[6] Twenty or thirty thousand years ago, Paleolithic people painted on cave walls (see exhibit 18.4). Scientists believe these drawings communicated rituals related to hunting. These paintings are beautiful, but since they can't be reproduced or moved, they have limited communication value.

Communication technology improved when Mesopotamian and Egyptian civilizations introduced written alphabets using cuneiform letters and hieroglyphics about 5,000 years ago (see exhibit 18.5). This period also saw some of the first symbols for mathematical expression, based on

EXHIBIT 18.4 Cave Painting *Source*: Corbis Corporation.

physical tokens. These crude alphabets were a large step in the right direction but remained cumbersome. Typically, only the elite in these societies were literate.

The Chinese developed characters that allowed for greater standardization (see exhibit 18.6). A simpler form of symbolic communication, this alphabet allowed the Chinese to print books using wood blocks roughly 500 years before Gutenberg invented the printing press in Europe.

The Greeks simplified many sounds into just a few letters, which serve as the basis for the twenty-six-letter Roman alphabet used in many western languages today. We can combine these letters to represent almost any concept. This alphabet helped contribute to a sharp rise in literacy and improved the world's standard of living.

But shortly before World War II, another language came to prominence—the language of 1s and 0s. Binary or digital language allows us to encode almost any information possible—from words, to music, to the map of the human genome (see exhibit 18.7).

Because digital language is simple, we can code, transmit, and decode it very quickly.[7] It also maintains remarkable fidelity and is easy to store.

EXHIBIT 18.5 Hieroglyphics—Syllabic Signs *Source*: Corbis Corporation.

EXHIBIT 18.6 "Consilient Observer" Written in Chinese

探求融会贯通的观察者

Source: Jean Yu.

EXHIBIT 18.7 "Consilient Observer" Written in Binary Code

0100001101101111
0110111001110011
0110100101101100
0110100101100101
0110111001110100
0010000001001111
0110001001110011
0110010101110010
0111011001100101
01110010

Source: http://nickciske.com/tools/binary.php.

EXHIBIT 18.8 Worldwide Storage of Original Information

Storage Medium	2002 Terabytes Upper Estimate	1999–2000 Terabytes Upper Estimate	% Change Upper Estimates
Paper	1,634	1,200	36%
Film	420,254	431,690	–3%
Magnetic	4,999,230	2,779,760	80%
Optical	103	81	28%
TOTAL	5,421,221	3,212,731	69%

Source: Lyman and Varian, "How Much Information? 2003." Reproduced with permission.

Exhibit 18.8 shows the change in information production from 1999 to 2002. Note the large increases in magnetic and optical storage mediums.

What does all of this mean for innovation? Because of the flexibility of digital language, we can now identify and manipulate building blocks like never before. Combine this with the growing inventory of building blocks, and the conclusion is that the rate of innovation is likely to accelerate. Changes in healthcare, for example, will likely be sweeping as scientists combine digitization, biological knowledge (the map of the genome), and increased computing power.

Creative Destruction—Here to Stay

Twenty-first-century Wright Brothers have unprecedented access to and ability to find combinatorial solutions. And wealth in the future is likely to follow those who create the useful ideas instead of those who execute those ideas.

19

Pruned for Performance
What Brain Development Teaches Us
About Innovation

I think that's exactly what you see going on here. Every
experiment [on the Internet] is getting tried. Many of them
are going to succeed, and many of them are going to fail.

—Jeff Bezos, Internet summit, 1999

Too Clever by Half

Whenever I start to feel smart, I take a good look at a three-year-old child.
That child is learning at a staggering pace. Research shows that preliterate children learn a new word every two hours they are awake on their way to knowing approximately 45,000 words by high school graduation.[1] Young children
have a remarkable ability to learn what is useful given their environment.

Adults, on the other hand, have a more difficult time absorbing so much
new information. Learning a second language, for instance, is much more
challenging for a middle-aged adult than for a young child. Why? The
answer is not only interesting from the standpoint of child development
but also provides a useful way to think about the process of innovation in
the business world.

From a child's birth to the age of three, there is a huge increase in the
number of synapses—connections between neurons—in the brain. In fact,
a toddler has roughly 1 quadrillion synaptic connections, twice as many as
an adult. Children have brains that are more active, more connected, and
more flexible than those of grownups.[2]

But following this synaptic proliferation is a significant *pruning* process. Through experience, useful synaptic connections are strengthened,
and those that aren't used get pruned (known as a Hebbian process after

psychologist Donald Hebbs).[3] Estimates suggest that young children lose approximately 20 billion synaptic connections each day.[4] This process fine-tunes the brain to survive in its particular environment. By the time we are adults, synaptic selection has shaped our brains to succeed.

This process of synaptic overproduction and pruning may not seem remarkable, except when you consider that it's an incredibly expensive tactic in terms of neural components and energy cost. Why has evolution allowed this wasteful process to persist? Nature is pretty smart. Models of neural networks show that the overproduction/pruning approach is very flexible and more reliable at preserving information than a feed-forward network. Starting with lots of alternatives and winnowing down to the most useful ones proves to be a robust process, even though it appears quite inefficient.[5]

Why should investors and businesspeople care about neural development? Neural overproduction and subsequent pruning appears to parallel closely what happens when a new industry emerges. An understanding of this process provides investors with three benefits. First, it is a model of innovation that is both theoretically sound and that researchers have tested empirically. Second, the process provides investors with a basis for understanding manias or bubbles. Finally, it shows that the innovation process often leads to investment opportunity.

The Dynamics of Innovation

In his thoughtful book *Mastering the Dynamics of Innovation*, James Utterback suggests three phases in industry innovation. The first is what he calls the fluid phase, a period in which there is a great deal of experimentation. This mirrors the upswing in synaptic connections. The transitional phase comes next, where evolutionary forces select the dominant product design. This phase is similar to the pruning process. The final phase is the specific phase, where changes in product or process are modest. That's what most of us adults face.

These phases suggest a consistent pattern of a sharp upswing in the number of companies in an industry when it is in the early stages followed by a sharp downswing as the pruning process takes hold. The process appears very wasteful when we see how many alternatives it dismisses. But ultimately the interplay between technical capabilities and market choices selects a product design that best suits the environment.

This pattern has played out over and over in the business world.[6] Take two giants in the annals of American industry—the automobile and television (see exhibit 19.1). In both cases, investors allocated capital liberally in the early phases as each industry's growth potential was significant but uncertain. But both industries saw steep declines in the number of competing firms over time, especially once the industry gravitated toward a dominant design.

The more recent history of the disk drive and personal computer industries shows the same pattern (see exhibit 19.2), although the pruning process occurs over a much shorter period. What took thirty years in the auto industry a century ago took fifteen years for the disk drive industry and more like a decade for the PC manufacturers.

The Internet, too, went through a similar process at the turn of the twenty-first century (see exhibit 19.3). Although the Internet is not an industry per se, there was a period of rampant experimentation through the late 1990s. The pruning process came forcefully in 2001; according to Webmergers.com, 544 Internet companies were shut down in 2001,

EXHIBIT 19.1 The Decline of Firms

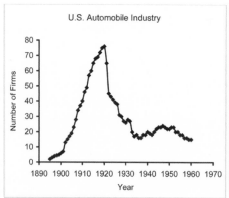

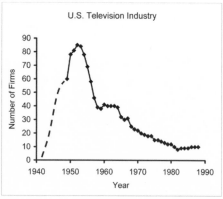

Source: Utterback, *Mastering the Dynamics of Innovation*, 35 and 38, and author estimates. Used by permission.

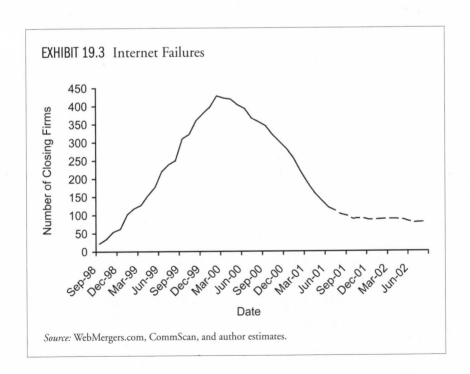

EXHIBIT 19.2 More Declines: Disk Drives and Computers

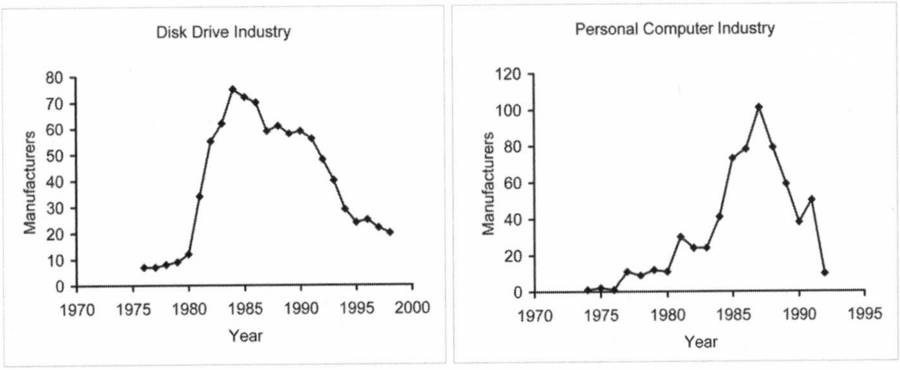

Source: DISK/TREND reports, *Management Science*, and author estimates.

EXHIBIT 19.3 Internet Failures

Source: WebMergers.com, CommScan, and author estimates.

up from 223 in 2000. Through the first half of 2002, shutdowns dropped almost 75 percent from the previous year's total.[7] While the excesses of the Internet and telecom booms in the late 1990s carried into the twenty-first century, this boom-and-bust pattern is by no means unique. I expect to see the same process unfold in the future.

As we transition from infants to adults, we trade vast mental flexibility for capabilities tailored to our environment. Skill and competence improve even as the number of synaptic connections declines. What occurs in the business world is comparable. An industry continues to grow even as the number of competitors shrinks as forces select a dominant design, process, or both (see exhibit 19.4).

Pundits often deride the boom-and-bust phenomenon as wasteful and speculative even though it provides the necessary platform for future growth. Further, over the 3 billion years of life on earth, nature has repeatedly settled on this process. In fact, paleontologist David Raup draws a direct analogy between the stock market and the fossil record.[8]

Investors: Use the Brain

Now that the picture has been filled out a little more, let's return to investor benefits. The first is a basic appreciation for the existence of the

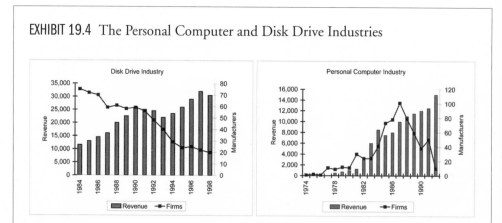

EXHIBIT 19.4 The Personal Computer and Disk Drive Industries

Source: DISK/TREND reports, *Management Science*, and author estimates.

boom-and-bust pattern and why it is so prevalent. In effect, when the environment is uncertain, it helps to start with lots of alternatives (e.g., synaptic connections) and then select (via pruning) the ones that are best given the environment. The process is undoubtedly costly because lots of energy and resources necessarily go to waste, but it's the best one going.

The second benefit is how this process plays into manias. Imagine a baby's brain as a market, with each synapse representing a company or entrant. When the baby is born, the market is buzzing because the brain is creating a lot of synapses and some will be wildly successful. Enthusiasm reigns. Introduce prices, and you have a foundation for a mania.

Investors use price as an important cue, among others, toward a business's potential success. As the price is bid up, humans naturally want to participate. A positive-feedback loop kicks in, which bootstraps a mania. But as we know, many synapses, or companies, don't make it. The path to innovation is paved with failure and waste.

Market participants must recognize, however, that because the business environment is generally fluid in periods of innovation, it's often hard to

EXHIBIT 19.5 OEM Hard Disk Drive Survivors

| Company | Market Capitalization (in thousands) | | History |
	12/31/1984	6/30/2000	
Miniscribe	$51,720		Bankrupt assets purchased by Maxtor
Masstor	$51,786		Bankrupt
Rodime	$53,095		Licensing patents only
Iomega	$106,068	$1,100,000	Ongoing
Cipher Data	$298,056		Acquired by Archive Corporation
Computer Memories	$35,685		Acquired by investor group
Onyx + IMI	$14,399		Acquired by Corvus Systems Inc.
Seagate	$220,795	$12,000,000	Ongoing
Quantum	$199,836		Split into two tracking stocks
DSS (Quantum)		$1,400,000	Ongoing
HDD (Quantum)		$888,000	Ongoing
Micropolis	$43,826		Purchased by Singapore Technologies
Priam	$77,682		Bankrupt assets purchased
Tandon	$304,710		Assets purchased by Western Digital
Total	$1,457,658	$15,388,000	

Source: Bygrave, Lange, Roedel, and Wu, "Capital Market Excesses," 13. Reproduced with permission.

know which businesses will succeed or fail. The payoff for the survivors can be significant, though, which leads to my final point.

Investors are wise to look around for survivors at the end of the pruning process because a portfolio of surviving companies often presents an opportunity for attractive shareholder returns. For example, an investment in the twelve hard-disk-drive companies that survived through the beginning of 1985, held through June 2000, would have generated an 11 percent annual compound return. Further, despite continued failures and brutal competition, investors who sold their winners at peak prices would have realized compound annual returns of 21 percent (see exhibit 19.5).[9] I found similar results with the PC stocks from 1989 to 2000.

While markets and businesses are social constructions, they exhibit features that have strong parallels in nature. The similarity between brain development and industry innovation is but one example.

20

Staying Ahead of the Curve
Linking Creative Destruction and Expectations

You know that you're over the hill when your mind makes a
promise that your body can't fill.

—Little Feat, "Old Folks Boogie"

Losing Pride

It's a familiar scene to anyone who's watched a nature show on TV. A young
and brash lion challenges the pride's imposing but aging leader. The elder
lion, using intimidation and measured force, succeeds in keeping the insur-
gent in check for a while. Eventually, though, the leader succumbs and the
younger and stronger lion succeeds him.[1]

One obvious observation is that while not all challengers become the
pride's new leader, the new leader of the pride is always a challenger.[2] In
business, as in the savanna, there is a never-ending struggle for leadership.
Success in nature means passing your genes to the next generation. Success
in business means that a company generates high economic returns and
total shareholder returns in excess of its peer-group average.

How does thinking about leader/challenger dynamics help investors?
These dynamics are not only a mental model for innovation but are also
useful because there appears to be a discernable pattern of investor reaction
to innovation. Investors tend to understate and overstate growth prospects.

The stock market adds a wrinkle to the innovation process because stock
prices are not about the here and now but rather reflect expectations for the
future.[3] Investors, using myriad means and methods, place a present value
on a company's future—more accurately, the present value of the company's
future cash flows. Stock prices reflect the collective expectations of investors.

So investors can't just consider innovation; they must assess how the market will consider innovation. Therein lies the potential opportunity.

Goldilocks Expectations: Too Cold, Too Hot, Just Right

There is substantial evidence that industry sales and earnings trace an S-curve after a discontinuity or technological change.[4] Growth starts slowly, then increases at an increasing pace, and finally flattens out (see exhibit 20.1). This diagram is useful for thinking about shifting expectations. Investors (indeed humans in general) often think linearly. So at point A, investors do not fully anticipate the growth and economic returns from an industry, and they extrapolate relatively low growth. Expectations for future financial performance are too low. Following a period of sustained growth (point B), investors naively extrapolate the recent growth into the indefinite future. Expectations are too high. Finally, at point C, investors reign in expectations and adjust stock prices to reflect a more realistic outlook.

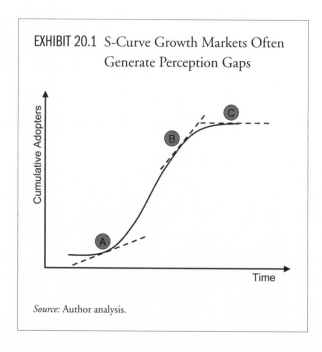

EXHIBIT 20.1 S-Curve Growth Markets Often Generate Perception Gaps

Source: Author analysis.

So the obvious goal for an investor is to buy a stock at point A and sell it at point B—avoiding the unpleasant downward expectations revision at the top of the S-curve. The work of technology strategist Geoffrey Moore—including the best-selling *Gorilla Game*—provides a framework to anticipate such an upward revision. Moore discusses the key issues involved in getting beyond point A, or the elbow in the S-curve, and articulates strategies to identify the potential winners. The difficulty, of course, is that many companies try, but few succeed in becoming the leader in a new industry. It's a jungle out there.

My goal is to document that the transition from point A to point B presents opportunities for excess returns and that the transition from point B to point C often spells poor stock-price performance. Recognizing these inflection points can be very useful for investors for a couple of reasons. First, accelerating innovation assures that industry and product life cycles are shortening.[5] Because the waves of innovation are coming faster and faster, there will be more A-to-B opportunities, and investors must be more nimble to anticipate the expectations revisions.

Second, humans often fall into automatic action when an experience "imprints" on them. For instance, stocks that have performed well in the recent past leave an imprint on the minds of many investors. As a result, following difficult periods investors want to go back to the stocks that drove their portfolio performance in the past.[6] These companies are often at point B and hence are generally the stocks that investors should avoid. In a fast-changing world, you're almost always better off betting on the new guard than the old. You may not know which new company will generate the excess returns, but you can be almost assured that the older company will not.

Out with the Old, In with the New

In their very important book, *Creative Destruction*, Richard Foster and Sarah Kaplan show that new entrants generate higher total return to shareholders (TRS) than their older and more established competitors (see exhibit 20.2). This represents the transition from point A to point B in exhibit 20.1. These data cover a time span in excess of thirty years and literally thousands of companies. All that the researchers required for a company to get into the sample was that it had to be in the top 80 percent of all companies by market capitalization and have 50 percent or more of its sales in the defined industry.

Admittedly, this analysis is skewed toward innovative industries. However, one can argue that the sharper rate of change in the global economy is tilting the challenger/incumbent balance even more dramatically in favor of the challengers. Foster articulated the process of innovation in his path-breaking 1986 book, *Innovation: The Attacker's Advantage*.

Specifically, the research shows that most of an entrant's excess shareholder returns versus its industry come in the first five years. In the subsequent fifteen years, the entrant delivers total shareholder returns that are roughly in line with the industry. Twenty years after entry, a company's stock tends to underperform its peers.

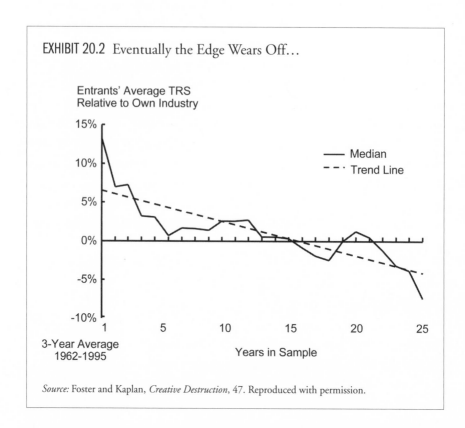

EXHIBIT 20.2 Eventually the Edge Wears Off...

Source: Foster and Kaplan, *Creative Destruction*, 47. Reproduced with permission.

Foster and Kaplan offer three reasons for this pattern. First, competitors imitate or improve on yesterday's innovations, leaving the original innovators with little opportunity to generate either returns above the cost of capital or meaningful growth. Second, the market reflects expectations more accurately for businesses that are more stable and that have longer operating histories than the challengers typically do. Finally, almost all companies eventually lose the innovative edge as the result of size, success, or established institutional routines (the authors call it "cultural lock-in").

Here's the crucial message: the companies that outperform the market are "temporary members of a permanent class." The aggregate returns of the stock market indexes belie an accelerating rate of change in the composition of those indexes as young innovators unseat their established competitors in the market-capitalization game. Corporate longevity is on the wane, and company-specific volatility is rising.[7] Both companies and investors face great opportunity and risk.

The Mind Makes a Promise That the Body Can't Fill

In 1998, the Corporate Strategy Board published a detailed study on what they called "stall points"—the inflection point at the top of the S-curve.[8] Stall points are the transitions from point B to point C in exhibit 20.1. The board found that 83 percent of the companies that reach the stall point grow sales at a rate in the mid-single digits or less in the subsequent ten years. Even more relevant for investors, they show that roughly 70 percent of these companies lose at least one-half of their equity market capitalization. This is evidence that investors extrapolate trends of the recent past into the foreseeable future, only to have those expectations revised down when growth slows.

The researchers also found that it is extremely rare for companies to generate double-digit (real) top-line growth when revenues reach roughly $20 billion (although the ceiling is slowly rising over time). The stock prices of some large technology companies still reflect expectations for strong double-digit growth today.[9]

A noteworthy parallel between the research in *Creative Destruction* and in *Stall Points* is that an inability to innovate and grow is the result of largely controllable organizational and strategic factors. Foster and Kaplan discuss in detail how corporate routines allow companies to slip into senescence, and the authors provide some useful guidelines for constant renewal. The Corporate Strategy Board report provides a detailed analysis of the cause of stall points and suggests that companies can attribute less than 20 percent of the explanation to factors outside of their control.

Expectations and Innovation

The research indicates that where there is innovation, there are winners and losers. The data show that challengers have the advantage and that incumbents often don't innovate enough to sustain leadership positions. Since stock prices reflect expectations, investors must not only consider the dynamics of innovation but also what the market anticipates. The evidence suggests that expectations for challengers are at first too low and then too high.

21

Is There a Fly in Your Portfolio?
What an Accelerating Rate of Industry Change Means for Investors

The results . . . provide strong evidence that periods of sustained competitive advantage, as evidenced by its consequence, superior economic performance, are growing shorter over time. These results hold across a wide range of sectors of the economy.

—Robert R. Wiggins and Timothy W. Ruefli, "Hypercompetitive Performance: Are the Best of Times Getting Shorter?"

I think the multiples of technology stocks should be quite a bit lower than stocks like Coke and Gillette, because we are subject to complete changes in the rules. I know very well that in the next ten years, if Microsoft is still a leader, we will have had to weather at least three crises.

—Bill Gates, *Fortune*, 1998

Fruit Flies and Futility

Geneticists and biologists love to work with *Drosophila melanogaster*, a common fruit fly, and have made it a staple of biological study. Indeed, insights from *Drosophila* research helped a trio of scientists win the 1995 Nobel prize in medicine. Thousands of researchers continue to study the *Drosophila* to better understand various genetic and developmental issues.

Drosophila is attractive to scientists because they understand its features and it is easy to handle. But the fly has another essential feature that scientists covet: its life cycle. *Drosophila* go from embryo to death in about two weeks. This rapid rate of reproduction allows scientists to study hundreds of generations of the fly's development and mutations in a relatively short time. *Drosophila's* fast evolution provides scientists with important clues about evolution in other species, which generally evolve at a relatively glacial pace.[1]

Why should businesspeople care about *Drosophila*? A sound body of evidence now suggests that the average speed of evolution is accelerating in the business world. Just as scientists have learned a great deal about evolutionary change from fruit flies, investors can benefit from understanding the sources and implications of accelerated business evolution.

The most direct consequence of more rapid business evolution is that the time an average company can sustain a competitive advantage—that is, generate an economic return in excess of its cost of capital—is shorter than it was in the past. This trend has potentially important implications for investors in areas such as valuation, portfolio turnover, and diversification.

Speed Trap?

In his book *Clockspeed: Winning Industry Control in the Age of Temporary Advantage*, Charles Fine defines clockspeed, a measure of cycle time, on multiple levels.[2] The first is product clockspeed. Consistent with intuition, product clockspeed considers how quickly an industry launches new products and how long products live. Evidence of accelerating new product activity is everywhere. For example, *Technology Review* reports that General Motors has reduced the time it takes to develop and build a new vehicle from forty-eight to twenty-one months. In fact, GM is launching a new vehicle every twenty-three days, on average.[3]

Next is what Fine calls process clockspeed, which deals with the process for creating and delivering a good or service. One way to measure process clockspeed is to look at average asset lives. The HOLT database shows that the average asset life (which includes R&D capitalization) of the top 1,800 industrial companies in the United States has gone from approximately fourteen years in 1975 to under ten years currently. Today's companies need to generate economic returns on investment over a shorter time horizon than they did a generation ago. Exhibit 21.1 shows Fine's estimates of product and process clockspeeds for a host of industries.

EXHIBIT 21.1 Clockspeeds in Sample Industries

Industry	Product Clockspeed	Process Clockspeed
Fast-Clockspeed Industries		
Personal computers	< 6 months	2–4 years
Toys and games	< 1 year	5–15 years
Semiconductors	1–2 years	3–10 years
Cosmetics	2–3 years	10–20 years
Medium-Clockspeed Industries		
Automobiles	4–6 years	10–15 years
Fast food	3–8 years	5–25 years
Machine tools	6–10 years	10–15 years
Pharmaceuticals	7–15 years	5–10 years
Slow-Clockspeed Industries		
Commercial aircraft	10–20 years	20–30 years
Tobacco	1–2 years	20–30 years
Petrochemicals	10–20 years	20–40 years
Paper	10–20 years	20–40 years

Source: Fine, *Clockspeed*, 239. Reproduced with permission.

That average clockspeeds are shortening does not mean that all sectors are changing equally rapidly. One of the factors underlying the average change is a shift in the composition of public companies. Eugene Fama and Kenneth French show that the number of companies in the Compustat database rose 70 percent between the mid-1970s and the mid-1990s. Most of the new companies, launched via initial public offerings, were smaller and faster growing than the existing companies.[4] Since more fast-clockspeed companies have been added to the market mix over the past twenty-five years or so, the average clockspeed has shrunk. But the evidence shows that some companies can and do sustain high economic returns for a long time.[5]

Investors care about clockspeed because of its close link to sustainable competitive advantage. Robert Wiggins and Timothy Ruefli did an empirical study of the sustainability of excess returns. They defined persistent superior economic performance as "statistically significant above average performance relative to a reference set that persists over a long period of calendar time."[6] While they measured performance using accounting numbers (return on assets and Tobin's q) rather than sound economic numbers, I suspect the size of their sample (nearly 6,800 firms in forty industries) and the time period (twenty-five years, 1972 to 1997) were sufficient to yield representative results.

Wiggins and Ruefli propose and test four hypotheses:

1. *Periods of persistent superior economic performance are decreasing in duration over time.* Their analysis supports the hypothesis, showing that the probability of leaving the "superior performance stratum" has increased over time.

2. *Hypercompetition is not limited to high-technology industries but will occur through most industries.* Here, the evidence supports the hypothesis by showing that while nontechnology companies had a higher probability of staying in the superior-performance stratum than technology companies did, the probability of leaving the stratum did increase over time.

3. *Over time, firms increasingly seek to sustain competitive advantage by concatenating a series of short-term competitive advantages.* The idea here is that successful companies string together a series of short-lived competitive advantages. The data support this hypothesis, too. The researchers show that the pattern of one-period superior performance is more prevalent in the study's later time periods.[7]

4. *Industry concentration, large market share, or both are negatively associated with chance of loss of persistent superior economic performance in an industry.* The research did not support the final hypothesis. Neither a concentrated industry nor large market shares is empirically consistent with sustainable competitive advantage.

The Wiggins and Ruefli work is consistent with other recent research, including Foster and Kaplan's *Creative Destruction* and the finding of Campbell et al. that firm-specific volatility has been rising steadily since the mid-1970s.[8] An accelerating rate of innovation is causing a greater rate of dislocation for individual companies.

Two factors lead me to believe that the trend of faster clockspeed will persist. The first is the increase in information technology, which will likely have an ongoing, significant microeconomic effect.[9] Technology increases clockspeed by allowing companies to improve processes and provides consumers with greater transparency. Second, an ongoing shift from physical to knowledge assets provides greater flexibility in resource allocation. Companies can change employee tasks more readily than they can change a factory's output.

Investor Evolution

Faster clockspeed affects investors in a number of ways. First, shortening periods of sustainable excess returns have important implications for valuation. Shorter product and process life cycles undermine the usefulness of historical multiples (especially price/earnings, which weren't very useful to begin with), because the basis of comparison is different. I believe there has been a trade-off: higher economic returns for shorter periods are increasingly replacing lower economic returns for longer periods. Whether or not I am right, simplistic valuation assumptions invite danger.

Another possible valuation pitfall comes with terminal valuations in discounted cash-flow models. Many discounted cash-flow models assume perpetual growth beyond an explicit forecast period, hence embedding an assumption of long-term value creation. In a world of shortening sustainable advantages, such an assumption appears particularly inappropriate.[10]

Clockspeed also has implications for portfolio turnover. Just as companies must string together a series of competitive advantages, optimal portfolio turnover is higher today than in the past. That said, I still suspect that aggregate portfolio turnover, which has risen sharply over the past twenty-five years, is too high. But extremely low portfolio turnover (less than 20 percent) may not provide sufficient flexibility to capture the market's dynamics.

In addition, faster clockspeed suggests the need for greater diversification. If competitive advantages are coming and going faster than ever, investors need to cast a wider net in order to assure that their portfolios reflect the phenomenon. (Ideally, of course, investors would only focus on the winners and avoid the losers. This is practically very difficult.) The data show evidence for this increased diversification.

Finally, the rate of change in the business world demands that investors spend more time understanding the dynamics of organizational change. Success and failure at fast-changing companies may provide investors with some useful mental models for appreciating change at the slower evolving companies. The business world is going the way of *Drosophila*.

22

All the Right Moves
How to Balance the Long Term with the Short Term

Strategy in complex systems must resemble strategy in board games. You develop a small and useful tree of options that is continuously revised based on the arrangement of pieces and the actions of your opponent. It is critical to keep the number of options open. It is important to develop a theory of what kinds of options you want to have open.

—John H. Holland, presentation at the
2000 CSFB Thought Leader Forum

Managing for the Long Term

At a business forum I attended, a senior executive of a Fortune 100 company proclaimed that his company manages "not for the next quarter, but for the next quarter century." Ugh. Such platitudes do not instill confidence in investors. Most managers don't have any idea what's going to happen in the next five years, much less the next twenty-five years. How do you manage for an ambiguous future?

Yet managers must clearly strike some balance between the short term and the long term. It's like speeding down the highway in a car. If you focus just beyond the hood, you're going to have a hard time anticipating what's coming. Look too far ahead, on the other hand, and you lose perspective on the actions that you need to take now to navigate safely. There's a tradeoff between the short term and the long term, and the appropriate focal point shifts as conditions warrant.

The notion that managers should only focus on the long term is nonsensical. Have you ever heard of a company that blew twenty straight quarters but had a great five years? It doesn't happen; the long term is, by definition, an aggregation of short terms. So what's the best way to think about managing for the long term in a complex environment?

Deep Blue's Lessons

The strategies of chess grandmasters provide us with some very important clues about how to approach business strategy. Even with a relatively small number of rules and an eight-by-eight board, chess games are very complex and have perpetually novel outcomes. Even though chess is not too mathematically complicated, assessing all (or most) potential positions requires staggering computational power.

Deep Blue, IBM's chess-playing supercomputer, demonstrated this computational brute force when it beat world champion Garry Kasparov in a six-game match in 1999. The $3 million computer evaluated 200 million positions a second—over 35 billion in the three minutes allotted to a single move—compared with Kasparov's approximately three positions a second. Deep Blue also had a database of grandmaster opening games over the last hundred years.[1]

The strategic lesson in Deep Blue's victory is not machine over man but rather that pure computational power can succeed in a well-defined game. Add a small amount of complexity to the game, however, and the number of options rises dramatically, rendering even the most powerful computers useless. For example, no computer program comes close to the best humans in the game of Go, which also has simple rules but a larger nineteen-by-nineteen board.[2]

Since the business world is vastly more complex than any board game, it's impossible to understand all possible future positions, much less assess them. So success for humans in either chess or business is not about crunching numbers; it's about developing strategies to achieve a long-term goal.

Strategies for Winners

So how do great chess players approach the game? Chess master Bruce Pandolfini observes four behaviors that are consistent among chess champions and useful in thinking through the short-term/long-term debate.[3]

1. *Don't look too far ahead:* Most people believe that great players strategize by thinking far into the future, by thinking 10 or 15 moves ahead. That's just not true. Chess players look only as far into the future as they need to, and that usually means thinking just a few moves ahead. Thinking too far ahead is a waste of time: The information is uncertain.

2. *Develop options and continuously revise them based on the changing conditions (see exhibit 22.1):* Great players consider their next move without playing it. You should never play the first good move that comes into your head. Put that move on your list, and then ask yourself if there's an even better move. If you see a good idea, look for a better one—that's my motto. Good thinking is a matter of making comparisons.

3. *Know your competition:* Being good at chess also requires being good at reading people. Few people think of chess as an intimate, personal game. But that's what it is. Players learn a lot about their opponents, and exceptional chess players learn to interpret every gesture that their opponents make.

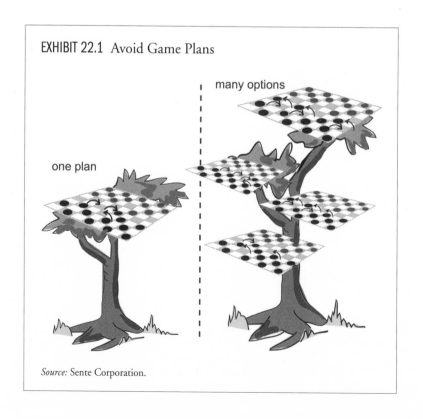

EXHIBIT 22.1 Avoid Game Plans

many options

one plan

Source: Sente Corporation.

4. *Seek small advantages:* You play for seemingly insignificant advantages—advantages that your opponent doesn't notice or that he dismisses, thinking, "Big deal, you can have that." It could be slightly better development, or a slightly safer king's position. Slightly, slightly, slightly. None of those "slightlys" mean anything on their own, but add up seven or eight of them, and you have control.

Pandolfini stresses to his students that his goal is not to make them great chess players but great thinkers:

My goal is to help them develop what I consider to be two of the most important forms of intelligence: the ability to read other people, and the ability to understand oneself. Those are the two kinds of intelligence you need to succeed at chess—and in life.[4]

There are limits to the business-as-chess analogy. Besides the added complexity of business, the most significant limitation is that chess is a zero-sum game: for every winner, there's a loser. The business world is not zero-sum, and the game between players has an unspecified tenure. So how can we apply these lessons from chess to the business world?

Strategy as Simple Rules

One of the characteristics of a complex system is that highly variable outcomes emerge from simple rules. Unless you deliberately replay a chess game, you'll never see the same game twice. Herein lies the key to resolving the tension between the short term and the long term.

Companies should develop long-term decision rules that are flexible enough to allow managers to make the right decisions in the short term. In this way, the company is managing for the long run even when it has no information about what the future holds. No company knows how the business landscape will develop—just as chess players don't know how the board will develop—but decision rules provide action guidelines no matter what happens.

Kathy Eisenhardt and Don Sull call this "strategy as simple rules."[5] They argue that companies, especially in fast-changing markets, should not embrace complex strategies but rather adopt and stick to "a few straightforward, hard-and-fast rules that define direction without containing it."

Eisenhardt and Sull specifically suggest five types of rules:

1. *How-to rules* spell out key features of how a company should execute a process. It answers the question, What makes our process unique?

2. *Boundary rules* focus managers on which opportunities they should pursue and which are outside the pale.

3. *Priority rules* help managers rank the opportunities they accept.

4. *Timing rules* synchronize managers with the pace of opportunities that emerge in other parts of the company.

5. *Exit rules* help managers decide when to pull out of yesterday's opportunities.

Eisenhardt and Sull argue that a company should have somewhere between two and seven rules, that young companies typically have too few, and that more mature businesses have too many. A decision rule to maintain accounting integrity (i.e., to avoid managing earnings per share versus managing the business) might also help reduce undue short-termism.

This "strategy as simple rules" approach is not only strongly analogous to successful chess playing, but it also resonates with other complex adaptive systems. Most important, it puts to rest the nonproductive debate about whether companies should manage for the short or long term. Companies that embrace simple rules can manage *both* for the next quarter and the next quarter century.

23

Survival of the Fittest
Fitness Landscapes and Competitive Advantage

> It is not the strongest of the species that survives, nor the most intelligent, but the one most responsive to change.
>
> —Charles Darwin, *The Origin of Species*

A Peek at Another Peak

In the spring of 1997, Tiger Woods didn't just win the prestigious Masters golf tournament; he dominated it. Competing with the best golfers in the world, he sprinted away from the pack, winning by a record twelve strokes. To put this achievement in perspective, Woods had joined the tour less than a year earlier, and was still the tender age of twenty-one. He had already won four of the fifteen PGA Tour tournaments he had entered. Golf aficionados started favorably comparing him to Jack Nicklaus, widely considered the best golfer ever.

How did Woods react to his extraordinary success? He didn't assume he had reached his potential. He didn't sit back and enjoy. Instead, he carefully studied the videotape of his Masters performance and came to a surprising conclusion: "My swing really sucks."[1]

Woods called his coach, Butch Harmon, to help revamp his swing. Harmon was sure Woods could take his game to an even higher level but knew that the results would not come instantly. Woods would have to risk getting worse in the short term in order to get better for the long term. He didn't hesitate. Working with Harmon, Woods improved his strength and changed his grip, allowing him to maintain his power while gaining more control.

Even as Woods managed to win only one Tour event from July 1997 to February 1999, he insisted he was a better golfer than before. "Winning is not always the barometer of getting better," he asserted. In the spring of 1999, the new swing gelled. Woods went on to win ten of the next fourteen events in 1999, including eight PGA Tour victories. He tacked on another nine PGA Tour wins in 2000, and after capturing the 2001 Masters, he was the first golfer to be the reigning champion in all four majors simultaneously.

Fitness Landscapes

This story is a useful introduction to the idea of fitness landscapes. Evolutionary biologists originally developed fitness landscapes to help them understand evolution—in particular, how a species increases its fitness.[2] Along the way, the framework has spawned useful ideas for corporate strategists.[3]

What does a fitness landscape look like? Envision a large grid, with each point representing a different strategy that a species (or a company) can pursue. Further imagine that the height of each point depicts fitness. Peaks represent high fitness, and valleys represent low fitness. From a company's perspective, fitness equals value-creation potential. Each company operates in a landscape full of high-return peaks and value-destructive valleys.[4] The topology of the landscape depends on the industry characteristics.

As Darwin noted, improving fitness is not about strength or smarts but rather about becoming more and more suited to your environment—in a word, adaptability. Better fitness requires generating options and "choosing" the "best" ones. In nature, recombination and mutation generate species diversity, and natural selection assures that the most suitable options survive.[5] For companies, adaptability is about formulating and executing value-creating strategies with a goal of generating the highest possible long-term returns.

Since a fitness landscape can have lots of peaks and valleys, even if a species reaches a peak (a local optimum), it may not be at the highest peak (global optimum). To get to a higher altitude, a species may have to reduce its fitness in the near term to improve its fitness in the long term. We can say the same about companies. This is a good metaphor for the Tiger Woods experience.

Fitness landscapes are a rich way to think about businesses. For any individual company, you have to answer two questions. First, what does the fitness landscape look like from the company's perspective? Of course, not only are a company's decisions influenced by its fitness landscape, but the decisions themselves help define the landscape. Second, is the company pursuing the right strategies to improve its fitness (i.e., economic value) over time given its landscape?

It's important to note, though, that you can't focus solely on the evolution of one company or industry because of the central role of coevolution. Actions trigger reactions. Sometimes companies cooperate with one another, sometimes they conflict. Nothing happens in a void—companies are always jockeying to improve their position.[6] Further, the more dynamic the fitness landscape, the greater the necessary rate of adaptation.

To help answer the first question, here are three broad types of landscapes: stable, coarse, and roiling (see exhibit 23.1):

- *Stable.* These are industries where the fitness landscape is reasonably stable. In many cases, the landscape is relatively flat, and companies generate excess economic returns only when cyclical forces are favorable. Examples include electric and telephone utilities, commodity producers (energy, paper, metals),

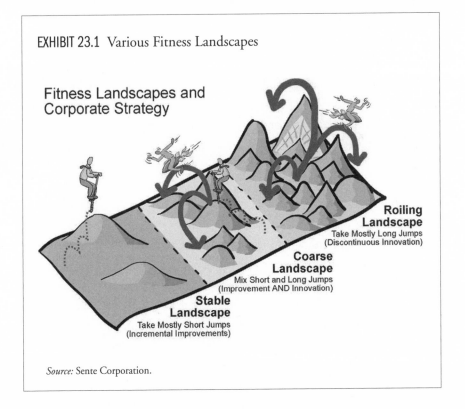

EXHIBIT 23.1 Various Fitness Landscapes

Source: Sente Corporation.

capital goods, consumer nondurables, and real estate investment trusts. Companies within these sectors primarily improve their fitness at the expense of their competitors. These are businesses that tend to have structural predictability (i.e., you'll know what they look like in the future) at the expense of limited opportunities for growth and new businesses.

- *Coarse.* The fitness landscape is in flux for these industries, but the changes are not so rapid as to lack predictability. The landscape here is rougher. Some companies deliver much better economic performance than do others. Financial services, retail, health care, and more established parts of technology are illustrations. These industries run a clear risk of being unseated (losing fitness) by a disruptive technology.[7]

- *Roiling.* This group contains businesses that are very dynamic, with evolving business models, substantial uncertainty, and ever-changing product offerings. The peaks and valleys are constantly changing, ever spastic. Included in this type are many software companies, the genomics industry, fashion-related sectors, and most start-ups. Economic returns in this group can be (or can promise to be) significant but are generally fleeting.

You can make a good case that the combination of an accelerating pace of innovation, ongoing deregulation, and globalization is causing the global fitness landscape to contort more than it has in the past.[8] Once you have a general sense of what the fitness landscape looks like for a company—and whether it is becoming more or less stable—you can consider the appropriate strategy process to maximize long-term value.

Look Before You Leap?

Consultant Eric Beinhocker suggests two general strategies to improve fitness. He calls the first "short jumps," small incremental steps toward a peak. Most process-improvement initiatives are short jumps. He labels the other "long jumps," discontinuous moves that may catapult a company to a higher peak or may leave it in a lower valley. Long jumps include meaningful acquisitions in unrelated fields and investing in nascent products. I believe that a company's fitness landscape largely defines the appropriate balance between short and long jumps.[9]

For example, the focus in stable industries is often process optimization—continual small jumps. Long jumps are potentially costly and distracting, and therefore do not yield much value. This is not to say, for example, that technology will not touch these industries. It has and it will. However, the technological improvements are generally incremental and replicable.

To go to the opposite extreme, companies that compete in roiling fitness landscapes must focus more on long jumps—pursuit of the next big thing—because even if they find themselves at a peak, the shifting landscape assures that the peak quickly disappears. Since product life cycles are short, adaptation is more important than optimization.[10]

Companies that compete in coarse fitness landscapes quite logically need to find a blend between short and long jumps. Indeed, models show that this mix is the best search strategy for a correlated landscape.[11]

Tools of the Trade-Off

Just as a different mix of short and long jumps is appropriate for different fitness landscapes, so too are different financial tools and organizational structures. Traditional discounted cash flow analysis is well suited for businesses that compete in stable fitness landscapes. A centralized management approach is effective, as industry activities are often clearly defined.

A coarse fitness landscape requires a blend of traditional cash flow tools and strategic options. Strategic options are the right, but not the obligation, to pursue potentially value-creating business opportunities.[12] Finally, companies that compete in roiling industries must lean more on strategic options to assess their current and potential fitness. Further, these companies are well served to adopt a "strategy by simple rules" approach. This decentralized approach has agreed-upon decision rules but lets individuals make decisions at the local level as they see fit.[13]

Fitness landscape	Financial tool	Organizational structure
Stable	Discounted cash flow	Centralized
Coarse	DCF plus strategic options	Loose centralization
Roiling	Strategic options	Decentralized

Tiger Woods showed that change, while sometimes painful in the short term, is necessary to improve fitness in the long term. Fitness landscapes can help you evaluate whether a company is pursuing the right potential strategies and has the appropriate organization. The analysis also points to the appropriate financial tools to assess various businesses.

24

You'll Meet a Bad Fate If You Extrapolate
The Folly of Using Average P/Es

For past averages to be meaningful, the data being averaged have to be drawn from the same population. If this is not the case—if the data come from populations that are different—the data are said to be nonstationary. When data are nonstationary, projecting past averages typically produces nonsensical results.

—Bradford Cornell, *The Equity Risk Premium*

Intangible assets . . . surpass physical assets in most business enterprises, both in value and contribution to growth, yet they are routinely expensed in the financial reports and hence remain absent from corporate balance sheets. This asymmetric treatment of capitalizing (considering as assets) physical and financial investment while expensing intangibles leads to biased and deficient reporting of firms' performance and value.

—Baruch Lev, *Intangibles*

Social Versus Security

Ernest Ackerman was one lucky hombre. The first reported applicant for Social Security payment, Ackerman retired one day after the program was launched in 1937. During his day of participation in Social Security, his employer withheld one nickel from his pay. Upon retirement, Ackerman collected a lump-sum payment of seventeen cents.

Future Social Security recipients may not be as fortunate. Even though the government has made significant changes to Social Security over the past sixty-plus years, the system faces severe challenges. In large part, these challenges reflect a change in the demographics of the U.S. population.

For example, the government originally set the retirement age at sixty-five because actuarial studies showed that "using age 65 produced a manageable system that could easily be made self-sustaining with only modest levels of payroll taxation."[1] But from 1940 to today, the average percentage of men that survive from age twenty-one to age sixty-five leaped from 54 percent to 72 percent, the male life expectancy at sixty-five swelled from 12.7 to 15.3 years, and the fertility rate dipped nearly 10 percent. As a result, the worker per retiree ratio has plunged from forty-two to one in 1940 to about three to one today.

A look at Social Security's evolution illustrates a crucial point: It is really hard to manage a system when the underlying data are constantly changing. You can't draw conclusions from past averages because they don't accurately represent today's averages.

This lesson carries over directly to investing. One instance that stands out is when investors blithely apply historical-average price-earnings ratios to value either today's market or an individual stock. Past-ratio averages are only applicable to the degree that they capture current circumstances. Just as no policymaker would dream of using old demographic data to assess the future of Social Security, investors should not casually rely on past price-earnings ratios to understand today's market.

Nonstationarity and Historical P/Es

Nonstationarity is a crucial concept in any time-series analysis, and it is especially relevant for fields like climatology and finance. The basic idea is that for averages to be comparable over time, the statistical properties of the population must be the same, or stationary. If the properties of the population change over time, the data are nonstationary. When data are nonstationary, applying past averages to today's population can lead to misleading conclusions.

Theoretical and empirical analysis of price-earnings ratios suggests that they are probably nonstationary.[2] In fact, research shows that there has been no statistically significant relationship between a price-earnings ratio at the beginning of a year and the subsequent twelve- and twenty-four-month returns over the past 125 years.[3] More bluntly, the historical-average price-earnings ratio provides investors little or no guidance about market returns over the typical investment horizon.

While recognition that price-earnings ratios are likely nonstationary is critical, knowing *why* they are nonstationary provides more practical insight. Three big drivers of price-earnings ratio nonstationarity are the role of taxes and inflation; changes in the composition of the economy; and shifts in the equity-risk premium.

Why the Past May Not Be Prologue

A bedrock concept in finance is that investors price assets to generate an appropriate return (adjusted by perceived risk) net of taxes, inflation, and transaction costs. Accordingly, changes in tax law and inflation rates have a material effect on the appropriate value of the market, and hence price-earnings ratios.

The role of taxes is conceptually straightforward. Increases in dividend and capital gains taxes require investors to earn a higher pretax return to generate comparable returns. So all things equal, lower tax rates lead to higher multiples, and vice versa.

Tax rates have been anything but stable since the 1960s (see exhibit 24.1). The government taxed dividends at a nearly 90 percent rate in the early 1960s, and the rate has trended down to 15 percent in 2003, where it remains today. Capital gains taxes have seesawed between 20 and 35 percent before dipping to 15 percent in the early twenty-first century.

The interplay between tax rates and inflation is also important. Investors who seek real, after-tax returns increase their pretax-return requirements when they expect rising inflation. Exhibit 24.2 shows annual inflation (including forecasts) and rolling five-year trailing inflation from 1960 through 2006. The combination of high inflation and high nominal capital gains tax rates spurred very high discount rates—and very low price-earnings ratios—during the 1970s. Inflation also distorts financial statements. So price-earnings ratios vary significantly from one tax and inflation scenario to the next.

A second factor that shapes price-earnings ratios is the global economy's shift from a reliance on tangible to intangible capital. Companies recognize tangible investments, such as new factories, on their balance sheets and

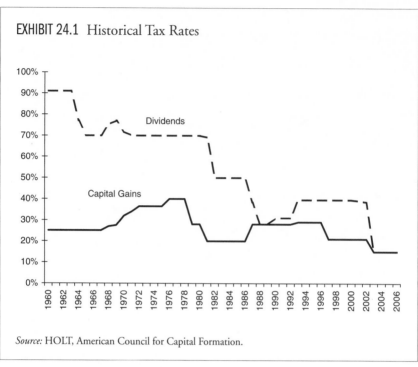

EXHIBIT 24.1 Historical Tax Rates

Source: HOLT, American Council for Capital Formation.

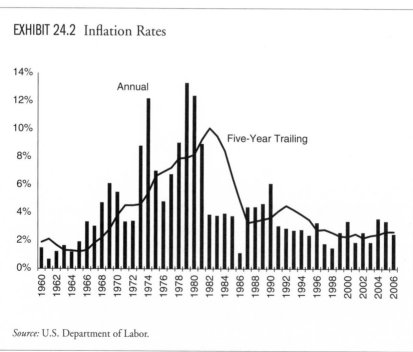

EXHIBIT 24.2 Inflation Rates

Source: U.S. Department of Labor.

depreciate the assets over their useful life. In contrast, companies immediately expense intangible investments like research and development or advertising.

So it's the form of investment, not just the magnitude of investment, that dictates the earnings a company reports. A tangible-oriented and an intangible-oriented business may invest an identical amount with the same return on investment and still have significantly different earnings. In general, intangible-reliant companies have a higher cash-flow-to-net-income ratio.

To illustrate this point, I take two samples from the Dow Jones Industrial Average. The first, which I call the tangible group, includes Alcoa, Caterpillar, United Technologies, and Wal-Mart. The intangible group comprises Altria, Coca-Cola, Microsoft, and Procter and Gamble. Over the five reported fiscal years that ended with 2006, the tangible group had a cash-flow-to-net-income ratio of 28 percent, versus a 111 percent ratio for the intangible group.

There is pervasive evidence that the global economy is moving from a reliance on tangible to intangible assets, including market-to-book ratios, workforce allocation, and the rising significance of education. Further, because intangible-reliant businesses have few assets on their balance sheets, they tend to show high returns on capital. With other factors held constant, higher cash-flow-to-net-income ratios and returns on capital support higher price-earnings ratios.[4]

The final factor that dictates the price-earnings ratio is the equity-risk premium, or the return that equity investors demand above and beyond a risk-free security. (The equity-risk premium itself appears to be nonstationary.)[5] While a number of factors come into play to determine the risk premium, including future growth estimates, the aggregate risk appetite of investors is certainly important. In periods of general optimism, equity-risk premiums shrink, and premiums expand when investors are cautious. The ebb and flow of investor risk appetite likely contributes to the nonstationarity of multiples.

Bounded Parameters

The market's price-earnings ratio has averaged just over fourteen over the past 130 years or so, and the multiple has zigzagged across this level many times during that period.[6] Isn't this proof enough that fourteen is the multiple to which the market reverts?

The answer, I believe, is a qualified no. In all likelihood, two of the three drivers of nonstationarity—taxes/inflation and equity risk premium—are probably bounded. That is, they vacillate within reasonably defined, albeit large, channels. These drivers might average out over the very long term (i.e., a decade or more), but they are the source of significant, and legitimate, multiple differences over many decades.

Absent a change in our accounting system, the third driver, the evolving economy, argues for higher price-earnings multiples, all else being equal. The simple basis for this conclusion is that companies that expense their investments tend to have higher cash-flow-to-net-income ratios than companies that capitalize their investments. This is likely a secular trend.

Offsetting this upward bias, though, is the fact that the period of sustainable competitive advantage may well be shorter for service and knowledge businesses than it was for the physical capital businesses of the past. So the warranted price-earnings ratio, net of these countervailing forces, may not be much different than historical averages. But the underlying economic rationale for the ratio has changed substantially.

Unpacking the (Mental) Baggage

Because price-earnings ratios are likely nonstationary, investors should use them sparingly and cautiously, if at all. The attraction of a ratio, of course, is that it is often a useful rule of thumb. I argue, however, that investors who insist on using multiples will find them much more useful if they unpack the embedded assumptions. This unpacking reveals how and why circumstances are different today (e.g., growth, inflation, taxes, risk appetite, the structure of the economy) than they were in the past and what that means for the multiple.

25

I've Fallen and I Can't Get Up
Mean Reversion and Turnarounds

> The key finding of this research . . . is that the demonstrated rarity of achieving sustained superior economic performance implies that it is extremely difficult to achieve. An associated finding . . . is that even if superior performance is achieved and sustained for a period of time, the probability of slipping from that lofty perch is relatively high.
>
> —Robert R. Wiggins and Timothy W. Ruefli,
> "Sustained Competitive Advantage"

Returns and Growth

Finance professor Josef Lakonishok argued that the stock market had many "pockets of craziness" in a 2004 *New York Times* article.[1] Lakonishok's case was based on the relationship between growth and price-earnings ratios, and he suggested that the market was implying unrealistically rapid earnings-growth rates for some companies with lofty price-earnings multiples. Research he conducted with a pair of colleagues showed that very few companies sustain high growth rates.[2]

But what really determines a price-earnings ratio? A company's value is a function of the market's expectations for its growth rate *and* its economic returns. This fundamental concept explains why looking at growth in isolation can be so misleading. Growth can be good (when a company earns returns in excess of the cost of capital), bad (when returns are below the cost of capital), or neutral (when returns equal the cost of capital).

You must first have a clear sense of whether a company is earning appropriate returns before you can judge the effect of growth. Companies can, and do, grow their way to bankruptcy.[3] Likewise, some low-growth, high-return businesses consistently carry premium valuations. Studying growth in isolation of economic returns is an invitation to failure.

Gaining a firm grasp of a company's prospects for economic returns requires a thorough understanding of competitive strategy.[4] The goal of strategic analysis is to address three fundamental questions:

1. Is the company generating returns on investment above the cost of capital, or is there good reason to believe it will earn attractive returns in the future?

2. If returns do exceed the cost of capital, for how long can the company sustain its excess returns?[5]

3. Once a company's returns dip below the cost of capital, what's the probability it can stage a sustained recovery to above-required returns?

In this piece I take a closer look at the latter two questions, drawing on empirical data from the technology and retail industries to bring the points to life.

Death, Taxes, and Reversion to the Mean

One microeconomic theory that is well documented empirically is the notion that a company's return on investment reverts to the cost of capital over time.[6] The theory, and intuition, is straightforward. Companies that generate high returns attract competition and capital, which drive returns toward opportunity-cost levels. Similarly, capital flees poor-return industries—through bankruptcy, disinvestment, or consolidation—lifting returns back to the cost of capital.

Exhibit 25.1 shows this process for a sample of over 450 technology companies from 1979 to 1996. (The analysis stops at 1996 to avoid issues related to the Internet bubble.)[7] Credit Suisse ranked companies by quartiles based on their cash flow return on investment (CFROI), and followed the return patterns. Because CFROI is a real, after-tax measure, the time series is unaffected by the potentially distorting shifts in interest rates and inflation.

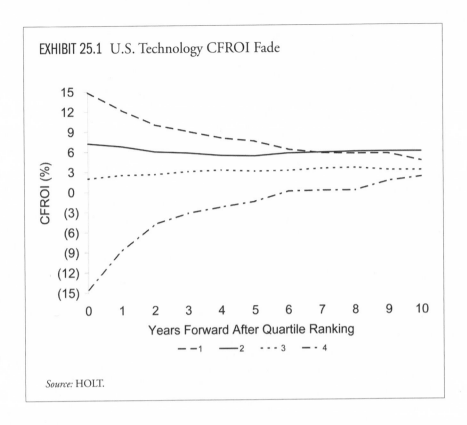

EXHIBIT 25.1 U.S. Technology CFROI Fade

Years Forward After Quartile Ranking

— — 1   —— 2   · · · 3   — · 4

Source: HOLT.

The top group earned an average CFROI of 15 percent during the initial period and declined to 6 percent after only five years. The worst group went from 15 percent negative returns to almost zero (still well below the cost of capital) within five years. The middle two quartiles showed relative stability around cost-of-capital levels. The return gap between the highest and lowest quartiles went from 3,000 basis points at the first measurement period to just 300 basis points after ten years. While ten years is insufficient to complete the reversion-to-the-mean process, much of the progression is evident within that time frame.

Consistent with theory, attrition plays a central role in the improvement of lowest-quartile returns. Just 60 percent of the lowest-quartile companies were active after five years, as many of the poor performers went bankrupt or were acquired. This attrition creates a survivorship bias, allowing returns to rise during the decade. In contrast, 85 percent of the firms in the highest-return quartile were active after five years. Attrition rates across all quartiles tend to average out after five years.

One consistent feature across the many mean-reversion studies is that some companies (albeit not many) can and do earn persistently high returns. In the study of nearly 700 retailers from 1950 to 2001, 14 percent of the companies never earned below their cost of capital.[8] Of the 1,700 technology companies in the sample from 1960 to 1996, 11 percent sustained an unblemished record of positive excess returns.

Sustaining high returns is a huge potential source of wealth. Given two companies with the same initial returns and future growth rates, the business that can sustain above-cost-of-capital returns longer will be significantly more valuable and hence will trade at a much higher valuation multiple.[9]

A strategic assessment of a business earning high returns should reveal the source of the excess spread—typically either a consumer or production advantage—and provide some framework to consider the longevity of that advantage. Further, some businesses (especially those in network and knowledge businesses) enjoy increasing returns as they grow.[10] A company's strategic strengths, and the economics that result, are essentially overlooked by a singular focus on growth.

I've Fallen and I Can't Get Up

Stock prices reflect expectations, and the key to generating superior long-term returns is to successfully anticipate expectation revisions. An important corollary is that neither a good (i.e., high-return) business nor a bad (low-return) business is inherently attractive or unattractive. Investors need to assess the stocks of all companies versus expectations.[11]

In this spirit, it's worth looking at a particular class of companies—those that have realized a downturn. Here, a downturn is defined as two consecutive years of CFROI below the cost of capital following two years of returns above the cost of capital.

This analysis is particularly important for value investors, who often buy companies that are statistically inexpensive in the hope that economic returns improve. The classic value trap is buying a cheap company that deserves to be cheap based on poor economic returns. But buying a company that is cheap because of a temporary downturn is potentially very attractive if the market does not anticipate the turnaround.

Exhibit 25.2 shows what happens to companies that realize a downturn. The sample includes almost 1,200 companies from the technology and retail sectors. The data for the two industries are strikingly similar, and not particularly encouraging: Only about 30 percent of the sample companies were able to engineer a sustained recovery. (Credit Suisse defined a sustained recovery as three years of above-average returns following two years of below-cost-of-capital results.) Roughly one-quarter of the companies produced a non-sustained recovery. The balance—just under half the population—either saw no turnaround or disappeared. Companies can disappear gracefully (get acquired) or disgracefully (go bankrupt).

EXHIBIT 25.2 I've Fallen and I Can't Get Up

	Technology[a] (%)	Retail[b] (%)
No turnaround	45	48
Nonsustained turnaround	26	23
Sustained turnaround	29	29

[a] Sample of 712 companies from 1960 to 1996.
[b] Sample of 445 companies from 1950 to 2001.
Source: HOLT.

This analysis also shows how long companies experienced downturns. For both retailers and technology companies, roughly 27 percent of downturns lasted only two years, and for both sectors over 60 percent of downturns lasted for less than five years. In other words, the destiny of most firms that live through a downturn is determined rather quickly.

These mean-reversion and turnaround data underscore how strong and consistent competitive forces are. Most stocks that are cheap are cheap for a reason, and the likelihood that a business earning poor returns resumes a long-term, above-cost-of-capital profile is slim.

Yet the evidence that high-return persistence does occur (and the likelihood that markets misprice this persistence) suggests that investors with a strong grasp of competitive dynamics and a sufficient investment horizon have an opportunity to realize superior returns.

26

Trench Cooperation
Considering Cooperation and Competition
Through Game Theory

What the Prisoner's Dilemma captures so well is the tension
between the advantages of selfishness in the short run versus
the need to elicit cooperation from the other player to be successful over the longer run. The very simplicity of the Prisoner's Dilemma is highly valuable in helping us to discover and
appreciate the deep consequences of the fundamental processes
involved in dealing with this tension.

—Robert Axelrod, *The Complexity of Cooperation*[1]

The live-and-let-live system was endemic in trench warfare. It
flourished despite the best efforts of senior officers to stop it,
despite the passions aroused by combat, despite the military
logic of kill or be killed, and despite the ease with which the
high command was able to repress any local efforts to arrange
a direct truce.

—Robert Axelrod, *The Evolution of Cooperation*[2]

The War Metaphor—Death or Life?

Executives and investors often use war metaphors to describe business.[3] You
hear discussions of "winning the market share battle," "make a killing,"
"locking up customers," and "outflanking the competition" all the time. In
fact, the word strategy comes from the Greek *strategia*, which means "command of a general."

We generally think of business, like war, as zero-sum: One side's victory is the other side's loss. And many games of strategy—like chess and

checkers—*are* zero-sum. Not surprisingly, early researchers focused their efforts on the best way to play these games. That thinking also spilled over to competitive strategy, which often assumes clear-cut winners and losers. In such settings, the war metaphor certainly appears appropriate.

But is war always zero-sum? No, as one extraordinary example illustrates. The Western Front, a five-hundred-mile line in France and Belgium, was the scene of some of World War I's most horrific fighting. Enemy units were hunkered down in trenches one to four hundred yards apart, and the payoff from a bloody encounter was often just a few yards of territory. From these dismal circumstances, cooperation—a live-and-let-live strategy—emerged. Both sides learned that there would be proportionate retaliation for any aggression, so when one side showed restraint, the other side learned to reciprocate.[4]

In retrospect, it looks like the cooperation got started at mealtimes. When the quartermasters brought food to the front, each side stopped shooting. From there, the soldiers arranged additional truces by shouts or signals. When battalions rotated to the front lines every eight days, the outgoing group would provide fresh troops with the details of the tacit understanding with the enemy. As one soldier leaving the front said to his replacement: "Mr. Bosche ain't a bad fellow. You leave'im alone; 'e'll leave you alone."[5]

This story is relevant for executives and investors because it provides clues about what circumstances are necessary for cooperation to prevail over brutal competition. There are two areas where competitive cooperation is especially valuable: pricing and capacity additions. I will use some basic ideas from game theory to show how cooperation can emerge and why it's so hard to achieve. This tool is especially useful for industries where two competitors largely dictate industry actions.

Why a Date and a Marriage Are So Different

Game theory is the study of interactions among players trying to maximize their payoff. What makes the analysis tricky is that the actions (and reactions) of the players determine the payoff. So game theory forces executives to think not only about their own choices but also how those choices will affect the choices of their competitors. Not all executives naturally put themselves in their competitors's shoes. Consider the following quotation from the former chief financial officer of a leading multinational paper company:

> If you're thinking about building a new paper facility, you're going to base your decision on some assumptions about economic growth . . . What we never seem to factor in, however, is the response of our competitors. Who else is going to build a plant or machine at the same time?[6]

One simple yet powerful model in game theory is the prisoner's dilemma.[7] Consider a case where two competing commodity producers must decide whether or not to add capacity at a cyclical peak. Exhibit 26.1 shows the payoffs. If competitor B adds capacity and A does not (upper right corner), B gets a disproportionate payoff. Alternatively, if A adds and B doesn't (lower left corner), A gets most of the spoils. If both add capacity (lower right corner), the aggregate payoff drops and neither A nor B do as well as if only they had added capacity. Finally, the industry payoffs are the highest if neither company adds capacity (upper left corner), but each

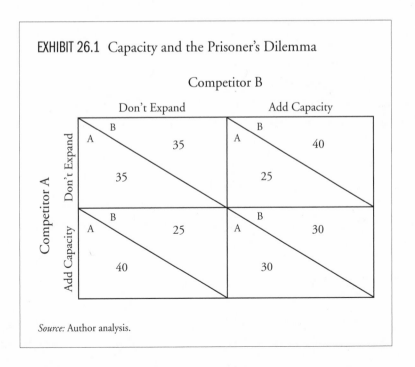

EXHIBIT 26.1 Capacity and the Prisoner's Dilemma

Source: Author analysis.

company's payoff is not as high as it would have been if only one had added capacity.

So what should a company do if it plays the game once? Suppose you're company A and you believe company B won't add capacity. Your best strategy is to add capacity. But let's say you believe company B will add capacity. Your best choice, again, is to add capacity yourself. So no matter what competitor B does, if you play the game once it pays for you to add capacity.[8] The scenario that optimizes total value, though, is for neither company to add capacity. Among other things, game theory shows that the rational solution for a company is not always the solution that is optimal for the industry in total.

In business, as in our trench warfare example, the interaction is not one time but continual. So instead of playing the prisoner's dilemma once, companies effectively play it over and over. Cooperation is much more likely to evolve in an iterated prisoner's dilemma because companies "learn" to work together.

In the 1980s, political scientist Robert Axelrod held a tournament to determine which strategy was most effective in an iterated prisoner's dilemma (each game comprised two hundred moves). The strategy that won was tit-for-tat, which starts by cooperating and then uses its competitor's prior move as its next move. Tit-for-tat assumes the best to start, provides clear negative feedback for defection, and is quick to forgive.[9]

Cooperative behavior in the business world breaks down, or doesn't get started, for a host of reasons. One important factor is the quality of the signals. Sometimes companies try to signal their intentions to their competitors, but those signals are simply too ambiguous or are misread. Another factor is corporate memory. Even though two cyclical companies may compete day to day, when a top-of-the-cycle capacity addition decision presents itself, executives may treat the situation as a one-time prisoner's dilemma because they often don't think over long enough time scales (both past and prospective).

Price and Quantity

For three decades prior to 1974, the two afternoon newspapers serving Sydney, Australia, the *Sun* and *Daily Mirror*, raised prices consistently and in effective lockstep. The *Sun* led these price increases. In 1975, things changed. The *Sun* raised its price from 10 to 12 cents, but the Rupert Murdoch-owned *Daily Mirror* stood pat. The lower price allowed the *Mirror* to gain circulation share and hence increase its advertising rates, driving higher profits. *Sun* profits, in contrast, fell. Finally, in 1979, the *Sun* dropped its price back to 10 cents.[10]

This is but one example of where game theoretic analysis might have been useful. A tit-for-tat strategy would have encouraged the *Sun* to immediately drop its price back to 10 cents, eliminating the *Daily Mirror's* payoff from choosing the negative strategy.

Executives and investors can use tit-for-tat to analyze dynamic pricing rivalry.[11] Cases where these tools have been useful include the U.S. film business, the U.S. ready-to-eat cereal business, and the Costa Rican cigarette market. And while the framework is likely most relevant in cases where there are two clear competitors, it is also relevant provided there is sufficient industry concentration.

Game theory is also useful for evaluating capacity additions. In many cyclical businesses—including autos, chemicals, papers, airlines, and energy—companies tend to evaluate capacity additions at cyclical peaks. This analysis comes at the peak because demand is robust and companies typically have the financial wherewithal to add the capacity.

As noted in the earlier example, though, capacity additions by all companies dampen the payoff at the peak and lead to greater excess capacity during the ensuing trough. In their book focused on game theory, *Co-opetition*, Brandenburger and Nalebuff argue that the benefits of limiting supply outstrip the costs.[12]

The main message is that competitive markets need not be zero-sum. Under the right conditions, executives can see their situation as an iterated prisoner's dilemma and make pricing and capacity decisions that maximize long-term value. Because tit-for-tat can deal with negative competitive action (e.g., price cut or capacity addition) quickly and unequivocally, it incorporates a policing component. Investors can use this framework to judge management's thought process and degree of corporate memory.

27

Great (Growth) Expectations
On the Limits of Corporate Growth

> Castles in the air—they are so easy to take refuge in. And so easy to build too.
>
> —Henrik Ibsen, *Master Builder*

> I see more predictions of future earnings growth at high rates, not less. A few people have taken the abstinence pledge, but it's very few.
>
> —Charlie Munger, *Outstanding Investor Digest*[1]

Compounding and Confounding

Managers and investors generally consider growth to be an absolute good. Managers routinely discuss stretch objectives and sometimes even embrace "big, hairy audacious" goals to motivate their employees and to impress their shareholders. Growth investors routinely seek companies that promise rapid, sustainable increases in sales and earnings.

But most investors do not intuitively understand the power, and onus, of compounding. To see how you stack up, take this little quiz:

One dollar today becomes how much when compounded over twenty years? Write the amount in the space provided.

Starting amount	Compounded at (%)	Becomes how much after 20 years?
$1	2	_____
$1	7	_____
$1	15	_____
$1	20	_____

For most of us, these calculations do not come naturally. A 2 percent compounded annual growth rate (CAGR) over twenty years turns $1 into $1.49. A 7 percent growth rate equals $3.87. A 15 percent rate—a common earnings growth goal among large companies—implies a value of $16.37. And finally, $1 compounded at a 20 percent rate becomes $38.34.

How did you do? If you are like most people, you had difficulty properly gauging the relationship between the growth rate and the ending value. For example, it is not intuitive to most investors that an increase from 15 to 20 percent growth implies more than a doubling in value after twenty years. That's why Albert Einstein called compounding the "eighth wonder of the world." The trick for investors is to make the compounding work *for* them, not *against* them.

Reality Check

In the insightful book, *Profit from the Core*, Bain & Company consultant Chris Zook reveals a study of the companies that actually achieved sustained growth in the 1990s.[2] The sample drew from over 1,800 companies in seven countries that had sales in excess of $500 million.

Zook set three hurdles:

- 5.5 percent real (inflation adjusted) sales growth.
- 5.5 percent real earnings growth.
- Total shareholder returns in excess of the cost of capital.

Notably, these targets are well below what most strategic plans suggest. In fact, Bain found that two-thirds of the companies it examined had double-digit nominal growth rates built into their plans.

Exhibit 27.1 shows the study results. As it turns out, only about 25 percent of all companies achieve the sales growth rate, and just one in eight meets all criteria for sustained growth. Notably, these results are against one of the most buoyant economic backdrops in a generation. The vast majority of companies seek (and plan!) to grow at a double-digit rate and the vast majority do not.

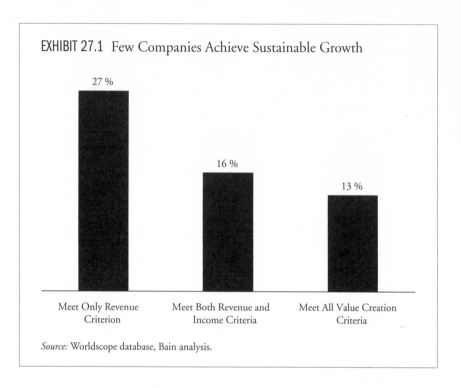

EXHIBIT 27.1 Few Companies Achieve Sustainable Growth

27 %

16 %

13 %

Meet Only Revenue
Criterion

Meet Both Revenue and
Income Criteria

Meet All Value Creation
Criteria

Source: Worldscope database, Bain analysis.

How acute is the potential gap between perception and reality? To check that, I first looked at the distribution of ten-year sales growth rates (1997–2006) for U.S. companies with base-year revenues in excess of $500 million (see exhibit 27.2). The average growth rate for that group was 6.2 percent, and less than one-third of the companies sustained double-digit nominal top-line growth. Further, these growth rates do not adjust for acquisitions, so the organic growth rate is almost surely lower.[3]

Next, I layered in projected three-year earnings growth for all companies with sales in excess of $500 million (2006 base). Even though the earnings growth has been historically roughly 100 basis points higher than sales growth, the analytical point is unchanged. The average expected growth rate for this group, at 13.4 percent, is still roughly double the rates that companies achieved in the recent past (see exhibit 27.3). Also noteworthy is that the distribution of expected growth doesn't include any negative rates.

What is the significance of a 13 percent growth rate versus a 6 percent rate? Our compounding exercise shows that after twenty years at the 13 percent rate, the end value is nearly *four times higher*. As companies get larger,

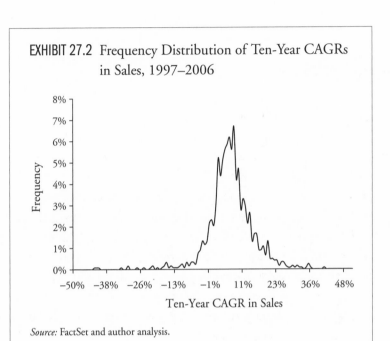

EXHIBIT 27.2 Frequency Distribution of Ten-Year CAGRs in Sales, 1997–2006

Source: FactSet and author analysis.

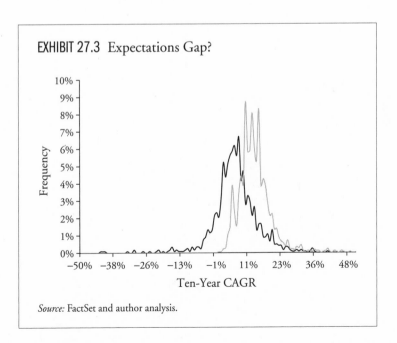

EXHIBIT 27.3 Expectations Gap?

Source: FactSet and author analysis.

sustaining double-digit rates becomes very difficult. So if past is prologue, the expected growth rates for many companies will have to come down.

The Bigger They Are, the Slower They Grow (or Don't Grow)

The entire population of company sizes, like city sizes, tends to follow a distinct distribution.[4] In models that replicate this distribution, scientists note that *average* growth rates are independent of size and that the growth rate *variance* declines with size. Call it the cone of growth.

Exhibit 27.4 shows this graphically. Here I looked at the ten-year compounded annual sales growth rate for over 2,600 U.S. companies. The horizontal axis is on a log scale. The chart shows that while the average growth rate for small and large companies is approximately the same, there is less likelihood that a large company will grow or shrink rapidly. Investors often call this the law of large numbers—big companies can't grow as fast as small companies—but it's more accurate to say that big company growth doesn't vary much from the average growth rate.[5]

Readers who have gotten to this point may have the impression that all companies with high growth rate expectations are poor investments. Nothing

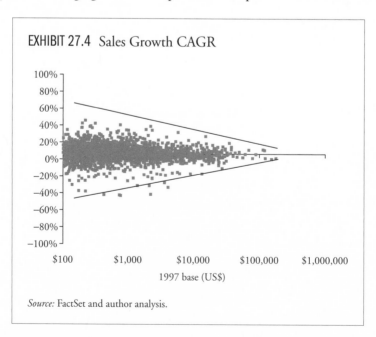

EXHIBIT 27.4 Sales Growth CAGR

Source: FactSet and author analysis.

could be further from the truth! The problem is that while we know that some companies *will* grow rapidly in the future, spurring upside revisions and attractive shareholder returns, we have no *systematic* way to identify those companies. Therein lies a great opportunity.

To demonstrate that growth is good but that it's hard to take advantage of it, we turn to Jeremy Siegel's excellent analysis of the Nifty Fifty in his investment classic *Stocks for the Long Run*.[6] The Nifty Fifty were the leading growth stocks in the early 1970s and had high growth rate expectations and price/earnings (P/E) multiples in excess of forty. In the subsequent bear market of 1973–1974, these stocks as a group dropped sharply.

Siegel asks a basic question: Were the Nifty Fifty overvalued in 1972 based on their subsequent total shareholder returns? Based on his analysis, the answer is no. While some stocks did much better than the market (Philip Morris, Gillette, and Coca-Cola) and others did much worse (Burroughs, Polaroid, and Black & Decker), on balance they delivered a return consistent with that of the overall market. Siegel's point is that based on ensuing performance, the warranted P/E in 1972 was much *higher* for some companies and much *lower* for others. But on average, the P/E was just about right.

Refuse Refuge in Castles in the Air

That there's a gap between expectations and reality is not new. For example, bottom-up estimates of S&P 500 earnings have consistently been more optimistic than the top-down appraisal. But today, the issue seems compounded by the earnings expectations game.[7] Managers and investors engage in an expectations-bar-raising ritual. Executives work to meet or beat Wall Street's forecasts, which encourages analysts to increase their expectations, and compels the executives to deliver even more growth—by whatever means possible.[8]

Investors and managers must have reasonable expectations. The evidence shows that sustaining rapid growth is very difficult, especially for large corporations. Furthermore, while there is nothing wrong with growth stocks, the indications are that it is very difficult to know which companies will exceed expectations and which will disappoint. Investors should continue to focus on investment ideas where the expected value is favorable—where the upside opportunity outstrips the downside risk.

Part 4

Science and Complexity Theory

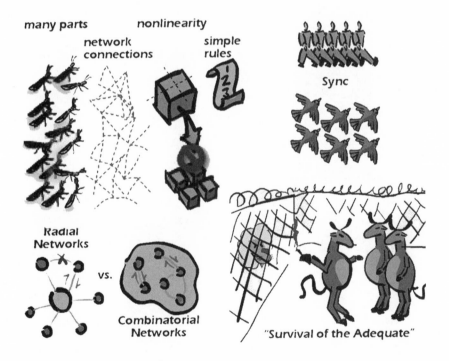

many parts   nonlinearity

network connections

simple rules

Sync

Radial Networks

vs.

Combinatorial Networks

"Survival of the Adequate"

One of my first calls after the major East Coast power blackout in August 2003 was to my friend Duncan Watts, then a Columbia University sociology professor. I peppered him with questions about the failure: what might have caused it, how it progressed, and by what means could we avoid future similar events.

Now you might ask, why would you call a sociologist to answer questions about a power failure? Watts, who has a Ph.D. in theoretical and applied mechanics, is one of the world's experts in network theory. It so happens he practices his craft in a social science department, but he's totally comfortable straddling the physical and social sciences. In our far-ranging discussion, he drew parallels between the blackout, Harry Potter's success, stock market booms, and flu epidemics.

The hard and social sciences are typically housed in different buildings on university campuses, but the real distance is philosophical rather than geographic. In recent years, a handful of scientists—like Duncan Watts—have shown the value of multidisciplinary thinking. Physicists, psychologists, and complexity theorists have all added to our understanding of financial markets.

Science has much to teach investors. The essays in this part are valuable because they offer some important mechanisms that explain how markets are efficient (and inefficient), delve into important empirical results that standard finance doesn't handle well, and show why it's futile to make simple cause-and-effect links in markets.

Social insects, like ants and bees, are fascinating because they show us how decentralized groups coordinate effectively to solve problems. This part looks at various forms of collective problem solving, from a honeybee waggle dance to the Hollywood Stock Exchange.

One of the best examples of a complex adaptive system—generically, a system that emerges from the interaction of lots of heterogeneous agents—is the stock market. Research suggests that when investors err independently, markets are functionally efficient. What's more, defining the conditions under which markets are efficient provides us with a template to consider when markets are inefficient.

Many models in standard finance theory assume that stock price changes are normally distributed around the well-known bell curve. A normal distribution is a powerful analytical tool, because you can specify the distribution with only two variables, the mean and standard deviation.

The model, despite its elegance, has a problem: it doesn't describe real world results very well. In particular, the model is remiss in capturing "fat tails": infrequent but very large price changes. The failure of risk-management models to fully account for fat tails has led to some high-profile debacles, including the 1998 demise of the hedge fund Long Term Capital Management.

Fat tails are closely associated with power laws, a mathematical link between two variables characterized by frequent small events and infrequent large events. Power laws are fascinating, and they empirically represent relationships as diverse as city sizes, earthquakes, and income distribution. While scientists still don't have a firm grasp on the mechanisms behind power laws, their very existence provides investors with good insight.

Humans have a deep-seated desire to link cause and effect. Unfortunately, markets do not easily satisfy this desire. Unlike some mechanical systems, you can't understand markets by looking at the parts. Reductionism doesn't work. Yet we often turn to individuals to explain the workings of the market. Just as an ant relying on local information and local interaction has no clue what's going on at the colony level, explaining all but the most mundane market moves is beyond the ability of market mavens.

Complex adaptive systems have another feature that is difficult to grasp: the magnitude of an outcome is not necessarily proportionate to the size of the perturbation. Sometimes small perturbations lead to large changes, and vice versa. We have to let go of our conventional notions of proportionality when we study markets.

In recent years, scientists have renewed their efforts to find connections between the hard and social sciences. Investors in the stock market can benefit from looking beyond their narrow discipline.

28

Diversify Your Mind
Thoughts on Organizing for Investing Success

The more that you read,
the more things you will know.
The more that you learn,
the more places you'll go.

—Dr. Seuss, *I Can Read With My Eyes Shut!*

Ant Brain

In the fall of 2000, I gathered a small group of leading investors to hear from various finance, strategy, and business luminaries. While these presenters were terrific, none got the award for creating the most buzz. That honor went to Los Alamos National Laboratory scientist Norman Johnson, who opened his talk in a seemingly inauspicious way: "I've been asked here to talk about what's wrong with experts—as an expert in this area—in a subject area, finance, that I know almost nothing about."[1]

What did Johnson say to cause these smart investors to slide forward in their chairs? Simply put, he showed how diverse groups of "average" people, acting together, solve problems better than experts do. Johnson illustrated his point by discussing the behavior of social insects, including ants and bees. It was the incredible performance of these insects, above all, that sparked the imaginations of the listeners.

Most of Johnson's talk was at the macro level, or how the collective solves problems. This has obvious relevance for understanding how market efficiency arises.[2] My focus here is on the micro level, or how investors, *as individuals*, should organize for investment success. While the unit of analysis is different, the message is the same: diverse information and perspectives can help improve investment performance.

Now think carefully for a moment about your information sources. Do you read the same newspapers, talk to the same people, and review the same type of research reports over and over? Or do you allocate time to entertain new ideas, even at the risk of wasting time on intellectual cul-de-sacs? There is strong evidence to suggest that the leading thinkers in many fields—not just investing—benefit from input diversity.

A-Mazing

Before dwelling on the individual, I would like to show how diversity leads to better answers and how a lack of diversity can create inefficiencies. Johnson demonstrates how the collective is better than the average individual with a maze problem:

- First, he asks individuals of identical capabilities to solve a maze. Because the individuals have no global sense of the problem, they simply explore until they find a solution.
- Next, he asks the individuals to solve the problem again. With some learned information, they tend to improve.
- Finally, he constructs a linear combination of each individual's experiences and uses the same rules to find a collective solution.

Because each individual's initial search is random, a collection of individuals reflects diverse experience (maze regions), preferences (preferred paths), and performances (path lengths).[3] So the collective is really just a normal individual with super information. Because of this diverse information, the collective solution is vastly more robust than the average individual solution (see exhibit 28.1).

The power of this collective effect has not been lost on nature. This is where Johnson's stories about ants come in. How do the ants do it? Foraging ants depart the nest with one job in mind, to find and retrieve food. They also have the ability to leave and follow chemical trails. At first, they disperse randomly. When the ants that find food come back to the nest, they leave a chemical trail that their sisters can follow. Studies show that this process allows ants to consistently find the shortest path to the food.[4]

EXHIBIT 28.1 The Collective Beats the Individual

The insert in the figure shows the demonstration maze. The main figure shows the effect on the collective solution as more individuals contribute to it, for two different sets of random numbers. The number of steps of the collective is normalized by the average number of steps of the individuals contributing to the collective solution.

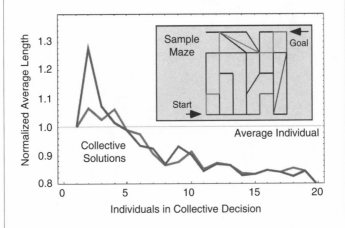

Source: Norman L. Johnson. See http://www.ishi.lanl.gov/symintel.html.

Once researchers understood this collective ability, they decided to play a trick on the ants. In a controlled setting, the scientists placed two food sources at identical path lengths from the nest. As it turned out, the ants ended up using just one of the paths, although they chose at random. Why? Because they follow chemical trails, a couple more ants going down one path will attract other ants, triggering a positive feedback loop. So instead of finding an optimal solution, the ants have one crowded path and an equally long empty path.

Amazingly, though, nature anticipated this problem as well. As it turns out, ants periodically break from the main path and begin a random search process again. The ants are "programmed" to strike a balance between exploiting a known food source and exploring for the next food source (see exhibit 28.2). Johnson calls this the "wild hair" alternative. The ants are hard-wired to seek diversity.

EXHIBIT 28.2 The Wild Hair Alternative

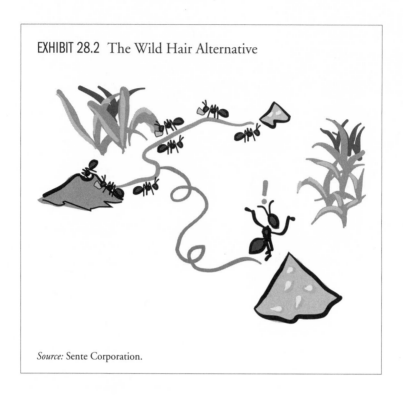

Source: Sente Corporation.

Getting a Diversity Degree

What do mazes and ants have to do with the challenging job of managing money? A lot, as it turns out. Physiologist Horace Barlow says that intelligence is all about making a guess that discovers some new underlying order. This includes solving a problem, seeing the logic of an argument, or finding an appropriate analogy.[5] Where does investment intelligence come from?

Here is where Norman Johnson's message is so important for investors. In well-defined systems, experts are useful because they can provide rules-based solutions. But when a system becomes complex, a collection of individuals often solves a problem better than an individual—even an expert. This means that the stock market is likely to be smarter than most people most of the time, a point the empirical facts bear out.

To be an expert in a complex system like the stock market, Johnson continues, you need two essential features. First, you must be able to create a "simulation" in your head, allowing you to conceive and select strategies.[6]

A description of the legendary hedge fund manager George Soros illustrates the point:

> [Gary] Gladstein, who has worked closely with Soros for fifteen years, describes his boss as operating in almost mystical terms, tying Soros's expertise to his ability to visualize the entire world's money and credit flows. "He has the macro vision of the entire world. He consumes all this information, digests it all, and from there he can come out with his opinion as to how this is going to be sorted out. He'll look at charts, but most of the information he's processing is verbal, not statistical."[7]

In addition, you must populate your mental system with information from diverse sources. While the ability to simulate may be largely hardwired (although you can improve your skills in this area), the pursuit of diverse ideas is within your control.

Psychologist Donald Campbell describes the situation in similar terms, referring to the process of creative thinking as "blind variation and selective retention." In other words, creative thinkers seek a variety of ideas but only choose those that are useful given their current goals.

Idea diversity allows you to find what Johnson calls "weak signals." A weak signal may be the start of a trend away from the dominant path (such as new technology or development) or the right piece of information at the right time from an unexpected source. In fact, a recent study suggests that informal learning fulfils up to 70 percent of learning needs inside some organizations.[8] It's often difficult to know where the next beneficial idea will come from. The evidence suggests that exposure to diverse information sources can improve the likelihood of finding a useful idea.

Creativity and Investing

In a classic article, former Merrill Lynch Investment Managers president Arthur Zeikel argued that superior investment performance requires key personnel within the firm to be creative.[9] He suggested that creative people are:

- Intellectually curious
- Flexible and open to new information

- Able to recognize problems and define them clearly and accurately
- Able to put information together in many different ways to reach a solution
- Antiauthoritarian and unorthodox
- Mentally restless, intense, and highly motivated
- Highly intelligent
- Goal-oriented

Diversity is the fuel for many natural and cognitive processes. Investors that have investment approaches, or information sources, that are too narrow risk missing out on the power of diversity. The downside, of course, is that entertaining diverse ideas means sorting through lots of potentially useless input. But on balance diversity seems to enrich the investment performance—and the lives—of thoughtful investors.

29

From Honey to Money
The Wisdom and Whims of the Collective

The most thought-provoking feature of a honey bee colony is
its ability to achieve coordinated activity among tens of thousands of bees without central authority.

Coherence in honey bee colonies depends . . . upon mechanisms of decentralized control which give rise to natural selection processes . . . analogous to those that create order in the
natural world and in the competitive market economies of
humans.

—Thomas D. Seeley, *The Wisdom of the Hive*

[Decision markets] pool the information that is known to
diverse individuals into a common resource, and have many
advantages over standard institutions for information aggregation, such as news media, peer review, trials, and opinion polls.
Speculative markets are decentralized and relatively egalitarian,
and can offer direct, concise, timely, and precise estimates in
answer to questions we pose.

—Robin D. Hanson, *Decision Markets*

Smart Ant

In his wonderful book *The Wisdom of the Hive*, Cornell biologist Thomas
Seeley explains that returning honey bee foragers do a little dance to tell
their colony mates where the food is. But what's remarkable is that the duration of the dance reflects not only the richness of the foraging site the bees
are advertising but also the colony's need for the commodity in question.

In other words, each bee's communication dance considers both the colony's opportunities *and* its needs. As a result, a bee colony's overall allocation pattern is appropriate even though no one bee is in control.[1]

Ants also demonstrate remarkable collective behavior. Leading ant researcher Deborah Gordon shows that ants place their cemeteries at the point furthest from the colony. But it gets better, because they place their trash heaps at the spot that maximizes its distance from the cemetery and the colony.[2] Without awareness, the ants solve a tricky spatial problem worthy of a standardized intelligence test.

What makes the behavior of social insects like bees and ants so amazing is that there is no central authority, no one directing traffic. Yet the aggregation of simple individuals generates complex, adaptive, and robust results. Colonies forage efficiently, have life cycles, and change behavior as circumstances warrant. These decentralized individuals collectively solve very hard problems, and they do it in a way that is very counterintuitive to the human predilection to command-and-control solutions.

I look at three systems that depend on collective behavior—social insects, decision markets, and the stock market—and consider the similarities and differences to gain better insights into how markets work. I conclude that collectives are very effective in a host of circumstances, but that there are substantive differences between these systems.

Traveling Salesman? Follow the Ant . . .

After describing the workings of a honey bee colony in some detail, Seeley summarizes the main features of colony organization. When scanning this list, consider your notion of how to optimally allocate resources and the parallels between a colony and a market. Main honey bee colony features include:[3]

1. Division of labor based on temporary specializations
2. Absence of physical connections between workers
3. Diverse pathways of information flow
4. High economy on communication
5. Negative feedback
6. Coordination without central planning

The comings and goings of bees and ants may be a source of fascination, but what can we humans learn from them? Social insect organization may provide useful insight into how to solve a set of problems that are difficult to tackle deductively.

One example is the famous traveling salesman problem, which researchers consider a benchmark challenge in combinatorial optimization. The goal is to figure out how to route the salesman from city to city using the shortest path possible. Scientists have demonstrated that the ant algorithm—based on ant-foraging patterns—provides as good or better results than more standard approaches.[4]

Delphic Decision Markets

One lesson we can draw from social insects is that the whole is often greater than the sum of the parts. Yet we humans often rely on experts in all sorts of fields, including medicine, politics, finance, and public policy. Do experts give us the best answers, or is there a way to tap the collective knowledge of many individuals?

Recent years have seen a rise in decision markets, where individuals bet on the outcomes of questions of interest and make or lose money based on whether or not they're right. These decision markets have proven to be uncannily accurate and, like the social insect colonies, their success relies on distributed intelligence.

The best known decision market is the Iowa Electronic Markets, founded in 1988.[5] The IEM allows for bets on what percentage of the election vote individual candidates will receive. The market's record is enviable: in the four presidential elections, the IEM's market price was a better predictor of the election results than the polls (nearly 600 of them) three-quarters of the time. The IEM also hosts other markets.[6]

Decision markets have proliferated well beyond the political sphere. Want to gauge the opening weekend box office receipts for a movie? Check the Hollywood Stock Exchange, where traders have been consistently more accurate than movie-industry pundits. This exchange also does a good job of predicting Oscar nominations and currently allows you to bet on future stars from the TV show *American Idol*.[7]

One of the most liquid markets is BetFair, which allows bets on everything from sports to politics to the stock market. Investors can observe—and bet on—the market's assessment of specific outcomes across a wide range of domains.[8]

Why do decision markets work so well? First, individuals in these markets think they have some edge, so they self-select to participate. Second, traders have an incentive to be right—they can take money from less insightful traders. Third, these markets provide continuous, real-time forecasts—a valuable form of feedback. The result is that decision markets aggregate information across traders, allowing them to solve hard problems more effectively than any individual can.

The Stock Market—the Ultimate Hive?

Stock markets share many of the same features as social insect colonies and decision markets. Markets emerge from the interaction of many individual investors. We've seen that both colonies and decision markets solve problems effectively. To gain better insight into the workings of these systems, we need to look at the differences as well as the similarities.

Perhaps the biggest differences between the hive and the market are incentives and the role of prices. In a colony, each bee acts not to maximize its own well-being but rather the well-being of the colony (evolution shaped this behavior). In markets, each trader seeks to maximize his own utility. This difference may make colonies more robust than markets because colonies are not as susceptible to the positive feedback that creates market fragility.

Also, hives do not have prices. Prices are important in a free-market economic system because they help individuals determine how to allocate resources. Bees convey information through their dances, but prices in markets often go beyond informing investors to influencing them, spurring unhealthy imitative behavior.

Decision markets are also very different than stock markets because they have finite time horizons and defined outcomes. This specificity creates outcome boundaries that effectively limit speculative imitation. In other words, momentum strategies don't work. Further, in stock markets, the performance of the stock can influence the company's fundamental outlook.[9] In decision markets, the outcome and the market are independent.

Swarm Smarts

Investors can draw a few messages from this discussion. First, decentralized systems, even with parts of limited intelligence, are often very effective at solving complex problems. The significance of distributed smarts will continue to rise as we create cheaper ways to harness the wisdom of the collective.[10]

Next, while we may be tempted to lump together all decentralized problem-solving systems, important distinctions exist—and those distinctions shape system performance. For example, stock prices tend to be efficient when investors are heterogeneous. But when heterogeneity does not prevail and investor errors become nonindependent, markets become subject to excesses.[11] Markets are more prone to excesses than colonies and decision markets.

Finally, decentralized systems tend to be robust. Despite episodic excesses, markets adapt well to change. This perspective shifts the onus of rationality away from individual investors and suggests that allocative efficiency arises from the structure of the market itself. Market smarts are the result of the aggregation of local information. That's why it is so hard to beat well-functioning markets.

30

Vox Populi

Using the Collective to Find, Solve, and Predict

We must show how a solution is produced by interactions of people each of whom possesses only partial knowledge. To assume all the knowledge to be given to a single mind in the same manner in which we assume it to be given to us as the explaining economists is to assume the problem away and to disregard everything that is important and significant in the real world.

—Freidrich Hayek, "The Use of Knowledge in Society"

Even when traders are not necessarily experts, their collective judgment is often remarkably accurate because markets are efficient at uncovering and aggregating diverse pieces of information. And it doesn't seem to matter much what markets are being used to predict.

—James Surowiecki, "Damn the Slam PAM Plan!"

The Accuracy of Crowds

Most investors do not associate group behavior with sparkling outcomes. An Amazon book review crows that Charles MacKay's classic *Extraordinary Popular Delusions and the Madness of Crowds* "shows that the madness and confusion of crowds knows no limits, and has no temporal bounds." Throwing vital problems at a diverse group doesn't look like an obvious way to generate satisfactory solutions.

But in recent years social scientists have started to gain a greater appreciation for the information-aggregation ability of markets. Recognition of this ability, when combined with the Internet's connectivity, has opened up new ways to find solutions to hard-to-answer questions, to solve complex problems, and to improve on predictions.

Of course, the stock market is no panacea. There's no question that markets periodically zoom to excesses when investors correlate their behavior. Yet on the whole, most investors and executives don't realize how and why markets are so good at generating accurate answers.

Not all collectives operate in the same way. In some situations, the challenge is to find a specific solution—typically knowledge or expertise held by an individual—to a specific problem. Other cases tap groups as information aggregators, where the group's collective judgment solves a problem or predicts an outcome better than almost any individual can.

Investors should take note of the accuracy of crowds for two reasons. First, information aggregation lies at the core of market efficiency. Here, I define efficiency as the inability of an individual to systematically exploit the market for superior returns. Second, companies that take advantage of the information embedded in collectives might be able to gain a competitive edge. I'll describe a few companies that are trying to do just that.

Needle in a Haystack

A recent *McKinsey Quarterly* article opened with the story of a manager at a biotechnology company seeking technical knowledge of a particular protein. After scouring internally for weeks, the manager concluded the expert didn't exist. Three days later, while in an elevator explaining the problem to a coworker, a woman next to the manager interjected, "I wrote my doctoral thesis on that protein. What do you need to know?"[1]

An ability to cost-effectively solve specific research questions is increasingly critical in our knowledge-based economy. Consider the pharmaceutical industry as an example. Research and development investment has nearly doubled as a percentage of sales over the past twenty years, and it costs roughly $800 million to shepherd a drug from development to full FDA approval and rollout.

Part of the challenge of an R&D-intensive company is to find experts in the lab who can solve tough research problems. Now think for a moment what would happen if a pharmaceutical company could present some of its tricky research problems to *all* capable scientists in the world, not just those on the company's payroll. Could the company solve its problems faster? Cheaper? With less risk?

In mid-2001, executives at Eli Lilly tried to answer these questions by launching a new company, Innocentive (see www.innocentive.com). In 2006, Innocentive had nearly forty "seeker" companies and a community of 95,000 scientist "solvers." After paying a membership fee, seeker companies post research problems along with a cash reward for the solution. Solvers come from all over, half from outside the United States.

Does Innocentive work? It may be too early to say, but some early results are encouraging. Take Procter & Gamble, which in 2002 had a $1.7 billion R&D budget and roughly 9,500 R&D employees, including 1,200 Ph.D.'s. Larry Huston, head of R&D, explains that he uses Innocentive because "these are difficult problems we cannot solve inside [the company]." At Innocentive, P&G enjoyed about a 45 percent solution success rate for the first set of its problems, above the one-third target it set.

P&G's success underscores the importance of a diverse solver group. Says Huston, "Our first problem was solved by a patent attorney in North Carolina who does patent law by day and chemistry at home by night while his wife reads romance novels—at least that's what he told us. Our second problem was solved by a graduate student in Spain, the third by a person in Bangalore (India), the fourth by a freelance chemist-consultant."[2]

It's not hard to imagine other areas where matching problems and solutions might be useful. In spite of some real hurdles like intellectual property rights and improper dissemination of inside or competitive information, the Innocentive model looks like a great step toward finding the idea needle in the diverse haystack.[3]

Weighing the Ox with the Vox

Creating a market from a collective is another powerful way to aggregate information and solve problems. Here, rather than matching a problem with a unique solution, the group solves a problem better than any single individual—even an expert.

Victorian polymath Francis Galton was one of the first to thoroughly document this group-aggregation capability. In a 1907 *Nature* article, "Vox Populi," Galton describes a contest to guess the weight of an ox at the West of England Fat Stock and Poultry Exhibition in Plymouth. He collected 787 participants who each paid a sixpenny fee to participate. (A small cost to deter practical joking.) According to Galton, some of the competitors were butchers and farmers, likely expert at guessing the weight. He surmised that many others, though, were guided by "such information as they might pick up" or "by their own fancies."

Galton calculated the median estimate—the vox populi—as well as the mean. He found that the median guess was within 0.8 percent of the correct weight, and that the mean of the guesses was within 0.01 percent. To give a sense of how the answer emerged, Galton showed the full distribution of answers. Simply stated, the errors cancel out and the result is distilled information.[4]

Subsequently, we have seen the vox populi results replicated over and over. Examples include solving a complicated maze, guessing the number of jellybeans in a jar, and finding missing bombs.[5] In each case, the necessary conditions for information aggregation to work include an aggregation mechanism, an incentive to answer correctly, and group heterogeneity.

Estimating Printers with Populi

In the prior example, the aggregation of individuals determined a particular state—the ox's weight, the number of jellybeans, the location of the bomb—but did not make a *prediction* of a future state. Is there any difference between estimating what is and estimating what is going to be?

Well, solid evidence exists to suggest that the vox populi is pretty good at anticipating the future. Scientists at Hewlett-Packard have demonstrated that even small groups can predict results better than individuals. Apparently, the internal market that Hewlett-Packard set up to predict sales was more accurate than its official internal forecasts.[6]

And Now, For the Real World

So collectives have proven adept at matching seekers and solvers and determining current or future states. How does all of this apply to the stock market?

The stock market is different than the markets I've described because there is no answer—stocks have no specified time horizon or value. (The exception is when a company has agreed to be acquired, in which case the stock price tends to very accurately represent the ultimate value.) As a result, stock investors are susceptible to imitation because they can earn excess profits by selling to someone else willing to pay a higher price. Said differently, one or more of the three conditions for proper information aggregation—group heterogeneity—is violated.

However, I would argue that extraordinary popular delusions and the madness of crowds are exceptions, not the rule. Investors who appreciate how and why markets are efficient will have better insight into how and why markets are inefficient. Further, investors who identify companies intelligently using collectives—the vox populi—may gain an investment edge.

31

A Tail of Two Worlds
Fat Tails and Investing

[Victor Niederhoffer] looked at markets as a casino where people act as gamblers and where their behavior can be understood by studying gamblers. He regularly made small amounts of money trading on that theory. There was a flaw in his approach, however. If there is a . . . tide . . . he can be seriously hurt because he doesn't have a proper fail-safe mechanism.

—George Soros, *Soros on Soros*

In statistical terms, I figure I have traded about 2 million contracts . . . with an average profit of $70 per contract. This average profit is approximately 700 standard deviations away from randomness, a departure that would occur by chance alone about as frequently as the spare parts in an automotive salvage lot might spontaneously assemble themselves into a McDonald's restaurant.

—Victor Niederhoffer, *The Education of a Speculator*

On Wednesday Niederhoffer told investors in three hedge funds he runs that their stakes had been "wiped out" Monday by losses that culminated from three days of falling stock prices and big hits earlier this year in Thailand.

—David Henry, *USA Today*, October 30, 1997

Much of the real world is controlled as much by the "tails" of distributions as by means or averages: by the exceptional, not the mean; by the catastrophe, not the steady drip; by the very rich, not the "middle class." We need to free ourselves from "average" thinking.

—Philip Anderson, Nobel Prize recipient in physics, "Some Thoughts About Distribution in Economics"

Experience Versus Exposure

In his 2001 letter to shareholders, Warren Buffett distinguishes between experience and exposure. Although Buffett's comments are in the context of Berkshire Hathaway's insurance business, his point is valid for any exercise with subjective probabilities. Experience, of course, looks to the past and considers the probability of future outcomes based on occurrence of historical events. Exposure, on the other hand, considers the likelihood—and potential risk—of an event that history (especially recent history) may not reveal. Buffett argues that in 2001 the insurance industry assumed huge terrorism risk without commensurate premiums because it was focused on experience, not exposure.

Investors, too, must discern between experience and exposure. The high-profile failures of Long Term Capital Management and Victor Niederhoffer give witness to this point. Remarkably, however, standard finance theory does not easily accommodate extreme events. Financial economists generally assume that stock price changes are random, akin to the motion of pollen in water as molecules bombard it.[1]

In a triumph of modeling convenience over empirical results, finance theory treats price changes as independent, identically distributed variables and generally assumes that the distribution of returns is normal, or lognormal. The virtue of these assumptions is that investors can use probability calculus to understand the distribution's mean and variance and can therefore anticipate various percentage price changes with statistical accuracy. The good news is that these assumptions are reasonable for the most part. The bad news, as physicist Phil Anderson notes above, is that the tails of the distribution often control the world.

Tell Tail

Normal distributions are the bedrock of finance, including the random walk, capital asset pricing, value-at-risk (VaR), and Black-Scholes models. Value-at-risk models, for example, attempt to quantify how much loss a portfolio may suffer with a given probability. While there are various forms of VaR models, a basic version relies on standard deviation as a measure of risk. Given a normal distribution, it is relatively straightforward to measure standard deviation, and hence risk. However, if price changes are not normally distributed, standard deviation can be a very misleading proxy for risk.[2]

The research, some done as far back as the early 1960s, shows that price changes do not follow a normal distribution. Exhibit 31.1 shows the frequency distribution of S&P 500 daily returns from January 1, 1978, to March 30, 2007, and a normal distribution derived from the data. Exhibit 31.2 highlights the difference between the actual returns and the normal distribution. Analyses of different asset classes and time horizons yield similar results.[3] The figures show that:

- Small changes appear more frequently than the normal distribution predicts
- There are fewer medium-sized changes than the model implies (roughly 0.5 to 2.0 standard deviations)
- There are fatter tails than what the standard model suggests. This means that there is a greater-than-expected number of large changes

The fat tails, in particular, warrant additional comment. These extreme value changes happen considerably more frequently than the standard model implies and can have a substantial influence on portfolio performance—especially for leveraged portfolios. For example, during the October 1987 crash, which I excluded from my figures for presentation purposes, the S&P 500 plummeted over 20 percent, a change that is twenty standard deviations from the mean. Roger Lowenstein notes:

Economists later figured that, on the basis of the market's historical volatility, had the market been open every day since the creation of the Universe, the odds would still have been against its falling that much in a single day. In fact, had the

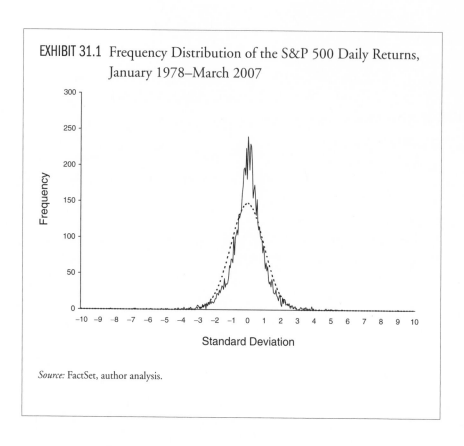

EXHIBIT 31.1 Frequency Distribution of the S&P 500 Daily Returns, January 1978–March 2007

Source: FactSet, author analysis.

life of the Universe been repeated *one billion times*, such a crash would still have been theoretically "unlikely."[4]

The pattern of many small events and few large events is not unique to asset prices. Indeed, it is a signature of systems in the state of "self-organized criticality." Self-organization is the result of interaction between individual agents (in this case, investors) and requires no leadership. A critical state is one where small perturbations can lead to events of many types. Self-organized criticality marks systems as varied as earthquakes, extinction events, and traffic jams.[5]

Is there a mechanism that can help explain these episodic lunges? I think so. As I have noted in other essays, markets tend to function well when a sufficient number of diverse investors interact.[6] Conversely, markets tend to become fragile when this diversity breaks down and investors act in a similar way (this can also result from some investors withdrawing). A burgeoning

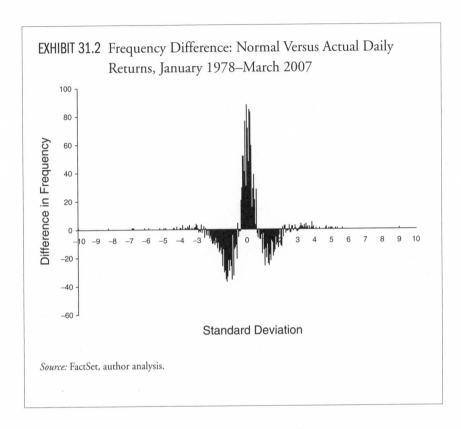

EXHIBIT 31.2 Frequency Difference: Normal Versus Actual Daily
Returns, January 1978–March 2007

Source: FactSet, author analysis.

literature on herding addresses this phenomenon. Herding is when many
investors make the same choice based on the observations of others, independent of their own knowledge. Information cascades, another good illustration of a self-organized critical system, are closely linked to herding.[7]

What Fat Tails Mean for Investors

OK: Big changes in prices appear more frequently than they are supposed
to. What does this mean for investors from a practical standpoint? I believe
there are a few important implications:

• *Cause and effect thinking.* One of the essential features of self-organized
critical systems is that the size of the perturbation and that of the resulting event

may not be linearly linked. Sometimes small-scale inputs can lead to large-scale events. This dashes the hope of finding causes for all effects.

• *Risk and reward.* The standard model for assessing risk, the capital-asset-pricing model, assumes a linear relationship between risk and reward. In contrast, nonlinearity is endogenous to self-organized critical systems like the stock market. Investors must bear in mind that finance theory stylizes real world data. That the academic and investment communities so frequently talk about events five or more standard deviations from the mean should be a sufficient indication that the widely used statistical measures are inappropriate for the markets.

• *Portfolio construction.* Investors that design portfolios using standard statistical measures may understate risk (experience versus exposure). This concern is especially pronounced for portfolios that use leverage to enhance returns. Many of the most spectacular failures in the hedge fund world have been the direct result of fat-tail events. Investors need to take these events into consideration when constructing portfolios.

A useful means to navigate a fat-tailed world is to first measure the current expectations underlying an asset price and then contemplate various ranges of value outcomes and their associated probabilities. This process allows investors to give some weight to potential fat-tail events.[8]

Standard finance theory has advanced our understanding of markets immensely. But some of the theory's foundational assumptions are not borne out by market facts. Investors must be aware of the discrepancies between theory and reality and adjust their thinking (and portfolios) accordingly.

32

Integrating the Outliers
Two Lessons from the St. Petersburg Paradox

The risk-reducing formulas behind portfolio theory rely on a number of demanding and ultimately unfounded premises. First, they suggest that price changes are statistically independent from one another. . . . The second assumption is that price changes are distributed in a pattern that conforms to a standard bell curve.

Do financial data neatly conform to such assumptions? Of course, they never do.

—Benoit B. Mandelbrot,
"A Multifractal Walk down Wall Street"

The very fact that the Petersburg Problem has not yielded a unique and generally acceptable solution to more than 200 years of attack by some of the world's great intellects suggests, indeed, that the growth-stock problem offers no hope of a satisfactory solution.

—David Durand,
"Growth Stocks and the Petersburg Paradox"

Bernoulli's Challenge

Competent investors take great pride in their ability to place an appropriate value on a financial claim. This ability is the core of investing: markets are just vehicles to trade cash for future claims, and vice versa.

OK, here's a cash-flow stream for you to value: Say the house flips a fair coin. If it lands on heads, you receive two dollars and the game ends. If it lands on tails, the house flips again. If the second flip lands on heads, you get four dollars; if it lands on tails, the game continues. For each successive round, the payoff for landing on heads doubles (i.e., $2, $4, $8, $16, etc.) and you progress to the next round until you land on heads. How much would you pay to play this game?

Daniel Bernoulli, one of a family of distinguished mathematicians, first presented this problem to the Russian Imperial Academy of Sciences in 1738.[1] Bernoulli's game, known as the St. Petersburg Paradox, challenges classical theory, which says that a player should be willing to pay the game's expected value to participate. The expected value of this game is infinite. Each round has a payoff of one dollar (probability of $1/2^n$ and a payoff of 2^n, or $1/2 \times 2, $1/4 \times 4, $1/8 \times 8, etc.) So,

$$\text{Expected value} = 1 + 1 + 1 + 1 \ldots = \infty$$

Naturally, very few people would be willing to pay even twenty dollars to play the game. Bernoulli tried to explain the paradox with the marginal utility of money. He argued that the amount you would be willing to pay is a function of your resources—the greater your resources, the more you would be willing to pay. Still, Bernoulli's explanation is not altogether satisfactory. The St. Petersburg Paradox has kept philosophers, mathematicians, and economists thinking for over two and a half centuries.[2]

Philosophical discourse aside, the St. Petersburg Paradox helps illuminate two very concrete ideas for investors. The first is that the distribution of stock market returns does *not* follow the pattern that standard finance theory assumes. This deviation from theory is important for risk management, market efficiency, and individual stock selection.

The second idea relates to valuing growth stocks. What do you pay today for a business with a low probability of an extraordinarily high payoff? This question is more pressing than ever in a world with violent value migrations and increasing returns.

What's Normal?

Asset price distributions are of great practical significance for portfolio managers. Standard finance theory assumes that asset price changes follow a normal distribution—the well-known bell curve. That this assumption is roughly accurate most of the time allows analysts to use very robust probability statistics. For example, for a sample that follows a normal distribution, you can identify the population average and characterize the likelihood of variance from that average.

However, much of nature—including the manmade stock market—is not normal.[3] Many natural systems have two defining characteristics: an ever-larger number of smaller pieces and similar-looking pieces across the different size scales. For example, a tree has a large trunk and a number of ever-smaller branches, and the small branches resemble the big branches. These systems are fractal. Unlike a normal distribution, no average value adequately characterizes a fractal system. Exhibit 32.1 contrasts normal and fractal systems visually and shows the probability functions that represent the data. Fractal systems follow a power law.[4]

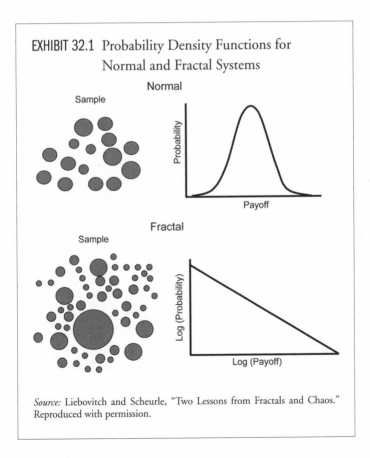

EXHIBIT 32.1 Probability Density Functions for Normal and Fractal Systems

Source: Liebovitch and Scheurle, "Two Lessons from Fractals and Chaos." Reproduced with permission.

Using the statistics of normal distributions to characterize a fractal system like financial markets is potentially very hazardous. Yet theoreticians and practitioners do it daily.[5] The distinction between the two systems boils down to probabilities and payoffs. Fractal systems have few, very large observations that fall outside the normal distribution. The classic example is the crash of 1987. The probability (assuming a normal distribution) of the market's 20-plus percent plunge in one day was so infinitesimally low it was practically zero. And still the losses were a staggering $2 trillion-plus.

A comparison of a normal coin-toss game and the St. Petersburg game illustrates the point. Assume that you toss a coin and receive $2 if it lands heads and nothing if it lands tails. The expected value of the game is $1, the amount you would be willing to pay to play the game in a fair casino. I simulated 1 million rounds of 100 tosses each, and plotted the payoffs in exhibit 32.2. Just as you would expect, I got a well-defined normal distribution.[6]

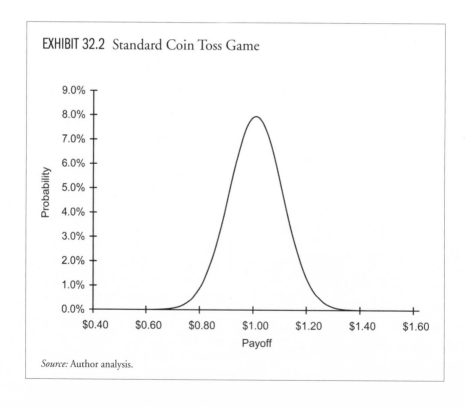

EXHIBIT 32.2 Standard Coin Toss Game

Source: Author analysis.

I then simulated the St. Petersburg game 1 million times and plotted that distribution (see exhibit 32.3). While the underlying process is stochastic, the outcome is a power law. For example, half the time the game only pays two dollars, and three-quarters of the time it pays four dollars or less. However, a run of thirty provides a $1.1 billion payoff, but this is only a 1-in-1.1 billion probability. Lots of small events and a few very large events characterize a fractal system. Further, the average winnings per game is unstable with the St. Petersburg game, so no average accurately describes the game's long-term outcome.

Are stock market returns fractal? Benoit Mandelbrot shows that by lengthening or shortening the horizontal axis of a price series—effectively speeding up or slowing down time—price series are indeed fractal. Not only are rare large changes interspersed with lots of smaller ones, the price changes look similar at various scales (e.g., daily, weekly, and monthly

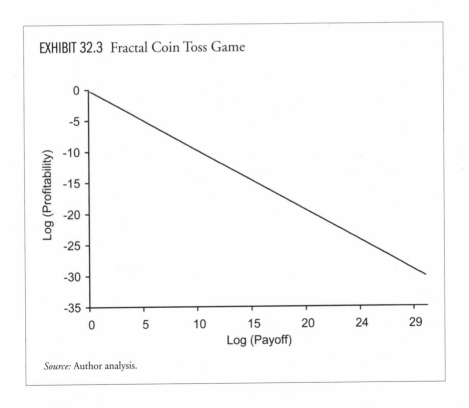

EXHIBIT 32.3 Fractal Coin Toss Game

Source: Author analysis.

returns). Mandelbrot calls financial time series multifractal, adding the prefix "multi" to capture the time adjustment.

In an important and fascinating book, *Why Stock Markets Crash*, geophysicist Didier Sornette argues that stock market distributions comprise two different populations, the body (which you can model with standard theory) and the tail (which relies on completely different mechanisms). Sornette's analysis of market drawdowns convincingly dismisses the assumption that stock returns are independent, a key pillar of classical finance theory. His work provides fresh and thorough evidence of finance theory's shortcomings.[7]

St. Petersburg and Growth Stock Investing

The St. Petersburg Paradox also provides insight for growth stock valuation.[8] What should you be willing to pay for a very small probability that a company can grow its cash flows by a very significant amount forever?[9]

David Durand took up this question in his classic 1957 article, "Growth Stocks and the Petersburg Paradox."[10] He encourages a good deal of caution, emphasizing reversion-to-the-mean thinking and modeling. But if anything, the challenge of valuing the low probability of significant value is even more pressing today than it was when Durand took on the challenge almost fifty years ago.

Consider, for example, that of the nearly 2,000 technology-stock initial public offerings from 1980 through 2006, less than 5 percent account for over 100 percent of the $2-trillion-plus in wealth creation.[11] And even within this small wealth-generating group, only a handful delivered the bulk of the huge payoffs. Given the winner-take-most characteristics of many growth markets, there's little reason to anticipate a more normal wealth-creation distribution in the future.

In addition, the data show that the distribution of economic return on investment is wider in corporate America today than it was in the past.[12] So the spoils awaiting the wealth creators, given their outsized returns, are greater than ever before. As in the St. Petersburg game, the majority of the payoffs from future deals are likely to be modest, but some will be huge. What's the expected value? What should you be willing to pay to play?

Integrating the Outliers

The St. Petersburg Paradox may be centuries old, but its lessons are as fresh as ever. One of the major challenges in investing is how to capture (or avoid) low-probability, high-impact events. Unfortunately, standard finance theory has little to say about the subject.

33

The Janitor's Dream
Why Listening to Individuals Can Be Hazardous to Your Wealth

> In the existing sciences much of the emphasis over the past century or so has been on breaking systems down to find their underlying parts, then trying to analyze these parts in as much detail as possible. . . . But just how these components act together to produce even some of the most obvious features of the overall behavior we see has in the past remained an almost complete mystery.
>
> —Stephen Wolfram, *A New Kind of Science*

Beyond Newton

Where does consciousness come from? This question has bedeviled philosophers and scientists for centuries. We have cured diseases, put men on the moon, and probed many details of our physical world. Yet even the best thinkers today have difficulty defining consciousness, let alone explaining it. Why have we had so much success in some scientific realms and so little in others, such as unveiling the mysteries of consciousness?

Not all systems are alike, and we can't understand the workings of all systems on the same level. Let's start with the systems that we do understand. Many of science's triumphs over the past few centuries are rooted in Isaac Newton's principles. Newton's world is a mechanical one, where cause and effect are clear and systems follow universal laws. With sufficient understanding of a system's underlying components, we can predict precisely how the system will behave.

Reductionism is the cornerstone of discovery in the Newtonian world, the basis for much of science's breathtaking advance in the seventeenth through nineteenth centuries. As scientist John Holland explains, "The idea is that you could understand the world, all of nature, by examining smaller and smaller pieces of it. When assembled, the small pieces would explain the whole."[1] In many systems, reductionism works brilliantly.

But reductionism has its limits. In systems that rely on complex interactions of many components, the whole system often has properties and characteristics that are distinct from the aggregation of the underlying components. Since the whole of the system emerges from the interaction of the components, we cannot understand the whole simply by looking at the parts. Reductionism fails.

Neuroscientist William Calvin, who is in the thick of the consciousness dialogue, notes that we can approach the problem in various ways but that the key to understanding consciousness certainly is not in the "basement" of neural chemistry or the "subbasement" of quantum mechanics. There are too many layers of interaction in the brain. The parts don't explain the whole. Calvin calls the leap from the subbasement of quantum mechanics directly to the penthouse of consciousness the *janitor's dream*.[2]

Why should investors care about the janitor's dream? If the stock market is a system that emerges from the interaction of many different investors, then reductionism—understanding individuals—does not give a good picture of how the market works. Investors and corporate executives who pay too much attention to individuals are trying to understand markets at the wrong level. An inappropriate perspective of the market can lead to poor judgments and value-destroying decisions.

Sorting Systems

When a system has low complexity and we can define interactions linearly, reductionism is very useful. Many engineered systems fit this bill. A skilled artisan can take apart your wristwatch, study the components, and have a complete understanding of how the system works. Such systems also lend themselves to centralized decision making. Many companies in the industrial revolution were good examples of engineered systems—a product went down a manufacturing line, and each worker contributed to the end product. Through scientific refinement, managers could continually improve the system's performance.

On the other hand, centralized control fails for systems with sufficient complexity. Scientists call these "complex adaptive systems" and refer to the components of the system as agents. Complex adaptive systems exhibit a number of essential properties and mechanisms:[3]

Aggregation. Aggregation is the emergence of complex, large-scale behavior from the collective interactions of many less-complex agents.

Adaptive decision rules. Agents within a complex adaptive system take information from the environment, combine it with their own interaction with the environment, and derive decision rules. In turn, various decision rules compete with one another based on their fitness, with the most effective rules surviving.

Nonlinearity. In a linear model, the whole equals the sum of the parts. In nonlinear systems, the aggregate behavior is more complicated than would be predicted by totaling the parts.

Feedback loops. A feedback system is one in which the output of one iteration becomes the input of the next iteration. Feedback loops can amplify or dampen an effect.[4]

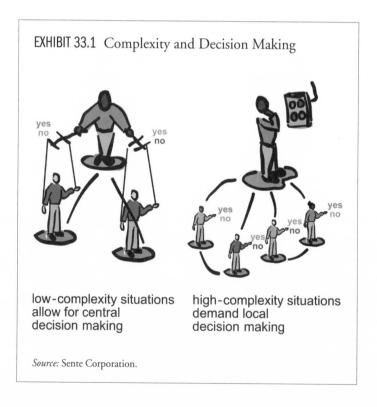

EXHIBIT 33.1 Complexity and Decision Making

yes
no   yes
                            no

yes
no   yes
                                no
        yes   no
        no

low-complexity situations
allow for central
decision making

high-complexity situations
demand local
decision making

Source: Sente Corporation.

Complex adaptive systems include governments, many corporations, and capital markets. Efforts to assert top-down control of these systems generally lead to failure, as happened in the former Soviet Union. Exhibit 33.1 contrasts the two types of systems.

Thinking about the market as a complex adaptive system is in stark contrast to classical economic and finance theory, which depicts the world in Newtonian terms. Economists treat agents as if they are homogenous and build linear models—supply and demand, risk and reward, price and quantity. None of this, of course, much resembles the real world.[5]

The Stock Market as a Complex Adaptive System

The stock market has all of the characteristics of a complex adaptive system. Investors with different investment styles and time horizons (adaptive decision rules) trade with one another (aggregation), and we see fat-tail price distributions (nonlinearity) and imitation (feedback loops). An agent-based approach to understanding markets is gaining broader acceptance. But this better descriptive framework does not offer the neat solutions that the current economic models do.

Investors who view the stock market as a complex adaptive system avoid two cognitive traps. The first is the constant search for a cause for all effects. Critical points, where large-scale reactions are the result of small-scale perturbations, are a characteristic of complex adaptive systems. So cause and effect are not always easy to link. Following the stock market crash of 1987, for instance, the government commissioned a study to isolate the "cause" of the crash. After an exhaustive study, the Brady commission was unable to find a particular cause. The point here is not that cause and effect don't exist but rather that not every effect has a proportionate cause. As humans like to identify a cause for every effect, this concept is difficult to internalize.

The second trap is to dwell on the input of any individual at the expense of understanding the market itself. For example, executives often question how it is that the empirical evidence shows the market follows cash flows when most investors talk about accounting results. The answer is that every individual operates with his or her own decision rules, while the market represents the aggregation of these rules. Further, studies of systems with sufficient complexity show that a collective of diverse individuals tends to solve problems better than individuals can—even individuals that are so-called experts.[6]

Using What You've Got

Time-pressured decision makers often rely on rules of thumb, or heuristics, for their decision making. While heuristics don't always lead to the best answer in a particular situation, they are often useful precisely because they save time for their users. However, heuristics can also lead investors to make biased decisions. One facet of successful decision making is gaining an understanding of these biases so as to mitigate their cost.[7]

The *availability heuristic* allows investors to assess the frequency or likely cause of an event by the degree to which similar events are "available" in memory. Ease of recall is one bias that emanates from the availability heuristic. In other words, investors or managers may place greater emphasis on information that is available than on information that is relevant.

I believe this bias is at the heart of the janitor's-dream problem. Investors and managers spend a lot of time focusing on information that is available, like current earnings and multiples, rather than on information that is more meaningful—that is, what the market reveals about expectations for future performance. Corporate managers see analyst reports that dwell on earnings and hence incorrectly assume that the market is a simple addition of these agents.

Investors and corporate managers trying to understand the market must recognize that it's a complex adaptive system. The market's action reflects the interaction of many agents, each with varying knowledge, resources, and motivation. So a disproportionate focus on individual opinions can be hazardous to wealth creation.

34

Chasing Laplace's Demon
The Role of Cause and Effect in Markets

[Our ancestors] must have felt uncomfortable about their inability to control or understand such [causeless] events, as indeed many do today. As a consequence, they began to construct, as it were, false knowledge. I argue that the primary aim of human judgment is not accuracy but the avoidance of paralyzing uncertainty.

We have a fundamental need to tell ourselves stories that make sense of our lives. We hate uncertainty and . . . find it intolerable.

—Lewis Wolpert, Faraday Lecture

We're accustomed to thinking in terms of centralized control, clear chains of command, the straightforward logic of cause and effect. But in huge, interconnected systems, where every player ultimately affects every other, our standard ways of thinking fall apart. Simple pictures and verbal arguments are too feeble, too myopic.

—Steven Strogatz, *Sync*

Evolution Made Me Do It

Most people know that the human brain has a left and a right hemisphere. The right hemisphere is superior at performing visual and spatial tasks, and the left brain specializes in language, speech, and problem solving. Right-brain-dominant people are known for their creativity, while the left brainers are the analytical types.

But the left-brain system does more than just calculate; it is constantly working to find relationships between events it encounters in the world. Dubbed "the interpreter" by neuroscientist Michael Gazzaniga, the left brain tries to tie life together in a coherent story.[1]

The corpus callosum, a bridge of nerve tissue, connects the left and right sides of the brain. To better understand the distinct roles of the two hemispheres, Gazzaniga and his colleague Joseph LeDoux studied patients with severed bridges between the left and right brain. The scientists knew that if one hemisphere received exclusive information, the information would be unavailable to the other side.

To test the interaction between hemispheres, Gazzaniga and LeDoux crafted a clever experiment. First, through visual cues they secretly instructed the right hemisphere to perform an action. The left side could observe the action but had no idea why it was going on. Next, the scientists asked the split-brain patient to explain why he was acting. Remarkably, the left hemisphere made up explanations for the actions. For example, if the scientists instructed the right hemisphere to laugh, the patient's left hemisphere would report that the scientists were funny guys. In LeDoux's words, "the patient was attributing explanations to situations as if he had introspective insight into the cause of the behavior when in fact he did not."[2] The interpreter at work.

Biologist Lewis Wolpert argues that the concept of cause and effect was a fundamental driver of human evolution. It is evolutionarily advantageous to understand the potential effects of a cause and the causes of an effect. Wolpert suggests that a combination of the concept of cause, language, and social interaction drove the increase in size and complexity of the human brain.[3]

So we humans are wired to make links between causes and effects. And making up causes for effects is not beyond us. The events with no clear causes that baffled us for most of human existence—illness, lightning, and volcanoes—are things that we now largely understand. Unsurprisingly, our ancestors turned to the supernatural to explain these effects.

Today, we comprehend many systems but remain vexed by large, interconnected systems—often called complex adaptive systems. We can't understand the global properties and characteristics of a complex adaptive system by analyzing the underlying heterogeneous individuals. These systems are not linear or additive; the whole does not equal the sum of the parts. As a result, cause and effect defies any simple explanation. The stock market is a perfect example of such a system.[4]

In investing, our innate desire to connect cause and effect collides with the elusiveness of such links. So what do we do? Naturally, we make up stories to explain cause and effect.

Why should investors care about cause and effect in the market? An appreciation of our need for explanation can be an inoculation against making mistakes. Investors who insist on understanding the causes for the market's moves risk focusing on faulty causality or inappropriately anchoring on false explanations. Many of the big moves in the market are not easy to explain.

Laplace's Demon

Two hundred years ago, determinism ruled in science. Inspired by Newton, scientists largely embraced the notion of a clockwork universe. The French mathematician Pierre Simon Laplace epitomized this thinking with a famous passage from *A Philosophical Essay on Probabilities*:

> An intellect which at any given moment knew all of the forces that animate Nature and the mutual positions of the beings that comprise it, if this intellect were vast enough to submit its data to analysis, could condense into a single formula the movement of the greatest bodies of the universe and that of the lightest atom: for such an intellect nothing could be uncertain; and the future just like the past would be present before its eyes.

Philosophers and scientists now call this "intellect" Laplace's demon. The notion that we can work out the past, present, and future through detailed calculations was, and remains, a very alluring concept precisely because it plays to our cause-and-effect bias.

But complex adaptive systems do not accommodate such simple calculations. We can describe many complex systems as being in the state of self-organized criticality. "Self-organized" means that there is no leader. The system arises from the interaction of many underlying individuals.

"Criticality" suggests nonlinearity. More specifically, the magnitude of a perturbation within the system (cause) is not always proportionate to its effect. Small perturbations can lead to large outcomes, and vice versa.

A sand-pile metaphor conveys this idea. Imagine sprinkling sand onto a flat surface. At first, not much happens, and the sand grains obey the basic laws of physics. But once the sand pile builds to a certain height and slope, it enters into a self-organized, critical state. A few additional grains sprinkled on the pile may lead to a small or a large avalanche. The size of the avalanche need not match the amount of sand the researcher sprinkles.

To make this metaphor more relevant to investors, replace sand grains with information. Sometimes a piece of information barely moves the market. At other times, seemingly similar information causes a big move. Models of information cascades provide some insight into why this happens.[5]

Interpreting the Market

Human desire to close the cause-and-effect loop combined with stock market movements that elude simple explanation can lead to some silly after-the-fact narrative. Researchers took the S&P 500 Index's fifty biggest daily price changes from 1941 through 1987 and examined what the press reported as the cause (see exhibit 34.1). They concluded that up to half of the variance of stock prices was the result of factors other than news on fundamentals. They write:

> On most of the sizable return days, however, the information the press cites as the cause of the market move is not particularly important. Press reports on subsequent days also fail to reveal any convincing accounts of why future profits or discount rates might have changed.[6]

I did a similar exercise for the market's biggest moves from late 2001 through March 2007 and found similar results (see exhibit 34.2). The press sounds a lot like a split-brain patient making up a cause for an effect, and we investors lap it up because the link satisfies a very basic need.

EXHIBIT 34.1 Top 30 S&P 500 Index Moves, 1941–1987

Date	Percent Change	Explanation
10/19/1987	−20.47	Worry over dollar decline and trade deficit; fear of U.S. not supporting dollar
10/21/1987	9.10	Interest rates continue to fall; deficit talks in Washington; bargain hunting
10/26/1987	−8.28	Fear of budget deficits; margin calls; reaction to falling foreign stocks
9/3/1946	−6.73	"No basic reason for the assault on prices"
5/28/1962	−6.68	Kennedy forces rollback of steel price hike
9/26/1955	−6.62	Eisenhower suffers heart attack
6/26/1950	−5.38	Outbreak of Korean War
10/20/1987	5.33	Investors looking for "quality stocks"
9/9/1946	−5.24	Labor unrest in maritime and trucking industries
10/16/1987	−5.16	Fear of trade deficit; fear of higher interest rates; tension with Iran
5/27/1970	5.02	Rumors of change in economic policy. "The stock surge happened for no fundamental reason"
9/11/1986	−4.81	Foreign governments refuse to lower interest rates; crackdown on triple witching announced
8/17/1982	4.76	Interest rates decline
5/29/1962	4.65	Optimistic brokerage letters; institutional and corporate buying; suggestions of tax cut
11/3/1948	−4.61	Truman defeats Dewey
10/9/1974	4.60	Ford to reduce inflation and interest rates
2/25/1946	−4.57	Weakness in economic indicators over past week
10/23/1957	4.49	Eisenhower urges confidence in economy
10/29/1987	4.46	Deficit-reduction talks begin; durable goods orders increase; rallies overseas
11/5/1948	−4.40	Further reaction to Truman victory over Dewey
11/6/1946	−4.31	Profit taking; Republican victories in elections presage deflation
10/7/1974	4.19	Hopes that President Ford would announce strong anti-inflationary measures
11/30/1987	−4.18	Fear of dollar fall
7/12/1974	4.08	Reduction in new loan demands; lower inflation previous month
10/15/1946	4.01	Mean prices decontrolled; prospects of other decontrols

(Continued)

EXHIBIT 34.1 Top 30 S&P 500 Index Moves, 1941–1987 (*Continued*)

Date	Percent Change	Explanation
10/25/1982	−4.00	Disappointment over Federal Reserve's failure to cut discount rates
11/26/1963	3.98	Confidence in Johnson after Kennedy assassination
11/1/1978	3.97	Steps by Carter to strengthen dollar
10/22/1987	−3.92	Iranian attack on Kuwaiti oil terminal; fall in markets overseas; analysts predict lower prices
10/29/1974	3.91	Decline in short-term interest rates; ease in future monetary policy; lower oil prices

Source: Cutler, Poterba, and Summers, "What Moves Stock Prices?" 8. Reproduced with permission.

Investor Risks

As this discussion illustrates, investors should be wary of explanations for market activity. Investors that actively seek explanations for the market's moves risk one of two pitfalls.

The first pitfall is confusing correlation for causality. Certain events may be correlated to the market's moves but may not be at all causal. In one extreme example, Cal Tech's David Leinweber found that the single best predictor of the S&P 500 Index's performance was butter production in Bangladesh.[7] While no thoughtful investor would use butter production for predicting or explaining the market, factors that are economically closer to home may also suggest faulty causation.

The second pitfall is anchoring. Substantial evidence suggests that people anchor on the first number or piece of evidence they hear to explain or describe an event. In one example, researchers asked participants to estimate the percentage of African countries in the United Nations. But before answering, the participants watched the research leader spin a wheel of fortune numbered one to one hundred. When the wheel landed on ten, one group of participants guessed 25 percent. When the wheel landed on sixty-five, another group guessed 45 percent.[8] This example may appear frivolous, but investors make serious financial decisions under the influence of similar anchors.

EXHIBIT 34.2 Top 30 S&P 500 Index Moves, September 2001–March 2007

Date	Percent Change	Explanation
07/24/2002	5.73	Investment community decides market overdue for at least a short-term rally; Congressional agreement on corporate-reform law
07/29/2002	5.41	Sense among investors that stocks have fallen too far
09/17/2001	−4.92	First day of trading following 9/11
10/15/2002	4.73	Better-than-expected corporate profits send stocks surging for fourth straight day
09/03/2002	−4.15	Market declines in Europe and Japan and weak U.S. and European manufacturing numbers; talk of more problems among Japanese banks
08/14/2002	4.00	Money moves from bonds to stocks; relief certification deadline passes, and short covering
10/01/2002	4.00	Positive earnings news; Iraq's agreement to let U.N. inspectors return, and strong economic news
10/11/2002	3.91	Another surge in Chicago Board Options Exchange volatility and short covering
09/24/2001	3.90	Foreign markets (except Japan) report gains; clear optimism in insurance and energy sectors; reduced fear of terrorism; and short covering
07/19/2002	−3.83	Continuing concern about accounting profits
05/08/2002	3.75	A gentle hint from Cisco Systems about a possible coming business recovery is enough to spark a monster stock rally
07/05/2002	3.67	Short covering
03/17/2003	3.54	News that the White House has dropped its sputtering diplomatic efforts and appears to be preparing for war with Iraq
03/24/2003	−3.52	Fears that the war in Iraq could be longer and more difficult than investors had anticipated
10/10/2002	3.50	Short covering; The Chicago Board Options Exchange's volatility index pushes above fifty— reflects exaggerated level of investor worry
02/27/2007	−3.47	Concern over high Chinese stock valuations and decision by People's Bank of China to drain liquidity from banking system cause strong sell off in Chinese market; spills over globally

(Continued)

EXHIBIT 34.2 Top 30 S&P 500 Index Moves, September 2001–March 2007 (*Continued*)

Date	Percent Change	Explanation
03/13/2003	3.45	United States expresses a willingness to delay until the following week a vote of using force to disarm Iraq
08/05/2002	−3.43	Weaker-than-expected U.S. employment report
07/10/2002	−3.40	Waning confidence in the market and in corporate integrity
01/02/2003	3.32	Anticipation of increased corporate spending; announcement that Bush's economic stimulus package will be released the following week
07/22/2002	−3.29	Bush affirms support for Treasury Secretary Paul O'Neill and takes some potshots at Wall Street
08/08/2002	3.27	Fed schedules monetary-policy meeting; IMF $30 billion bailout of Brazil; and Citigroup announces a series of corporate-governance measures
09/27/2002	−3.23	Lack of consumer confidence and negative earnings news
09/20/2001	−3.11	Political and economic uncertainty
09/19/2002	−3.01	Bad corporate news and housing construction falls for third straight month
08/06/2002	2.99	Anticipation of interest-rate cut
08/01/2002	−2.96	Report shows slowed manufacturing growth; unemployment worsening; government revises economic growth rates down
01/24/2003	−2.92	North Korea's nuclear threat; Mideast instability; the war against terrorism and rising tensions with European allies
06/17/2002	2.87	Bargain hunting in tech sector due to an oversold market
01/29/2002	−2.86	Accounting questions surface at more big companies

Source: Wall Street Journal, New York Times, author analysis.

The stock market is not a good place to satiate the inborn human desire to understand cause and effect. Investors should take nonobvious explanations for market movements with a grain of salt. Read the morning paper explaining yesterday's action for entertainment, not education.

35

More Power to You
Power Laws and What They Mean for Investors

In the last few years the concept of *self-organizing systems*—of complex systems in which randomness and chaos seem spontaneously to evolve into unexpected order—has become an increasingly influential idea that links together researchers in many fields, from artificial intelligence to chemistry, from evolution to geology. For whatever reason, however, this movement has so far largely passed economic theory by. It is time to see how the new ideas can usefully be applied to that immensely complex, but indisputably self-organizing system we call the economy.

—Paul Krugman, *The Self-Organizing Economy*

Zipf It

Here's an activity to offset ennui on a rainy afternoon. Take a text—say, James Joyce's *Ulysses*—and for all the words plot the rank (from the most widely used words to the least-used) and frequency (how often each word occurs).[1] If you express this word distribution on a proportional log scale, you will find a straight line from the upper left hand of the chart to the bottom right hand of the chart.[2]

George K. Zipf, a Harvard linguist, noticed this relationship in a number of systems in the 1930s and summarized them in his famous book *Human Behavior and the Principle of Least Effort*. Zipf's law, as scientists came to call it, is actually only one example among many of a "power law." To take language as an example, a power law implies that you see a few words very frequently and many words relatively rarely.

Zipf erroneously argued that his law distinguished the social sciences from the physical sciences. Since his work, scientists have discovered power laws in many areas, including physical and biological systems. For example, scientists use power laws to explain relationships between the mass and metabolic rates of animals, frequency and magnitude of earthquakes (the Gutenberg-Richter law), and frequency and size of avalanches. Power laws are also very prominent in social systems, including income distribution (Pareto's law), city size, Internet traffic, company size, and changes in stock price. Many people recognize power laws through the more colloquial "80/20 rule."[3]

Why should investors care about power laws? First, the existence of power law distributions can help reorient our understanding of risk. Most of finance theory—including models of risk—is based on the idea of normal or lognormal distributions of stock price changes. A power law distribution suggests periodic, albeit infrequent price movements that are much larger than the theory predicts. This fat-tail phenomenon is important for portfolio construction and leverage.

Second, the existence of power laws suggests some underlying order in self-organizing systems. Even though scientists haven't fully explained the mechanisms that lead to power laws in social systems, we have enough evidence that power laws *exist* to make some structural predictions about what certain systems will look like in the future.

Finally, standard economic theory does not easily explain these power laws. For example, neoclassical economics focuses on equilibrium outcomes and assumes that individuals are fully informed, rational, and that they interact with one another indirectly (through markets). In the real world, people are adaptive, are not fully informed, and deal directly with one another. So ideally we should seek to explain the empirical findings with an approach that fits how people really act.[4]

The More Things Change . . .

Zipf specified a very simple equation to express his law:

Rank × Size = Constant

This equation says that the quantity under study is inversely proportional to the rank. Given Zipf's equation, we can obtain a sequence by multiplying the constant by 1, 1/2, 1/3, 1/4, etc. Take the case of city-size distributions in Spain. If the largest city, Madrid, has 3 million inhabitants, the second-largest city, Barcelona, has one-half as many, the third-largest city, Valencia, one-third as many, and so forth. Zipf's law does describe some systems well, but is too narrow to describe the variety of systems that exhibit power laws.

The brilliant polymath Benoit Mandelbrot showed that two modifications to Zipf's law make it possible to obtain a more general power law.[5] The first modification is to add a constant to the rank. This changes the sequence to 1/(1 + constant), 1/(2 + constant), 1/(3 + constant), etc.

The second modification is to add a constant to the power of 1 in the denominator. This yields $1/(1 + \text{constant})^{1 + \text{constant}}$, $1/(2 + \text{constant})^{1 + \text{constant}}$, etc. The modified power can be a whole number or an intermediate value (e.g., $1/(1 + \text{constant})^{3/4}$). Zipf's law is the special case where both constants are set to zero.

Even with the introduction of these two parameters, the generalization from Zipf's law to a broader set of power laws remains very simple. That such an elementary equation describes such diverse phenomena certainly evokes wonder, especially since we have no unified explanation for how these power laws come about.

One of the interesting features of power laws in social systems is their robustness. For example, exhibit 35.1 shows the plot for the rank and size in U.S. cities from 1790 to 1990. Notwithstanding population growth and substantial geographic shifts, the relationship between rank and size remained remarkably consistent for 200 years.

Another example, and more directly applicable for investors, is company size. Exhibit 35.2 shows that the relationship between sales and frequency for U.S. companies in 1997 follows Zipf's law. Economist Rob Axtell created this chart based on U.S. Census Bureau data, which were not available until early 2001, based on 5.5 million firms and more than 100 million employees.

Axtell notes that the distribution of firm sizes is insensitive to changes in political and regulatory environments, waves of mergers and acquisitions, new firm and bankruptcy trends, and even large-scale demographic transitions within the workforce (e.g., women entering the U.S. workforce).[6] The implication is that there are important underlying mechanisms that create the order we see.

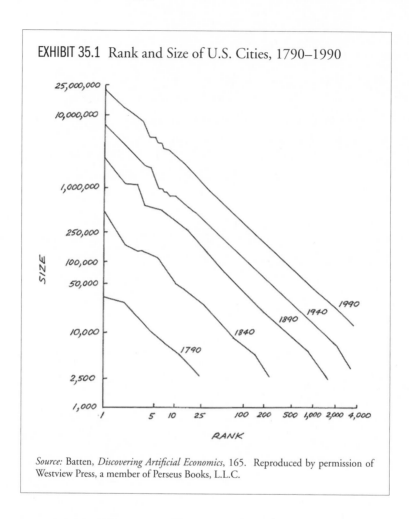

EXHIBIT 35.1 Rank and Size of U.S. Cities, 1790–1990

Source: Batten, *Discovering Artificial Economics*, 165. Reproduced by permission of Westview Press, a member of Perseus Books, L.L.C.

No one completely understands the mechanisms that yield power laws, but there are a number of models or processes that generate them.[7] Perhaps the best known is "self-organized criticality"—a model popularized by theoretical physicist Per Bak. Bak suggests a scene where a child is at a beach letting sand trickle down into a pile. At first the pile is relatively flat and the grains remain close to where they fall. Once the pile becomes steeper, additional grains will periodically trigger a little sand slide. A while longer and the sand slides will be as big as the pile itself. The system is in a "critical" state—between steady state and randomness. Once the pile is in a critical state, additional grains produce sand slides of varying magnitudes and the sizes of the sand slides follow a power law.[8]

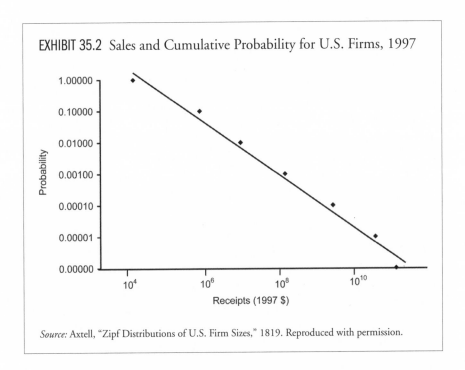

EXHIBIT 35.2 Sales and Cumulative Probability for U.S. Firms, 1997

Source: Axtell, "Zipf Distributions of U.S. Firm Sizes," 1819. Reproduced with permission.

There are aspects of the sand-pile metaphor that are useful for thinking about social systems. For one, the economic systems are clearly self-organizing. That is, most companies, cities, and countries are the result of interactions among individuals, not of central planning. Also, there is a sense of a critical state. In a physical system, a critical point is one where a small change produces a phase transition—for example, water freezes as the temperature drops below zero degrees centigrade. Economists do not define critical points as clearly for economic systems, but we do know that individuals neither stay at the same company forever (steady state) nor haphazardly jump from company to company (randomness). Axtell has captured these features through an agent-based model to explain firm and city sizes. His model yields results that are consistent with the empirical data.[9]

Catch the Power

There are a number of ways that an understanding of power laws helps investors. The first way builds off Axtell's work on company size. Given the evidence that power law distributions are robust over time, we have a good sense of what the distribution will look like in the future even though we have no idea where individual companies will fall within it.[10] But given reasonable assumptions for economic growth and inflation, we can derive a good estimate of the probabilities of companies being of a particular size.

We know ahead of time, for example, that a miniscule percentage of companies will be very large (e.g., > $200 billion sales). We can look at the imputed growth rates of large companies today and discern how many of them are projected, based on expected growth, to be very large. If the group projected to be very large vastly exceeds the percentage that will be large, we know there is the likelihood of substantial downward expectation revision.

Another way investors can use power laws is to understand the topology of the Internet. A classic example of a self-organizing network, the Internet has spawned a host of power law relationships—including the number of links per site, the number of pages per site, and the popularity of sites. These power laws suggest uneven benefits for companies that make heavy use of the Web.[11] The development of the Web may be instructive for the organization of future networks.

Power laws represent a number of social, biological, and physical systems with fascinating accuracy. Further, many of the areas where power laws exist intersect directly with the interests of investors. An appreciation of power laws may provide astute investors with a useful differential insight into the investment process.

36

The Pyramid of Numbers
Firm Size, Growth Rates, and Valuation

Growth is important because companies create shareholder value through profitable growth. Yet there is powerful evidence that once a company's core business has matured, the pursuit of new platforms for growth entails daunting risk. Roughly one company in ten is able to sustain the kind of growth that translates into an above-average increase in shareholder returns over more than a few years. . . . Consequently, most executives are in a no-win situation: equity markets demand that they grow, but it's hard to know how to grow.

—Clayton M. Christensen and Michael E. Raynor,
The Innovator's Solution

Analysts and investors seem to believe that many firms' earnings can consistently grow at high rates for quite a few years. The evidence suggests instead that the number of such occurrences is not much different from what might be expected from sheer chance.

—Louis K. C. Chan, Jason Karceski, and Josef Lakonishok,
"The Level and Persistence of Growth Rates"

Why Big Fierce Animals Are Rare

On the surface, the size and frequency distribution for species, cities, and company sizes may not seem like they would have a lot in common. Yet each follows a power law, which looks like a straight line when plotted on a log-log scale. Power laws indicate that there are lots of small occurrences and very few large ones.[1] In nature, there are lots of ants—the combined weight of ants is larger than the combined weight of humans—but very few elephants. Similarly, we have many small companies and a modest number of huge ones. Exhibit 36.1 shows examples of these distributions side by side.

Take species for a moment. Why are large carnivorous animals, like tigers, relatively rare, while small animals, like termites, are so abundant? Ecologists answer by pointing out that all animals have a niche—not just a physical location, but a real place in the grand scheme of things. A species must not only survive in its home; it must successfully interact with the other plant and animal species that share that home.

The niche idea, though, still doesn't explain why the distribution of species looks the way it does. That insight came from Oxford's Charles Elton, who noted that larger animals need smaller animals to sustain them. (Animals rarely prey on larger animals.) So, Elton reasoned, with every increment in body size, there should be an associated loss in numbers. He called this fact of life the "Pyramid of Numbers." Big fierce animals are rare because they have fewer sources of energy than smaller animals.[2] The species power law distribution is a natural outcome of interacting animals constrained by the laws of physics.[3]

What does this have to do with the stock market? Investors should pay attention to these distributions for three reasons. First, companies, like species, fit into niches. Thinking about these niches and how they change can provide some insight into a company's growth potential.

EXHIBIT 36.1 Distribution for Species, City, and Company Sizes

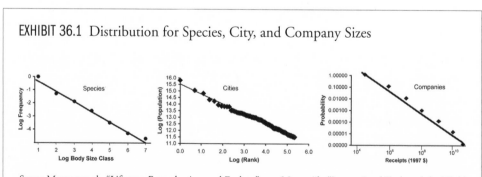

Source: Marquet et al., "Lifespan, Reproduction, and Ecology"; van Marrewijk, "International Trade and the World Economy," http://www.few.eur.nl/few/people/vanmarrewijk/international/zipf.htm; Axtell, "Zipf Distributions," 1819. Reproduced with permission.

Second, a strong body of evidence shows that the variance of growth rates is smaller for large firms than for small firms (even though the median growth rate is fairly stable across the population). Further, growth for large companies often stalls, leading to marked share-price underperformance as investors recalibrate their expectations.

Finally, investors often extrapolate past growth rates into the future, leading to disappointing shareholder returns for companies that cannot meet those expectations. Investors who are aware of patterns of growth may be able to avoid unfavorable expectations gaps.

Find Your Niche

The idea that companies find niches is certainly not new. For example, many aspects of competitive-strategy literature in general, and game theory in particular, address how and why companies should seek profitable niches. The main message here is that environments, and hence niches, change over time as the result of technological developments, regulatory shifts, and industry entry and exit.

Think of mini-mills versus integrated steel companies, or Internet-based retailers compared to brick-and-mortar competitors. New niches open, and new companies exploit them. A company's ability to adapt to a changing environment is critical—and the number of companies that can do so is small.

As a result, optimal firm size may not be fixed for a particular industry, and comparing the valuations of companies with different economic models doesn't make sense.

Dear CEO: We've Made It to the Fortune 50! You're Fired

Studies of firm size distributions and growth rates reveal four stylized facts:

1. *Firm-size distributions follow Zipf's law* (a specific class of power law).[4] What is crucial for investors is that this distribution is very robust in the face of significant economic change. This means that the proportion of very large companies to smaller companies is unlikely to vary much in the future.

2. *Variances of firm-growth rates decrease with size.*[5] My analysis suggests that median growth rates are stable across a large sample of U.S. public companies (sales of $100 million or more) but that the variance in growth narrows substantially (see exhibit 36.2). On one level, this observation is common sense—large companies represent a substantial percentage of the GDP, so it's unlikely that they will outstrip it to any meaningful degree. (The Fortune 50 represent about 35 percent of the GDP.) Yet companies that launch into the Fortune 50 are often those that have realized strong past growth, setting up a potential investor-expectations mismatch.

This empirical finding is consistent with stochastic models similar to Gibrat's law. This law, also known as the law of proportionate effect, says that a firm's growth rate is independent of its size. With some modifications, applying Gibrat's law to a sample of companies generates a Zipf distribution. Classical microeconomics has no satisfactory models to explain these findings.[6]

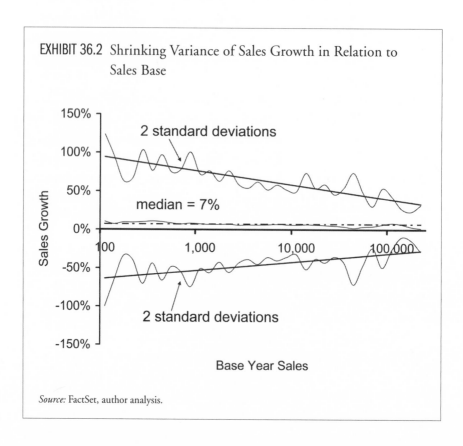

EXHIBIT 36.2 Shrinking Variance of Sales Growth in Relation to Sales Base

Source: FactSet, author analysis.

3. *The growth for large companies often stalls.* This was the conclusion of a detailed study by the Corporate Strategy Board.[7] The research argued that once companies reach a sufficient sales level, they see their growth rate stall. That stall level has risen over the decades but looked to be in the $20 to $30 billion area in the late 1990s.

Exhibit 36.3 shows the average annual growth rate for companies entering into the Fortune 50 (a ranking based on sales). The data show that companies often enjoy strong growth rates before making the top fifty but tend to have rather anemic growth once they attain that group. The high growth rate in the first year suggests that acquisitions catapult many companies into the Fortune 50.

4. *Most industries follow an identifiable life cycle.*[8] Early on, an industry tends to see substantial growth and entry, then meaningful exit and high economic returns (for the survivors), followed by gradual growth deceleration. In mature stages, companies have muted growth and economic returns close to competitive equilibrium. Large companies tend to be mature companies.

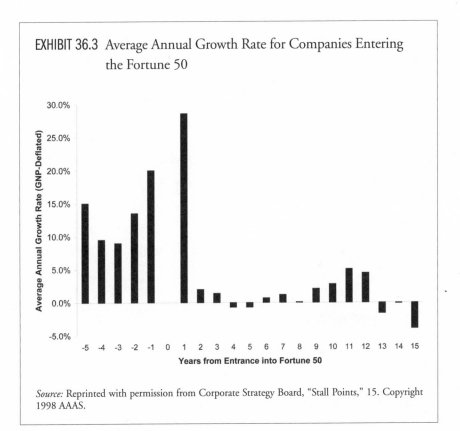

EXHIBIT 36.3 Average Annual Growth Rate for Companies Entering the Fortune 50

Source: Reprinted with permission from Corporate Strategy Board, "Stall Points," 15. Copyright 1998 AAAS.

Advising companies what to do in the face of slowing growth is an industry in and of itself. It is true that large companies have a difficult time innovating as successfully as smaller companies for a host of reasons. I enthusiastically recommend a book by Clayton Christensen and Michael Raynor, *The Innovator's Solution*, which provides managers with a useful innovation framework. But the truth is that not all companies can grow rapidly forever.

Extrapolative Expectations

A review of the evidence on firm size and growth rates suggests that investors should temper their growth expectations as companies get larger. But the reality is that investors tend to extrapolate from the recent past and hence miss declining growth rates. According to Chan, Karceski, and Lakonishok:

> Market valuation ratios have little ability to sort out firms with high future growth from firms with low growth. Instead, in line with the extrapolative expectations hypothesis, investors tend to key on past growth. Firms that have achieved high growth in the past fetch high valuations, while firms with low past growth are penalized with poor valuations.[9]

Data from the Corporate Strategy Board support this point. Its multidecade study shows that roughly two-thirds of the companies that hit

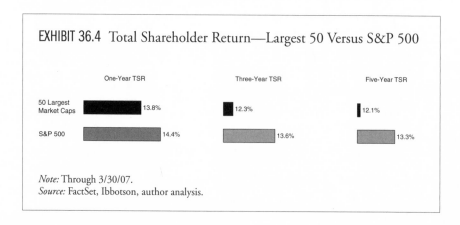

EXHIBIT 36.4 Total Shareholder Return—Largest 50 Versus S&P 500

Note: Through 3/30/07.
Source: FactSet, Ibbotson, author analysis.

EXHIBIT 36.5 Large Companies: Present Value of Cash Flows from Existing Assets Versus Future Investments

Company Symbol	Company	Market Cap in $ Millions	PV of CF from Existing Assets	NPV of CF from Future Investment
XOM	Exxon Mobil Corp.	429,567	92	8
GE	General Electric Co.	363,611	67	33
MSFT	Microsoft Corp.	272,912	47	53
C	Citigroup Inc.	254,030	75	25
T	AT&T Inc.	246,207	98	2
BAC	Bank of America Corp.	227,499	64	36
PG	Procter & Gamble Co.	199,294	51	49
WMT	Wal-Mart Stores Inc.	193,643	69	31
MO	Altria Group Inc.	184,396	57	43
PFE	Pfizer Inc.	178,761	80	20
AIG	American International Group Inc.	174,878	54	46
JNJ	Johnson & Johnson	174,451	49	51
BRK.A	Berkshire Hathaway Inc.	168,151	68	32
JPM	JPMorgan Chase & Co.	168,041	68	32
CVX	Chevron Corp.	159,408	91	9
CSCO	Cisco Systems Inc.	154,202	96	4
GOOG	Google Inc.	142,468	48	52
IBM	International Business Machines Corp.	141,911	80	20
WFC	Wells Fargo & Co.	116,026	62	38
COP	ConocoPhillips	112,374	86	14
	Average	$203,091	70%	30%

Note: As of April 2007.
Source: FactSet, HOLT.

the stall point lose 50 percent or more of their market value (relative to the Dow Jones Industrial Average) within a decade. Ninety-five percent underperform the DJIA by 25 percent or more.

I asked a similar, simple question: How would an equal-weighted portfolio of the largest fifty companies in market capitalization, purchased at year end, fare versus the S&P 500 in the subsequent one-, three-, and five-year periods? I ran the numbers from 1980 through 2006 and found that for each holding period, the S&P 500 outperformed the large cap portfolio (see exhibit 36.4). Again, it's hard for the largest companies to meaningfully outperform the market because they are such a large percentage of the market.[10]

Another way to look at expectations is to break down the percentage of shareholder value that comes from assets in place versus the value attributable to future investments. In early 2007, 30 percent of the value of the twenty largest U.S. companies was expected to come in the future (see exhibit 36.5).[11]

Economies and markets are certainly vibrant. But underneath the constant change lurk robust patterns of growth and firm-size distributions. Mindful investors should take these patterns into account as they assess the growth prospects of companies—especially large ones.

37

Turn Tale
Exploring the Market's Mood Swings

The conviction that the party is far from over is part of the reason . . . technology stocks soar ever higher. "I don't think anything could shake my confidence in this market," Mr. Allen says. Mr. O'Keefe adds: "Even if we do go down 30%, we'll just come right back."

"There was that bad stretch a little while back," he says. "Guys called me up and said, 'What do I do?' I told them, 'Buy more.'"

—"Tech-Stock Chit-Chat Enriches Many Cape Cod Locals"
The Wall Street Journal, March 13, 2000

"All they ever say is, 'Buy, buy, buy,' all the way down from $100 a share to bankruptcy," the burly 63-year-old barber said . . . Now, they give a stock tip and I stay as far away from it as I can. Nobody trusts anyone any more."

Indeed, while mostly avoiding investments in more stocks, Mr. Flynn has been driving to a casino in nearby Connecticut every Monday to play blackjack and poker. "I do better there than I do in the market," notes Mr. Flynn.

—"At Cape Cod Barber Shop, Slumping Stocks Clip Buzz,"
The Wall Street Journal, July 8, 2002

Hush Puppies and Dogs of the Dow

Sales of Hush Puppies, the nerdish suede shoes with crepe soles, hovered around 30,000 pairs in 1994. Indeed, the manufacturer of the once-popular shoes was considering phasing them out. But then, something remarkable happened: Hush Puppies suddenly became hip in downtown Manhattan. Sales of classic Hush Puppies reached 430,000 pairs in 1995 and over 1.7 million in 1996. Within a couple of years, Hush Puppies shook off their label as the dog of the footwear world and became a must-have item for the fashion cognoscenti.[1]

What does the story about Hush Puppies have to do with the stock market? In both cases, *sentiment* is a critical determinant of performance. The mechanism that made Hush Puppies hot is the same as what causes investors to go back and forth from extreme optimism to extreme pessimism.

I extracted the above quotations from two articles in *The Wall Street Journal* about a small-town barber, written less than two-and-one-half years apart. In the first article, the barber's faith in the market is unshakeable—his portfolio is approaching seven figures, he's doling out advice, and he's contemplating early retirement. In the second article, he's lost all faith in the stock market and investment professionals, and prefers casino gambling over investing. The barber's swing from manic to depressed resonates with us precisely because it reflects the change in sentiment among many investment professionals—those who are supposed to know better.

Ah Choo

If you want to understand how broadscale sentiment shifts occur, you can start by thinking about the flu—well, actually, how the flu *spreads*. There are two key dimensions, both intuitive. The first is the degree of contagiousness—how easily an idea spreads. The second is the degree of interaction—how much people bump into one another. If the flu is very contagious but carriers don't interact with others, it will not take off. If there's a lot of interaction but the flu strand is not contagious, it will not take off. But combine interaction with contagiousness and you've got an epidemic.[2]

As it turns out, the graphs of idea and disease propagation look the same. They both follow an S-curve (see exhibit 37.1). Not surprisingly, our biological analogy points to business world parallels. We can understand susceptibility, or contagiousness, as adoption thresholds. And we can model the degree of interaction with a "small-world" framework.

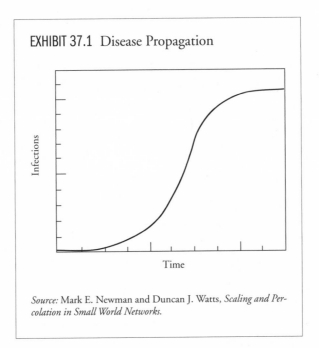

EXHIBIT 37.1 Disease Propagation

Source: Mark E. Newman and Duncan J. Watts, *Scaling and Percolation in Small World Networks.*

Ben Graham once said, "In the stock market, value standards don't determine prices; prices determine value standards."[3] Individuals don't construct value standards based on intrinsic principles but rather are influenced by what other people do. Stock prices reflect the collective actions of others. But we all don't have equal potential to be influenced. We all have what's called an adoption threshold, which is defined by how many other people must engage in an activity before we join in. Market extremes push the sentiment beyond the adoption threshold of nearly all investors. Such extremes can create, by definition, the conditions for a sentiment reversal.

Also, we interact more than ever. Scientists have made significant strides in understanding the small-world effect—colloquially known as six degrees of separation—in recent years.[4] One of the central ideas in the small-world model is clustering, or the degree to which connections to one node connect to another. For example, clustering expresses the likelihood that your friends are likely to know one another.

When modeling these networks, researchers discovered that just a few random links between local, clustered networks dramatically reduce the degrees of separation. Because of our modern, low-cost communications network, ideas can cascade through social clusters faster than ever. The mass media further reinforce our interconnectedness.

This biological analogy reveals that almost all investors succumb to strong sentiment—either bullish or bearish—sooner or later. Further, interaction is almost assured because of our ability to communicate. Sentiment swings are age old and there are no modern inoculations.

Economists, Meet Mr. Market

Economists have long understood the role of expectations in shaping economic outcomes, including the performance of the stock market and the robustness of capital spending. Yet most economic models presume rational agents, a convenient modeling assumption that also happens to be safely removed from reality. An agent-based model of markets not only offers results consistent with the empirical facts but also accommodates periodic deviations between price and value.[5]

Practitioners spanning the centuries have documented the role of sentiment in investing and speculation.[6] Perhaps the best way to think about sentiment is Ben Graham's Mr. Market metaphor. Graham suggested imagining market quotes coming from an accommodating fellow named Mr. Market, who never fails to show up and offer you a price to either buy or sell your interest in a business.

Warren Buffett describes Mr. Market's most important characteristic:

> Even though the business that the two of you own may have economic characteristics that are stable, Mr. Market's quotations will be anything but. For, sad to say, the poor fellow has incurable emotional problems. At times he feels euphoric and can only see the favorable factors favoring the business. When in that mood, he names a very high buy-sell price because he fears you will snap up his interest and rob him of imminent gains. At other times he is depressed and can see nothing but trouble ahead for both the business and the world. On these occasions he will name a very low price, since he is terrified that you will unload your interest on him.[7]

Buffett underscores that since Mr. Market does not mind if you ignore him, you should never fall under his influence. The message is that price and value may diverge from one another, but investors who focus too much on price may have an emotionally difficult time distinguishing between the two.

No Progress in Human Nature

In a lecture delivered in the mid-1940s, Ben Graham noted that while there had been many advances in the art of security analysis up to that date, in one "important respect" there was practically no progress at all: human nature. There is little in today's dismal market performance, swings in sentiment, and anxieties that is new. The small-town barber's fear and greed are symbolic of those investors who preceded him as well as those who are sure to follow.

The central role of sentiment comes through loud and clear in the first edition of Graham and Dodd's *Security Analysis*, written over seventy years ago. Here's what they said about the prevailing investor psychology in the late 1920s:

> The "new-era" doctrine—that "good" stocks (or "blue chips") were sound investments regardless of how high the price paid for them—was at bottom only a means of rationalizing under the title of "investment" the well-nigh universal capitulation to the gambling fever. We suggest that this psychological phenomenon is closely related to the dominant importance assumed in recent years by intangible factors of value, viz., good-will, management, expected earning power, etc. Such value factors, while undoubtedly real, are not susceptible to mathematical calculation; hence the standards by which they are measured are to a great extent arbitrary and can suffer from the widest variations in accordance with the prevalent psychology.[8]

Investors must bear in mind, too, that all sentiment extremes eventually pass, as Graham and Dodd remind us:

> But if past experience is any guide, the current critical attitude of the investor is not likely to persist; and in the next period of prosperity and plethora of funds for security purchases, the public will once again exhibit its ingrained tendency to forgive, and particularly to forget, the sins committed against it in the past.

Maintain Perspective

The stock market, like the bond market, is a discounting machine. This means investors should expect a mid- to high-single-digit nominal return over time under normal conditions. Sentiment swings, extreme optimism or pessimism, can distort these expected returns. (When investors *expect* returns to be highest is when they're likely to be the lowest, and vice versa.)

In difficult markets such as we had in the early 2000s, investors are well served to try to maintain perspective and avoid groupthink.[9] In particular, reflecting on history and carefully considering multiple scenarios can be helpful to provide necessary calibration. Buffett, with an emphasis on how easy it is to get swept up in emotion and a dismissal of overly quantitative approaches, comments:

> [A]n investor will succeed by coupling good business judgment with an ability to insulate his thoughts and behavior from the supercontagious emotions that swirl about in the marketplace.

38

Stairway to Shareholder Heaven
Exploring Self-Affinity in Return on Investment

> Nature uses only the longest threads to weave her pattern, so each small piece of the fabric reveals the organization of the entire tapestry.
>
> —Richard P. Feynman

I Could Do That

Life magazine created a stir in the late 1940s when it openly questioned whether Jackson Pollock (1912–1956) was "the greatest living painter in the United States." Pollock wasn't a standard paint-and-palette guy—he created his abstract art by dripping paint onto huge canvases. While some of his pieces sold for millions, one skeptic suggested his art is like "a mop of tangled hair I have an irresistible urge to comb out."[1] Some critics deridingly implied that they could recreate Pollock's work by randomly splashing paint on a surface.[2] Exhibit 38.1 shows a Pollock painting from the late 1940s.

Still, Pollock's work has draw. In an effort to understand the aesthetic appeal of Pollock's paintings, physicist Richard Taylor turned to the world of mathematics. He found that Pollock's paintings, while seemingly haphazard, exhibit pleasing fractal patterns. A fractal is "a geometric shape that can be separated into parts, each of which is a reduced-scale version of the whole."[3] In spite of the skeptical sneers, Taylor showed that fractal patterns are by no means an inevitable consequence of dripping paint.

Fractals are ubiquitous in nature—trees, clouds, and coastlines are but a few examples—and as a result are visually familiar to humans.[4] One critical feature of a fractal pattern is its fractal dimension—or degree of complexity

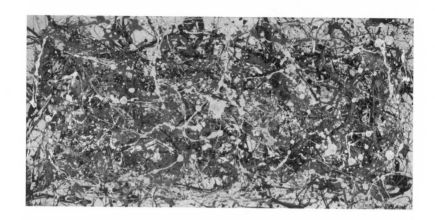

EXHIBIT 38.1 Jackson Pollock, *Number 8, 1949. Source:* Collection Neuberger Museum of Art, Purchase College, State University of New York, gift of Roy R. Neuberger. Photo by Jim Frank.

(a line has a fractal dimension of 1.0, while a filled space has a dimension of 2.0). Taylor and his collaborators found that humans have a preference for fractals with dimensions between 1.3 and 1.5, whether those fractals are natural or human-made. Many of Pollock's paintings fall within, or near, this range. As a consequence, scientists can quickly distinguish between a Pollock and non-Pollock.[5]

Because fractals are so common in nature, scientists often associate them with self-organized systems. Since economics deals largely with these types of systems, we might expect to see fractals in economic systems as well. And indeed, we do.

Just as we have to analyze a Pollock painting or a coastline to appreciate the underlying fractal pattern, we must take a fresh look at economic systems as well. Order is often hidden.[6]

Stairway to Shareholder Heaven

Self-affinity, or the resemblance of the parts to the whole, is another crucial feature of a fractal. Think of a cauliflower. The whole cauliflower, a large bump, and a small bump all visually resemble one another. Stock price changes are also fractal: after some adjustments, the data look the same whether you look at month-to-month, week-to-week, or day-to-day changes.[7]

Analysis shows that distributions of the spread between returns on investment and cost of capital show self-affinity across five levels: country, industry, company, firm, and division. The best way to assess this point is through visual inspection (see exhibit 38.2). Across all levels, we tend to see the same pattern of value creation, value neutrality, and value destruction. To be sure, some of the distributions skew toward value creation and others toward value destruction, but both sides of the spectrum are consistently represented.

While I show only one industry (diversified chemicals), we can look at any industry and see a similar array of value performance. Ditto for an individual company. So there is nothing unique about the country, industry, company, division, or business line we selected (besides availability of the data).

Making the Art Less Abstract

The usefulness of this observation may appear, on the surface, as abstract as a Pollock painting. But I believe these distributions present at least five concrete implications for investors:

1. *Consider why returns are less than the cost of capital.* Generating poor returns is clearly not desirable, but it is important to consider *why* the returns are low. For example, a company that is early in its life cycle may have depressed returns because it is investing heavily, but its economic future may be bright. Current weak returns may belie a strong outlook.

In contrast, a mature company may have poor returns because competitive forces have wrung out all the attractive opportunities, and the industry may be plagued with excess capacity.

Companies also invest in new businesses where they have little chance of gaining a competitive advantage. So some insight into the nature of poor returns is very useful.

2. *Look for changes in returns (both positive and negative) not anticipated by the market.* Empirical evidence shows that changes in returns are strongly correlated

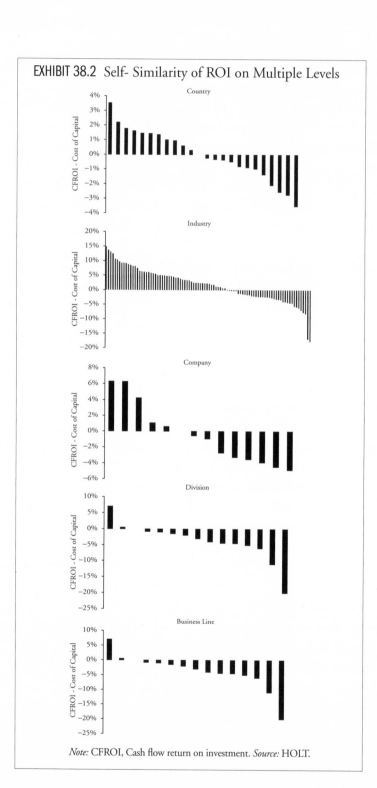

EXHIBIT 38.2 Self- Similarity of ROI on Multiple Levels

Note: CFROI, Cash flow return on investment. *Source:* HOLT.

to stock price changes. Companies with the greatest return improvement, on average, tend to significantly outperform the companies with the largest return degradation. These data suggest that the market does not fully anticipate the full degree of return changes.[8]

Investors should carefully gauge market expectations and try to determine whether or not those expectations are likely to change. Many investment processes fail to properly measure and consider market expectations.[9]

3. *Judge the likely longevity of excess returns.* Reversion to the mean is a powerful force with company-level returns. High-return businesses face competition that drives down their returns, and capital tends to flee low-return businesses, allowing returns to drift up. Discerning how long it is likely to take for excess returns to be competed away is essential.[10]

The stock market tends to equilibrate shareholder returns via valuation (allowing for risk differences). High-return businesses receive high price-to-book ratios, and low-return businesses garner low ratios. For this reason, good companies are not always good stocks.

4. *Strategy matters.* From a company's perspective, strategy is about pursuing a set of activities that allow it to generate returns above the cost of capital. Successful strategies typically put a company in a unique position, with either a differentiated offering or a low production cost. Strategy is about trade-offs—deciding what to do and what not to do.

One noteworthy finding of this work is that even the worst industries include value-creating companies, and the best industries, value-destroying companies. This evidence strongly suggests that competitive strategy matters. A thorough strategy assessment should be integral to a long-term investor's process.[11]

How does management allocate its time? Since exceptional, talented managers are so rare, investors must determine how a company allocates its managerial talent. Often, companies assign their best managers to turn around or fix ailing businesses, instead of letting them drive value at the strongest divisions. For this reason, investors should try to understand the value breakdown of various businesses (which may be in stark contrast to sales or operating income contributions) and judge whether or not the company is intelligently allocating managerial resources.

Order and Disorder

Better data and computational tools are allowing researchers to see order in systems previously perceived to be disorderly or random. I suspect that the self-affinity evident in return spreads is symptomatic of the self-organizing properties of global business. While this general observation is intellectually exciting, it also has practical, investment-related relevance. And you don't have to be a Jackson Pollock fan to see it.

Conclusion
The Future of Consilience in Investing

Since 1993, I have taught a course called Security Analysis at Columbia Business School. As you would expect, the course covers basic investing issues like valuation, financial-statement analysis, and competitive-strategy frameworks. However, in the first class of the semester every year I sound a warning for the students: this class will raise a lot more questions than it will answer.

For example, we don't really know how markets aggregate information and what that means for stock price efficiency. Our concept of risk remains incomplete, although we do know that the standard measure of risk is wrong. Most competitive strategy frameworks don't tell you what strategy is likely to succeed or fail under varying circumstances. And for sure, we still have lots to learn about how our brains work.

This long list of unanswered questions makes investing both exciting and frustrating. Exciting because we can expect to gain knowledge and improve our understanding in the years to come. Frustrating because we still understand so little, and the market consistently confounds even its smartest participants.

I firmly believe that consilience among disciplines will play a crucial role in advancing our investing knowledge. Financial economists often greet the investment-related work of physicists, psychologists, and sociologists with skepticism. No doubt, the lack of economic training can put these other scientists at a disadvantage. But ultimately, the insights that researchers gather from cross-disciplinary collaboration will provide the deepest insights—maybe even answers—into the workings of companies and markets.

Here are some quick thoughts about where a multidisciplinary approach might help our investing knowledge:

- *Decision making and neuroscience.* Throughout this book, I refer to Daniel Kahneman and Amos Tversky's prospect theory, which describes how people systematically make decisions that deviate from the theoretical ideal. Prospect theory catalyzed the field of behavioral finance, dedicated to the study of cognitive errors and decision-making biases in business and investing settings.

Though it represents a huge leap forward, prospect theory still fails to reveal why people make the decisions they do. Advances in neuroscience now allow researchers to peer into the brains of subjects, providing the first tantalizing glimpses of what's actually going on as people decide. Economist Colin Camerer likens the plunge into neuroscience to the first family on the block to have a television in the 1950s: the picture may be fuzzy and you may need to tweak the rabbit ears, but the new images and insights are exhilarating. The pictures will only get better with time.

- *Statistical properties of markets—from description to prediction?* When describing markets, financial economists generally assume a definable tradeoff between risk and reward. Unfortunately, the empirical record defies a simple risk-reward relationship. As Benoit Mandelbrot has argued, failure to explain is caused by failure to describe.

  Starting in earnest with Mandelbrot's work in finance in the early 1960s, statistical studies have shown that stock price changes are not distributed along a bell-shaped curve but rather follow a power law.[1] Practitioners acknowledged this fact long ago and have modified their models—even if through intuition—to accommodate this reality. Yet even if we can properly describe and categorize the market's statistical features, the challenge to figure out cause and effect remains.

- *Agent-based models.* Most economic models gloss over individual differences and simply assume average individuals. An agent-based model confers limited but varied abilities on individual agents, and lets them loose *in silico*. These models show that individual differences are important in market outcomes and that feedback mechanisms are rampant. For example, people often make decisions based on what other people decide. These simple models may dramatically improve on our intuition about why markets behave the way they do and eventually may lead to useful predictions.

- *Network theory and information flows.* Stanley Milgram is best remembered for his 1960s idea of six degrees of separation—you can connect any two people in the world through five intermediaries. The problem is that Milgram's research was shoddy at best. For decades, the six-degrees notion was popular but not proven.

In the late 1990s, a new generation of scientists addressed the problem using much more sophisticated analytical tools, including computers. They not only rigorously showed the validity of the six-degrees concept, they described the key features of network structure.[2]

Our improved understanding of networks has clearly been a multidisciplinary effort, with liberal exchange between the hard, biological, and social sciences. Network research intersects a number of areas, including epidemiology, psychology, sociology, diffusion theory, and competitive strategy. Network theory is likely to add substantially to our understanding of how product and capital markets develop and change.

- *Growth and size distribution.* The distribution of firm sizes in industrialized countries is highly skewed: there are very few large firms and many small ones. Scientists have observed this pattern for nearly a century. But no one has been able to explain the mechanism that leads to this distribution.

  The distribution of animal size and metabolic rate is also skewed, and in a very similar way to firm size. Notably, scientists have successfully explained the physical conditions between size and metabolic rate.[3] Extension of some of these biological and physical principles to the social sciences holds substantial promise.

- *Flight simulator for the mind?* I have always been very impressed by the flight simulators that pilots use for training. These sophisticated machines simulate myriad conditions, providing pilots with important experience and feedback in a realistic but safe setting.

  Is it possible to build a simulator that serves the same purpose for investors? One of the major challenges with investing—especially long-term-oriented investing—is feedback. Studies show that clear and consistent feedback helps professionals in probabilistic fields. While weather forecasters and handicappers get accurate and timely feedback, long-term investors don't. Maybe one day we'll create a simulator that provides investors the training they need to make better decisions. Of course, the result will be markets that are even harder to beat.

Trillions of dollars are exchanged in global markets every day. Yet despite the high stakes and considerable resources researchers have committed to understanding markets, there is much we do not grasp. This book celebrates the idea that the answers to many of these questions will emerge only by thinking across disciplines.

1. Be the House

1. J. Edward Russo and Paul J. H. Schoemaker, *Winning Decisions: Getting It Right the First Time* (New York: Doubleday, 2002), 3–10.

2. Alfred Rappaport and Michael J. Mauboussin, *Expectations Investing* (Boston, Mass.: Harvard Business School Press, 2001), 106–8. In this discussion, we assume investors running diversified portfolios are risk-neutral. For techniques to capture risk aversion, see Ron S. Dembo and Andrew Freeman, *Seeing Tomorrow: Rewriting the Rules of Risk* (New York: John Wiley & Sons, 1998).

3. Michael Steinhardt, *No Bull: My Life In and Out of Markets* (New York: John Wiley & Sons, 2001), 129.

4. Steven Crist, "Crist on Value," in Andrew Beyer et al., *Bet with the Best: All New Strategies From America's Leading Handicappers* (New York: Daily Racing Form Press, 2001), 64. Crist's chapter is one of the best descriptions of intelligent investing I have ever read. I also highly recommend Steven Crist, *Betting on Myself: Adventures of a Horseplayer and Publisher* (New York: Daily Racing Form Press, 2003).

5. From Robert Rubin's commencement address, University of Pennsylvania, 1999, http://www.upenn.edu/almanac/v45/n33/speeches99.html.

6. See chapter 5.

7. Sarah Lichenstein, Baruch Fischhoff, and Lawrence D. Phillips, "Calibration of Probabilities," in *Judgment Under Uncertainty: Heuristics and Biases*, ed. Daniel Kahneman, Paul Slovic, and Amos Tversky (Cambridge: Cambridge University Press, 1982), 306–34.

8. Peter Schwartz, *Inevitable Surprises: Thinking Ahead in a Time of Turbulence* (New York: Gotham Books, 2003).

9. Roger Lowenstein, *When Genius Failed: The Rise and Fall of Long-Term Capital Management* (New York: Random House, 2000); Nassim Nicholas Taleb, *The Black Swan: The Impact of the Highly Improbable* (New York: Random House, 2007).

10. Daniel Kahneman and Amos Tversky, "Prospect Theory: An Analysis of Decision Under Risk," *Econometrica* 47 (1979): 263–91.

11. Nassim Nicholas Taleb, *Fooled By Randomness: The Hidden Role of Chance in Markets and in Life* (New York: Texere, 2001), 89–90. Taleb takes to task the well-known investor Jim Rogers for arguing against investing in options because of the frequency of loss. Says Taleb, "Mr. Jim Rogers seems to have gone very far in life for someone who does not distinguish between probability and expectation."

12. See chapter 3.

13. Russo and Schoemaker, *Winning Decisions*, 123–24.

14. Rubin, commencement address, University of Pennsylvania, 1999.

2. Investing–Profession or Business?

1. Burton G. Malkiel, "The Efficient Market Hypothesis and Its Critics," *Journal of Economic Perspectives* 17, no. 1 (Winter 2003): 78. This is not a new finding. See also Burton G. Malkiel, "Returns from Investing in Equity Mutual Funds, 1971–1991," *Journal of Finance* 50, no. 2 (June 1995): 549–72; Michael C. Jensen, "The Performance of Mutual Funds in the Period 1945–1964," *Journal of Finance* 23 (1968): 389–416.

2. Special thanks to Gary Mishuris for creating the initial list and prompting this line of inquiry.

3. Jack Bogle, using John Maynard Keynes's terminology, contrasts *speculation* ("forecasting the psychology of the market") with *enterprise* ("forecasting the prospective yield of an asset"). Bogle argues that the turnover ratios suggest most investors are speculators. See John C. Bogle, "Mutual Fund Industry in 2003: Back to the Future," 14 January 2003, http://www.vanguard.com/bogle_site/sp20030114.html.

4. See Charles D. Ellis, "Will Business Success Spoil the Investment Management Profession?" *The Journal of Portfolio Management* (Spring 2001): 11–15, for an excellent exposition of this tension.

5. Bogle, "Mutual Fund Industry in 2003." Also see, "Other People's Money: A Survey of Asset Management," *The Economist*, July 5, 2003; John C. Bogle, "The Emperor's New Mutual Funds," *The Wall Street Journal*, July 8, 2003; and John C. Bogle, "The Mutual Fund Industry Sixty Years Later: For Better or Worse?" *Financial Analysts Journal* 61, no. 1 (January–February 2005): 15–24.

6. Ellis, "Will Business Success Spoil the Investment Management Profession?" 14.

3. The Babe Ruth Effect

1. I am not equating investing to gambling. In fact, long-term investing is really the opposite of gambling. In gambling, the more you play the greater the odds that you lose. In investing, the longer you invest, the greater the odds that you generate positive returns.

2. Daniel Kahneman and Amos Tversky, "Prospect Theory: An Analysis of Decision Under Risk," *Econometrica* 47 (1979): 263–91.

3. Nassim Nicholas Taleb, *Fooled By Randomness: The Hidden Role of Chance in Markets and in Life* (New York: Texere, 2001), 87–88.

4. Taleb points out that well-known investor Jim Rogers avoids options because "90 percent of all options expire as losses." Rogers is confusing frequency with how much money is made on average.

5. Brent Schlender, "The Bill and Warren Show," *Fortune*, July 20, 1998.

6. Charlie Munger, "A Lesson on Elementary, Worldly Wisdom As It Relates to Investment Management and Business" *Outstanding Investor Digest*, May 5, 1995, 50.

7. Warren Buffett, speech given at the Berkshire Hathaway Annual Meeting, 1989.

8. Alfred Rappaport and Michael J. Mauboussin, *Expectations Investing* (Boston, Mass.: Harvard Business School Press, 2001), 105–8.

9. Steven Crist, "Crist on Value," in Andrew Beyer et al., *Bet with the Best: All New Strategies From America's Leading Handicappers* (New York: Daily Racing Form Press, 2001), 63–64.

10. Edward O. Thorp, *Beat the Dealer* (New York: Vintage Books, 1966), 56–57.

4. Sound Theory for the Attribute Weary

1. See Mitchel Resnick, *Turtles, Termites, and Traffic Jams* (Cambridge, Mass.: MIT Press, 1994), 50–52. Also see, Steven Johnson, *Emergence: The*

Connected Lives of Ants, Brains, Cities, and Software (New York: Scribner, 2001), 12–13.

2. Professor Burton Malkiel: "It's like giving up a belief in Santa Claus. Even though you know Santa Claus doesn't exist, you kind of cling to that belief. I'm not saying that this is a scam. They generally believe they can do it. The evidence is, however, that they can't." *20/20*, ABC News, November 27, 1992. See http://www.ifa.tv/Library/Support/Articles/Popular/NewsShowTranscript.htm.

3. Clayton M. Christensen, Paul Carlile, and David Sundahl, "The Process of Theory-Building," *Working Paper, 02–016*, 4. For an updated version of this paper, see http://www.innosight.com/documents/Theory%20Building.pdf.

4. Phil Rosenzweig, *The Halo Effect: . . . and Eight Other Business Delusions That Deceive Managers* (New York: Free Press, 2006).

5. Peter L. Bernstein, *Capital Ideas: The Improbable Origins of Modern Wall Street* (New York: The Free Press, 1992), 129–30.

6. Richard Roll, "A Critique of the Asset Pricing Theory's Tests: Part 1: On Past and Potential Testability of the Theory," *Journal of Financial Economics* 4 (1977): 129–76.

7. Clayton M. Christensen, "The Past and Future of Competitive Advantage," *MIT Sloan Management Review* (Winter 2001): 105–9.

8. Kenneth L. Fisher and Meir Statman, "Cognitive Biases in Market Forecasts," *Journal of Portfolio Management* 27, no. 1 (Fall 2000): 72–81.

9. Mercer Bullard, "Despite SEC Efforts, Accuracy in Fund Names Still Elusive," *The Street.com*, January 30, 2001. See http://www.thestreet.com/funds/mercerbullard/1282823.html.

5. Risky Business

1. Gerd Gigerenzer, *Calculated Risks* (New York: Simon & Schuster, 2002), 28–29.

2. John Rennie, "Editor's Commentary: The Cold Odds Against Columbia," *Scientific American*, February 7, 2003.

3. Gigerenzer, *Calculated Risks*, 26–28.

4. Jeremy J. Siegel, *Stocks for the Long Run*, 3rd ed. (New York: McGraw Hill, 2002), 13.

5. Michael J. Mauboussin and Kristen Bartholdson, "Long Strange Trip: Thoughts on Stock Market Returns," *Credit Suisse First Boston Equity Research*, January 9, 2003.

6. See chapter 3.

6. Are You an Expert?

1. J. Scott Armstrong, "The Seer-Sucker Theory: The Value of Experts in Forecasting," *Technology Review* 83 (June–July 1980): 16–24.

2. Atul Gawande, *Complications: A Surgeon's Notes on an Imperfect Science* (New York: Picador, 2002), 35–37.

3. Paul J. Feltovich, Rand J. Spiro, and Richard L. Coulsen, "Issues of Expert Flexibility in Contexts Characterized by Complexity and Change," in *Expertise in Context: Human and Machine*, ed. Paul J. Feltovich, Kenneth M. Ford, and Robert R. Hoffman (Menlo Park, Cal.: AAAI Press and Cambridge, Mass.: MIT Press, 1997): 125–146.

4. R.J. Spiro, W. Vispoel, J. Schmitz, A. Samarapungavan, and A. Boerger, "Knowledge Acquisition for Application: Cognitive Flexibility and Transfer in Complex Content Domains," in *Executive Control Processes*, ed. B.C. Britton (Hillsdale, N.J.: Lawrence Erlbaum Associates, 1987), 177–99.

5. Robyn M. Dawes, David Faust, and Paul E. Meehl, "Clinical Versus Actuarial Judgment," in *Heuristics and Biases: The Psychology of Intuitive Judgment*, ed. Thomas Gilovich, Dale Griffin, and Daniel Kahneman (Cambridge: Cambridge University Press, 2002), 716–29.

6. Gawande, *Complications*, 44.

7. Katie Haffner, "In an Ancient Game, Computing's Future," *The New York Times*, August 1, 2002.

8. James Surowiecki, *The Wisdom of Crowds: Why the Many Are Smarter Than the Few and How Collective Wisdom Shapes Business, Economies, Societies and Nations* (New York: Doubleday, 2004).

9. Joe Nocera, "On Oil Supply, Opinions Aren't Scarce," *The New York Times*, September 10, 2005.

10. Philip E. Tetlock, *Expert Political Judgment: How Good Is It? How Can We Know?* (Princeton, N.J.: Princeton University Press, 2005), 68.

11. Ibid., 73–75.

7. The Hot Hand in Investing

1. Thomas Gilovich, Robert Valone, and Amos Tversky, "The Hot Hand in Basketball: On the Misperception of Random Sequences," *Cognitive Psychology* 17 (1985): 295–314.

2. Amos Tversky and Daniel Kahneman, "Belief in the Law of Small Numbers," *Psychological Bulletin* 76 (1971): 105–10. For an illustration, see Chris Wetzel, Randomness Web site, http://www.rhodes.edu/psych/faculty/wetzel/courses/wetzelsyllabus223.htm.

3. Adapted from Stephen Jay Gould, "The Streak of Streaks," *New York Review of Books*, August 18, 1988, available from http://www.nybooks.com/articles/4337, accessed 25 May 2005.

4. Stephen Jay Gould, *Triumph and Tragedy in Mudville* (New York: W. W. Norton & Company, 2003), 151–72. See http://mlb.mlb.com/mlb/history/rare_feats/index.jsp?feature=hitting_streaks.

5. Gould, "The Streak of Streaks."

6. Here's the math: DiMaggio had 7,671 plate appearances in 1,736 career games, or 4.42 plate appearances per game. He also had 2,214 career hits, for a 0.289 hit-per-plate appearance average. With a 0.289 hit-per-appearance average, DiMaggio would be expected to get a hit in 0.778 percent of his games. So the probability of getting a hit in fifty-six straight games is $(0.778)^{56}$, or 1-in-1.279 million. See Rob Neyer, ESPN Baseball Archives, January 2002, http://espn.go.com/mlb/s/2002/0107/1307254.html. For DiMaggio's career statistics, see Major League Baseball Historical Player Stats, http://mlb.mlb.com/NASApp/mlb/stats/historical/individual_stats_player.jsp?c_id=mlb&playerID=113376.

7. Amazingly, DiMaggio's fifty-six-game streak wasn't his longest. As a teenager in the Pacific Coast League, DiMaggio had a sixty-one-game streak. Of note, too, is immediately after DiMaggio's fifty-six-game streak was broken, he went on to a sixteen-game hitting streak. So he got a hit in seventy-two of seventy-three games during the course of the 1941 season.

8. Here's a sample of some references (there are too many to list exhaustively): Burton G. Malkiel, *A Random Walk Down Wall Street* (New York: W. W. Norton & Company, 2003), 191; Nassim Taleb, *Fooled By Randomness: The Hidden Role of Chance in Markets and in Life* (New York: Texere, 2001), 128–131; Gregory Baer and Gary Gensler, *The Great Mutual Fund Trap* (New York: Broadway

Books, 2002), 16–17; Peter L. Bernstein, *Capital Ideas: The Improbable Origins of Modern Wall Street* (New York: Free Press, 1992), 141–43.

9. Baer and Gensler, *The Great Mutual Fund Trap*, 17. Baer and Gensler only consider the streak's first ten years (even though the book came out after the eleventh year was complete). The difference between ten- and fifteen-year streaks is significant.

10. Miller also ran a second fund, Opportunity Trust, which has a different composition but beat the market for the six years ended 2005. The probability of beating the market twenty-one years consecutively (assuming a 44 percent fund outperformance rate) is roughly 1 in 31 million.

11. While the Value Trust streak is Miller's longest, it is not his only streak. In the six years that ended with 1993, Miller's Special Investment Trust beat the market every year.

8. Time Is on My Side

1. Paul A. Samuelson, "Risk and Uncertainty: A Fallacy of Large Numbers," *Scientia* 98 (1963): 108–13; reprinted at www.casact.org/pubs/forum/94sforum/94sf049.pdf. Shlomo Benartzi and Richard H. Thaler, "Myopic Loss Aversion and the Equity Premium Puzzle," *The Quarterly Journal of Economics* 110, no. 1 (February 1995): 73–92, available from http://gsbwww.uchicago.edu/fac/richard.thaler/research/myopic.pdf, write: "Specifically, the theorem says that if someone is unwilling to accept a single play of a bet at any wealth level that could occur over the course of some number of repetitions of the bet, then accepting the multiple bet is inconsistent with expected utility theory."

2. Daniel Kahneman and Amos Tversky, "Prospect Theory: An Analysis of Decision Under Risk," *Econometrica* 47 (1979): 263–91.

3. Nicholas Barberis and Ming Huang, "Mental Accounting, Loss Aversion, and Individual Stock Returns," *Journal of Finance* 56, no. 4 (August 2001): 1247–92.

4. Elroy Dimson, Paul Marsh, and Mike Staunton, "Global Evidence on the Equity Risk Premium," *Journal of Applied Corporate Finance* 15, no. 4 (Fall 2003): 27–38.

5. Benartzi and Thaler, "Myopic Loss Aversion."

6. This and following exhibits closely follow William J. Bernstein, "Of Risk and Myopia." See http://www.efficientfrontier.com/ef/102/taleb.htm. Also, see Nassim Nicholas Taleb, *Fooled By Randomness: The Hidden Role of Chance in the Markets and in Life* (New York: Texere, 2001), 56–59.

7. Michael J. Mauboussin and Kristen Bartholdson, "Long Strange Trip: Thoughts on Stock Market Returns," *Credit Suisse First Boston Equity Research*, January 9, 2003.

8. Benartzi and Thaler, "Myopic Loss Aversion," 80.

9. James K. Glassman and Kevin A. Hassett, *Dow 36,000: The New Strategy for Profiting from the Coming Rise in the Stock Market* (New York: Times Books, 1999).

10. Josef Lakonishok, Andrei Shleifer, and Robert W. Vishny, "Contrarian Investment, Extrapolation, and Risk," *Journal of Finance* 49, no. 5 (December 1994): 1541–78.

11. Bernstein, "Of Risk and Myopia."

9. The Low Down on the Top Brass

1. Berkshire Hathaway Annual Letter to Shareholders, 1993, http://berkshire-hathaway.com/letters/1993.html.

2. Jim Collins, *Good to Great* (New York: HarperBusiness, 2001), 21.

3. Meghan Felicelli, "2006 YTD CEO Turnover," *SpencerStuart*, December 31, 2006. Also, Chuck Lucier, Paul Kocourek, and Rolf Habbel, "CEO Succession 2005: The Crest of the Wave," *strategy+business*, Summer 2006.

4. When an interviewer recently asked Nokia CEO Jorma Ollila how he ensures that he knows all that he needs to know, he replied, "I think you just have to read a lot." (See David Pringle and Raju Narisetti, "Nokia's Chief Guides Company Amid Technology's Rough Seas," *The Wall Street Journal*, November 24, 2003.) Charlie Munger said it more bluntly, "In my whole life, I haven't known any wise person who didn't read all the time."

5. http://csfb.com/thoughtleaderforum/2003/harrington_sidecolumn.shtml.

6. Robert E. Rubin and Jacob Weisberg, *In an Uncertain World* (New York: Random House, 2003), 20.

7. Alfred Rappaport and Michael J. Mauboussin, *Expectations Investing* (Boston: Harvard Business School Press, 2001), 191–94.

8. Bethany McLean and Peter Elkind, *The Smartest Guys in the Room* (New York: Penguin Group, 2003), 132.

9. Take Pfizer as an example. From 1998 to 2002, roughly 85 percent of Pfizer's $192 billion in investments have been M&A related.

10. Berkshire Hathaway Annual Letter to Shareholders, 1987, http://berkshirehathaway.com/letters/1987.html.

10. Good Morning, Let the Stress Begin

1. Sapolsky has spent over twenty summers in Africa studying baboons to understand the link between stress and social hierarchy in primates. Writes Sapolsky: "The baboons work maybe four hours a day to feed themselves; hardly anyone is likely to eat them. Basically, baboons have about a half dozen solid hours of sunlight a day to devote to being rotten to each other. Just like our society . . . We live well enough to have the luxury to get ourselves sick with purely social, psychological stress." See Robert M. Sapolsky, *A Primate's Memoir* (New York: Scribner, 2001).

2. Robert M. Sapolsky, *Why Zebras Don't Get Ulcers: An Updated Guide to Stress, Stress-Related Disease, and Coping* (New York: W. H. Freeman and Company, 1994), 4–13.

3. Richard Foster and Sarah Kaplan, *Creative Destruction: Why Companies That Are Built to Last Underperform the Market—and How to Successfully Transform Them* (New York: Doubleday, 2001), 13.

4. John Y. Campbell, Martin Lettau, Burton Malkiel, and Yexiao Xu, "Have Individual Stocks Become More Volatile? An Empirical Exploration of Idiosyncratic Risk," *Journal of Finance* 54 (February 2001): 1–43.

5. This does not mean that stock prices reflect short-term expectations.

6. John C. Bogle, "Mutual Fund Directors: The Dog that Didn't Bark," January, 28, 2001, http://www.vanguard.com/bogle_site/sp20010128.html. Updated data are from John C. Bogle, "The Mutual Fund Industry Sixty Years Later: For Better or Worse?" *Financial Analysts Journal* (January–February 2005).

7. Kathryn Kranhold, "Florida Might Sue Alliance Capital Over Pension Fund's Enron Losses," *The Wall Street Journal,* April 23, 2002.

8. This is *not* to say that the stock market is short-term oriented. The research consistently shows that stocks reflect expectations for ten to twenty years of

value-creating cash flow. Increasingly, though, investors are making short-term bets on long-term outcomes.

9. Ernst Fehr, "The Economics of Impatience," *Nature*, January 17, 2002, 269–70.

10. John Spence, "Bogle Calls for a Federation of Long-Term Investors," *Index Funds, Inc.*, http://www.indexfunds.com/articles/20020221_boglespeech_com_gen_JS.htm. By my calculations, the weighted average return in 2001 was −4.8 percent for the funds with 20 percent turnover or less, −7.8 percent for the funds with turnover over 100 percent, and −10.5 percent for the funds that had over 200 percent turnover. See http://www.indexfunds.com/articles/20020221_boglespeech_com_gen_JS.htm.

11. Alice Lowenstein, "The Low Turnover Advantage," Morningstar Research, September 7, 1997, http://news.morningstar.com/news/ms/FundFocus/lowturnover1.html.

12. Russ Wermers, "Mutual Fund Performance: An Empirical Decomposition into Stock-Picking Talent, Style, Transaction Costs, and Expenses," *Journal of Finance* 55 (August 2000): 1655–1703.

13. Yahoo provides the risk classifications (above average, average, and below average) based on the standard deviation of portfolio performance. I quantified the three levels, allocating a value of 1 for funds with below-average risk, 2 for average-risk funds, and 3 for above-average-risk funds, in order to attain an average risk level for each turnover range. The numbers are on an asset-weighted basis.

11. All I Really Need to Know I Learned at a Tupperware Party

1. Robert B. Cialdini, "The Science of Persuasion," *Scientific American* (February 2001): 76–81.

2. Robert B. Cialdini, *Influence: The Psychology of Persuasion* (New York: William Morrow, 1993), 18.

3. See chapter 11.

4. For an interesting account of Asch's experiment, see Duncan J. Watts, *Six Degrees: The Science of a Connected Age* (New York: W. W. Norton & Company, 2003), 207–10.

5. Cialdini, *Influence*, 208–15. Also see Rod Dickinson, "The Milgram Reenactment," http://www.milgramreenactment.org/pages/section.xml?location=51.

6. Lisa W. Foderaro, "If June Cleaver Joined 'Sex and the City': Tupperware Parties for the Cosmo Set," *The New York Times*, February 1, 2003.

7. Cialdini, *Influence*, 37.

12. All Systems Go

1. Antonio R. Damasio, *Descartes' Error: Emotion, Reason, and the Human Brain* (New York: Avon Books, 1994), xi–xii.

2. Thomas A. Stewart, "How to Think With Your Gut," *Business 2.0*, November 2002.

3. Antonio R. Damasio, *The Feeling of What Happens: Body and Emotion in the Making of Consciousness* (New York: Harcourt Brace & Company, 1999), 301–3. Antoine Bechara, Hanna Damasio, Daniel Tranel, and Antonio R. Damasio, "Deciding Advantageously Before Knowing the Advantageous Strategy," *Science* 275 (February 28, 1997): 1293–95.

4. Daniel Kahneman, "Maps of Bounded Rationality: A Perspective on Intuitive Judgment and Choice," Nobel Prize Lecture, December 8, 2002, http://www.nobel.se/economics/laureates/2002/kahnemann-lecture.pdf.

5. Paul Slovic, Melissa Finucane, Ellen Peters, and Donald G. MacGregor, "The Affect Heuristic," in *Heuristics and Biases: The Psychology of Intuitive Judgment*, ed. Thomas Gilovich, Dale Griffin, and Daniel Kahneman (Cambridge: Cambridge University Press, 2002), 397–420.

6. Slovic, Finucane, Peters, and MacGregor, "The Affect Heuristic."

7. Donald G. MacGregor, "Imagery and Financial Judgment," *The Journal of Psychology and Financial Markets* 3, no. 1 (2002): 15–22.

13. Guppy Love

1. More accurately, the choice depends on how much the males diverged in coloration. When the difference was small, the females chose the less orange of the two. But if the male colors were sufficiently different, the females disregarded the cues from the others and went with the brighter hue. See Lee Alan Dugatkin and Jean-Guy J. Godin, "How Females Choose Their Mates," *Scientific American*, April 1998, 56–61.

2. Lee Alan Dugatkin, *The Imitation Factor* (New York: Free Press, 2000).

3. See Carl Anderson and John J. Bartholdi III, "Centralized Versus Decentralized Control in Manufacturing: Lessons from Social Insects," in *Complexity and Complex Systems in Industry*, ed. Ian P. McCarthy and Thierry Rakotobe-Joel (Warwick: University of Warwick, 2000), 92–105; http://www2.isye.gatech.edu/~carl/papers/cc.pdf.

4. For a discussion about the limits of arbitrage, see Andrei Shleifer, *Inefficient Markets: An Introduction to Behavioral Finance* (Oxford: Oxford University Press, 2000).

5. Investors should also note that feedback operates at different levels. There can be feedback at the product level, the company level, and the market level. Sometimes these layers of feedback are correlated; at other times they're not.

6. Sushil Bikhchandani and Sunil Sharma, "Herd Behavior in Financial Markets," *IMF Staff Paper* 47, no. 3 (2001), http://www.imf.org/External/Pubs/FT/staffp/2001/01/pdf/bikhchan.pdf.

7. Sushil Bikhchandani, David Hirshleifer, and Ivo Welch, "Informational Cascades and Rational Herding: An Annotated Bibliography," *Working Paper: UCLA/Anderson and Michigan/GSB* (June 1996).

8. Duncan J. Watts, "A Simple Model of Global Cascades on Random Networks," *Proceedings of the National Academy of Sciences* 99, no. 9 (April 30, 2002): 5766–71.

9. Anderson and Bartholdi, "Centralized Versus Decentralized Control."

10. Charles MacKay, *Extraordinary Popular Delusions and the Madness of Crowds* (1841; New York: Three Rivers Press, 1995).

11. Russ Wermers, "Mutual Fund Herding and the Impact on Stock Prices," *Journal of Finance* 54, no. 2 (April 1999): 581–622.

12. Ivo Welch, "Herding Among Security Analysts," *Journal of Financial Economics* 58, no. 3 (December 2000): 369–96.

13. Victor M. Eguiluz and Martin G. Zimmerman, "Transmission of Information and Herd Behavior: An Application to Financial Markets," *Physical Review Letters* 85, no. 26 (December 25, 2000): 5659–62.

14. J. Bradford DeLong, Andrei Shleifer, Lawrence H. Summers, and Robert J. Waldmann, "Positive Feedback Investment Strategies and Destabilizing Rational Speculation," *Journal of Finance* 45, no. 2 (June 1990): 379–95.

14. Beware of Behavioral Finance

1. Most experts agree that the starting point for the field came in 1985 with a landmark paper: Werner DeBondt and Richard Thaler, "Does the Stock Market Overreact?" *Journal of Finance* 40 (1985): 793–805.

2. See Alfred Rappaport and Michael J. Mauboussin, "Pitfalls to Avoid," at www.expectationsinvesting.com/pdf/pitfalls.pdf.

3. Hersh Shefrin, *Beyond Greed and Fear: Understanding Behavioral Finance and the Psychology of Investing* (Boston: Harvard Business School Press, 2000), 5.

4. Vernon L. Smith, "An Experimental Study of Competitive Market Behavior," *Journal of Political Economy* 70, no. 3 (June 1962): 111–37.

5. Andrei Shleifer, *Inefficient Markets: An Introduction to Behavioral Finance* (Oxford: Oxford University Press, 2000), 3. A few pages later, Shleifer is bolder: "It is this argument that the Kahneman and Tversky theories dispose of entirely" (12).

6. Sherry Sontag and Christopher Drew, *Blind Man's Bluff: The Untold Story of American Submarine Espionage* (New York: Perseus Books, 1998), 58–59.

7. Jack L. Treynor, "Market Efficiency and the Bean Jar Experiment," *Financial Analysts Journal* (May–June 1987), 50–53.

8. This is *not* true for corporate executives. Individual decision-making errors can have a significant negative effect on shareholder value. One good example is the winner's curse, where a company that wins an auction for an asset (winner) tends to overpay for the asset (curse).

9. See chapter 11.

15. Raising Keynes

1. W. Brian Arthur, "Inductive Reasoning and Bounded Rationality: The El Farol Problem," paper given at the American Economic Association Annual Meetings, 1994, published in *American Economic Review* (Papers and Proceedings) 84 (1994): 406–11, http://www.santafe.edu/arthur/Papers/El_Farol.html.

2. For a good discussion of expectation formation, see Karl-Erik Wärneryd, *Stock-Market Psychology* (Cheltenham, UK: Edward Elgar, 2001), 73–95.

3. See Bob Davis and Susan Warren, "How Fears of Impending War Already Take Economic Toll," *The Wall Street Journal*, January 29, 2003.

4. John Maynard Keynes, *The General Theory of Employment* (New York: Harcourt, Brace and Company, 1936), 162.

5. Ibid., 159.

6. John C. Bogle, "The Mutual Fund Industry in 2003: Back to the Future," remarks before the Harvard Club of Boston, January 14, 2003, http://www.vanguard.com/bogle_site/sp20030114.html.

7. This section relies heavily on Arthur, "Inductive Reasoning."

8. Corinne Coen and Rick Riolo, "El Farol Revisited: How People in Large Groups Learn to Coordinate Through Complementary Scripts," *Organizational Learning and Knowledge Management* conference proceedings, 4th International Conference, June 2001.

9. Max Bazerman, *Judgment in Managerial Decision Making*, 4th ed. (New York: Wiley, 1998), 36–39.

10. Hersh Shefrin, *Beyond Greed and Fear: Understanding Behavioral Finance and the Psychology of Investing* (Boston: Harvard Business School Press, 2000), 199.

16. Right from the Gut

1. Thomas A. Stewart, "How to Think with Your Gut," *Business 2.0*, November 1, 2002, http://money.cnn.com/magazines/business2/business2_archive/2002/11/01/331634/index.htm.

2. Ibid.

3. Peter L. Bernstein, *Against the Gods: The Remarkable Story of Risk* (New York: John Wiley & Sons, 1996), 99–100.

4. Raanan Lipshitz, Gary Klein, Judith Orasanu, and Eduardo Salas, "Taking Stock of Naturalistic Decision Making," Working Paper, July 15, 2000, http://organizations.haifa.ac.il/html/html_eng/raanan%20-%20taking.doc.

5. Robert A. Olsen, "Professional Investors as Naturalistic Decision Makers: Evidence and Market Implications," *The Journal of Psychology and Financial Markets* 3, no. 3 (2002): 161–67.

6. Ibid., 162–63.

7. Michael T. Kaufman, *Soros: The Life and Times of a Messianic Billionaire* (New York: Knopf, 2002), 141.

8. Gary Klein, *Sources of Power: How People Make Decisions* (Cambridge, Mass.: MIT Press, 1998), 161–66.

9. Stewart, "How to Think with Your Gut."

10. For more on the unconscious, see Frank Tallis, *Hidden Minds: A History of the Unconscious* (New York: Arcade Publishing, 2002), 95–109.

17. Weighted Watcher

1. http://www.brainyquote.com/quotes/authors/a/antoine_lavoisier.html.

2. http://www.phrases.org.uk/meanings/375700.html.

3. http://www.usdoj.gov/atr/cases/exhibits/20.pdf.

4. Dale Griffin and Amos Tversky, "The Weighing of Evidence and the Determinants of Confidence," in *Heuristics and Biases: The Psychology of Intuitive Judgment*, ed. Thomas Gilovich, Dale Griffin, and Daniel Kahneman (Cambridge: Cambridge University Press, 2002), 230–49.

5. Richard H. Thaler, *The Winner's Curse: Paradoxes and Anomalies of Economic Life* (Princeton, N.J.: Princeton University Press, 1994).

6. The 2003 sale of the Sears credit card portfolio is a vivid illustration of this point. Some investors were short the stock, believing the disposition price for the business would be below management guidance, and many potential buyers for the asset confirmed this view. But the buyer ended up paying more than what the average bidder thought the business was worth.

7. One example is of a former CSFB analyst, who in 2000 spent two days as a temporary employee, filling orders for an Amazon.com distribution center. Some generous math suggests he filled no more than $15,000 worth of orders in a quarter when the company generated $1 billion in sales. Yet the experience generated a research report and plenty of press.

8. Tarun Chordia, Richard Roll, and Avanidhar Subrahmanyam, "Evidence on the Speed of Convergence to Market Efficiency," Working Paper, April 29, 2002. Also Eugene F. Fama, Lawrence Fisher, Michael C. Jensen, and Richard Roll, "The Adjustment of Stock Prices to New Information," *International Economic Review* 10, no. 1 (February 1969); 1–21.

9. Stefano DellaVigna and Joshua Pollet, "Attention, Demographics, and the Stock Market," Working Paper, November 23, 2003, http://fisher.osu.edu/fin/dice/seminars/pollet.pdf.

10. See chapter 1.

11. http://www2.cio.com/techpoll/index.cfm.

12. Amos Tversky and Daniel Kahneman, "Extensional Versus Intuitive Reasoning: The Conjunction Fallacy in Probability Judgment," in *Heuristics and Biases: The Psychology of Intuitive Judgment*, ed. Thomas Gilovich, Dale Griffin, and Daniel Kahneman (Cambridge: Cambridge University Press, 2002), 19–48.

13. Sanford J. Grossman and Joseph E. Stiglitz, "On the Impossibility of Informationally Efficient Markets," *American Economic Review* 70 (1980): 393–408.

18. The Wright Stuff

1. Evolutionary economists Richard Nelson and Sidney Winters echo the same theme. They write, "Innovation in the economic system—and indeed the creation of any sort of novelty in art, science, or practical life—consists to a substantial extent of a recombination of conceptual and physical materials that were previously in existence. The vast momentum in scientific, technological, and economic progress in the modern world derives largely from the fact that each new achievement is not merely the answer to a particular problem, but also a new item in the vast storehouse of components that are available for use, in 'new combinations,' in the solution of other problems in the future." Richard R. Nelson and Sidney G. Winter, *An Evolutionary Theory of Economic Change* (Cambridge, Mass.: Harvard University Press/Belknap Press, 1982), 130.

2. Based on Romer's comments at a roundtable discussion held June 17, 1998, Pebble Beach, Calif., reproduced as Donald Lessand, moderator, "The Soft Revolution: Achieving Growth By Managing Intangibles," *The Journal of Applied Corporate Finance* 11, no. 2 (Summer 1998): 8–27.

3. Quoted in Stephen R. Waite, *Quantum Investing* (New York: Texere, 2002), 1–3.

4. The evolution of technique in sports shows the power of nonrival goods. Examples include the crawl swim stroke (which only became widespread within the past 200 years), overhand free-throw shots in basketball, and the Fosbury flop for high jumpers.

5. "Moore's law is the empirical observation that at our rate of technological development, the complexity of an integrated circuit, with respect to minimum component cost will double in about 24 months" (http://en.wikipedia.org/wiki/Moore's_Law).

6. Juan Enriquez, *As the Future Catches You* (New York: Crown Business, 2000), 62–65.

7. See http://nickciske.com/tools/binary.php.

19. Pruned for Performance

1. Steven Pinker, *The Language Instinct: How the Mind Creates Language* (New York: HarperCollins, 1994), 150–51.

2. Alison Gopnik, Andrew Meltzoff, and Patricia Kuhl, *The Scientist in the Crib: What Early Learning Tells Us About the Mind* (New York: First Perennial, 2001), 186–87.

3. Joseph LeDoux, *Synaptic Self: How Our Brains Become Who We Are* (New York: Viking, 2002), 79–81.

4. Robert Aunger, *The Electric Meme: A New Theory of How We Think* (New York: Free Press, 2002), 185.

5. Barbara Clancy and Barbara Finlay, "Neural Correlates of Early Language Learning," in *Language Development: The Essential Readings*, ed. Michael Tomasello and Elizabeth Bates (Oxford: Blackwell, 2001); an earlier version of the chapter is available from http://crl.ucsd.edu/courses/commdis/pdf/neuralcorrelateschapter-nofigures.pdf.

6. Michael J. Mauboussin and Alexander Schay, "Fill and Kill: Succeeding with Survivors Is Nothing New," *Credit Suisse First Boston Equity Research*, April 5, 2001.

7. See http://www.webmergers.com.

8. David M. Raup, *Extinction: Bad Genes or Bad Luck?* (New York: W. W. Norton, 1991), 32–33.

9. William D. Bygrave, Julian E. Lange, J. R. Roedel, and Gary Wu, "Capital Market Excesses and Competitive Strength: The Case of the Hard Drive Industry, 1984–2000," *Journal of Applied Corporate Finance* 13, no. 3 (Fall 2000), 8–19.

20. Staying Ahead of the Curve

1. In fact, one of the new leader's first actions is often to kill all of the cubs in the pride. This allows the new leader to sire new cubs that carry his genes.

2. See Richard Foster and Sarah Kaplan, *Creative Destruction: Why Companies That Are Built to Last Underperform the Market—and How to Successfully Transform Them* (New York: Doubleday, 2001), 47.

3. Alfred Rappaport and Michael J. Mauboussin, *Expectations Investing: Reading Stock Prices for Better Returns* (Boston: Harvard Business School Press, 2001).

4. See Foster and Kaplan, *Creative Destruction*; Everett Rodgers, *The Diffusion of Innovation* (New York: Free Press, 1995); and Geoffrey A. Moore, Paul Johnson, and Tom Kippola, *The Gorilla Game: Picking Winners in High Technology* (New York: HarperBusiness, 1999).

5. Michael J. Mauboussin and Alexander Schay, "Innovation and Markets: How Innovation Affects the Investing Process," *Credit Suisse First Boston Equity Research*, December 12, 2000.

6. Gregory Zuckerman, "Stars of the '90s Aren't Likely to Lead the Next Rally," *Wall Street Journal*, December 17, 2001.

7. John Y. Campbell, Martin Lettau, Burton G. Malkiel, and Yexiao Xu, "Have Individual Stocks Become More Volatile?" *Journal of Finance* 54 (February 2001): 1–43.

8. Corporate Strategy Board, "Stall Points: Barriers to Growth for the Large Corporate Enterprise," *Corporate Strategy Board* (March 1998).

9. Alfred Rappaport and Michael J. Mauboussin, "Exploiting Expectations," *Fortune*, January 21, 2002, 113–15.

21. Is There a Fly in Your Portfolio?

1. For readers with too much time on their hands, see: http://www.ceolas.org/fly/intro.html.

2. Charles H. Fine, *Clockspeed: Winning Industry Control in the Age of Temporary Advantage* (Reading, Mass.: Perseus Books, 1998).

3. Glenn Rifkin, "GM's Internet Overhaul," *Technology Review* (October 2002): 62–67.

4. Eugene F. Fama and Kenneth R. French, "Disappearing Dividends: Changing Firm Characteristics Or Lower Propensity To Pay?" *CRSP Working Paper 509*, June 2000; see http://papers.ssrn.com/sol3/papers.cfm?abstract_id=203092.

5. Robert R. Wiggins and Timothy W. Ruefli, "Sustained Competitive Advantage: Temporal Dynamics and the Incidence and Persistence of Superior

Economic Performance," *Organizational Science* 13, no. 1 (January–February 2002): 82–105.

6. Robert R. Wiggins and Timothy W. Ruefli, "Hypercompetitive Performance: Are The Best of Times Getting Shorter?" paper presented at the Academy of Management Annual Meeting 2001, Business Policy and Strategy (BPS) Division, March 31, 2001.

7. While I believe this hypothesis is likely true, I'm less convinced that the data support it. The main reason is that the later years of the study included historically high levels of write-offs and restructuring charges that likely distorted the accounting data.

8. Richard Foster and Sarah Kaplan, *Creative Destruction: Why Companies that are Built to Last Underperform the Market—and How to Successfully Transform Them* (New York: Doubleday, 2001); and John Y. Campbell, Martin Lettau, Burton G. Malkiel, and Yexiao Xu, "Have Individual Stocks Become More Volatile?" *Journal of Finance* 54 (February 2001): 1–43.

9. J. Bradford DeLong and Lawrence H. Summers, "The 'New Economy': Background, Historical Perspective, Questions, and Speculations", *Federal Reserve Bank of Kansas City Economic Review*, Fourth Quarter 2001. See http://www.kc.frb.org/PUBLICAT/ECONREV/Pdf/4q01delo.pdf.

10. Alfred Rappaport and Michael J. Mauboussin, *Expectations Investing: Reading Stock Prices for Better Returns* (Boston: Harvard Business School Press, 2001), 26–27, 36–38.

22. All the Right Moves

1. See "Frequently Asked Questions: Deep Blue," http://www.research.ibm.com/deepblue/meet/html/d.3.3.html.

2. Katie Haffner, "In an Ancient Game, Computing's Future," *New York Times*, August 1, 2002.

3. Anna Muoio, "All The Right Moves," *Fast Company*, May 1999; see http://www.fastcompany.com/online/24/chess.html.

4. This is reminiscent of Puggy Pearson's advice to gamblers. See Michael J. Mauboussin and Kristen Bartholdson, "Puggy Pearson's Prescription," *The Consilient Observer* 1, no. 11 (June 4, 2002).

5. Kathleen M. Eisenhardt and Donald N. Sull, "Strategy as Simple Rules," *Harvard Business Review* (January 2001): 107–16.

23. Survival of the Fittest

1. Dan Goodgame, "The Game of Risk: How the Best Golfer in the World Got Even Better," *Time*, August 14, 2000.

2. Stuart Kauffman, *At Home in the Universe* (Oxford: Oxford University Press, 1996).

3. Steve Maguire, "Strategy Is Design: A Fitness Landscape Framework," *Managing Complexity in Organizations: A View in Many Directions* (Westport, Conn.: Quorum Books, 1999), 67–104.

4. Eric D. Beinhocker, "Robust Adaptive Strategies," *Sloan Management Review* 40, no. 3 (Spring 1999): 95–106.

5. Daniel C. Dennett, *Darwin's Dangerous Idea: Evolution and The Meanings of Life* (New York: Simon & Schuster, 1995).

6. Robert Loest, "Fitness Landscapes and Investment Strategies, Parts 1 and 2," *Portfolio Manager Commentary—IPS Funds* (July and August 1998).

7. Clayton M. Christensen, *The Innovator's Dilemma: When New Technologies Cause Great Companies to Fail* (Boston: Harvard Business School Press, 1997).

8. Michael J. Mauboussin and Alexander Schay, "Innovation and Markets: How Innovation Affects the Investing Process," *Credit Suisse First Boston Equity Research*, December 12, 2000.

9. These can be recast as "exploit" versus "explore" strategies. See Robert Axelrod and Michael D. Cohen, *Harnessing Complexity* (New York: Free Press, 1999), 43–58.

10. W. Brian Arthur, "Increasing Returns and the New World of Business," *Harvard Business Review* (July–August 1996): 101–9.

11. General Electric, on Jack Welch's watch, effectively combined optimization with risk taking. For example, Welch gave the leaders of GE's largest businesses several hundred million dollars for discretionary spending with "no questions asked." See Warren Bennis, "Will the Legacy Live On?" *Harvard Business Review* (February 2002): 95–99.

12. Michael J. Mauboussin, "Get Real," *Credit Suisse First Boston Equity Research*, June 23, 1999.

13. Shona L. Brown and Kathleen M. Eisenhardt, *Competing on the Edge: Strategy as Structured Chaos* (Boston: Harvard Business School Press, 1998).

24. You'll Meet a Bad Fate If You Extrapolate

1. See http://www.socialsecurity.gov/history/hfaq.html.

2. Richard Roll, "Rational Infinitely-Lived Asset Prices Must be Non-Stationary," *Working Paper*, November 1, 2000; Bradford Cornell, *The Equity Risk Premium: The Long-Run Future of the Stock Market* (New York: Wiley, 1999), 45–55; Eugene F. Fama and Kenneth R. French, "The Equity Premium," *Journal of Finance* 57 (2002): 637–59; Jonathan Lewellen, "Predicting Returns with Financial Ratios," *MIT Sloan Working Paper 4374–02*, February 2002.

3. Kenneth L. Fisher and Meir Statman, "Cognitive Biases in Market Forecasts: The Frailty of Forecasting," *The Journal of Portfolio Management* 27, no. 1 (Fall 2000): 72–81.

4. Alfred Rappaport, "How to Avoid the P/E Trap," *Wall Street Journal*, March 10, 2003.

5. Cornell, *The Equity Risk Premium*, 59.

6. See http://www.econ.yale.edu/~shiller/.

25. I've Fallen and I Can't Get Up

1. Lakonishok, quoted in Mark Hulbert, "The Five-Year Forecast Looks Great, or Does It?" *New York Times*, January 25, 2004.

2. Louis K. C. Chan, Jason J. Karceski, and Josef Lakonishok, "The Level and Persistence of Growth Rates," *The Journal of Finance* 58, no. 2 (April 2003): 644–84. Also see chapter 30.

3. Michael J. Mauboussin and Kristen Bartholdson, "Whither Enron: Or—Why Enron Withered," *The Consilient Observer* 1, no. 1 (January 15, 2002).

4. Michael J. Mauboussin and Kristen Bartholdson, "Measuring the Moat: Assessing the Magnitude and Sustainability of Value Creation," *Credit Suisse First Boston Equity Research*, December 16, 2002.

5. Michael J. Mauboussin, Alexander Schay, and Patrick J. McCarthy, "Competitive Advantage Period (CAP): At the Intersection of Finance and Competitive Strategy," *Credit Suisse First Boston Equity Research*, October 4, 2001.

6. Ibid., 7–9.

7. Todd Erickson, Carin Cooney, and Craig Sterling, "US Technology Sector: Mean Reversion Analysis," *CSFB HOLT Research*, February 2, 2004.

8. HOLT analysts Christopher Catapano, Katie Dunne, and Craig Sterling performed the retail industry analysis.

9. To illustrate, we created a model with two companies that had 8 percent operating-income growth rates, initial returns on incremental invested capital of 100 percent, and identical costs of capital. We faded the first company's returns to zero over ten years, and the second company's returns to zero over twenty years. The second company—again, with identical growth—was 33 percent more valuable than the first, representing more than six price-earnings points.

10. W. Brian Arthur, "Increasing Returns and the New World of Business," *Harvard Business Review* (July–August 1996): 101–9.

11. See chapter 1.

26. Trench Cooperation

1. Robert Axelrod, *The Complexity of Cooperation: Agent-Based Models of Competition and Collaboration* (Princeton, N.J.: Princeton University Press, 1997), 6.

2. Robert Axelrod, *The Evolution of Cooperation* (New York: Basic Books, 1984), 74.

3. George Lakoff and Mark Johnson, *Metaphors We Live By* (Chicago, Ill.: The University of Chicago Press, 1980).

4. Axelrod, *The Evolution of Cooperation*, 73–87.

5. Ibid., 81. Axelrod quotes S. Gillon, *The Story of the 29th Division* (London: Nelson & Sons, n.d.). Eventually, the British, French, and German high commands undermined the live-and-let-live system by forcing raids, undermining the stability necessary to support the tacit agreements.

6. "Stern Stewart EVA Roundtable," *Journal of Applied Corporate Finance* 7, no. 2 (Summer 1994): 46–70.

7. For an excellent discussion, see William Poundstone, *Prisoner's Dilemma* (New York: Anchor Books, 1992).

8. The choice to add capacity gets both companies to the Nash equilibrium.

9. Axelrod, *The Evolution of Cooperation*, 27–54.

10. David Besanko, David Dranove, and Mark Shanley, *Economics of Strategy*, 2nd ed. (New York: John Wiley & Sons, 2000), 289–90.

11. Ibid., 293–302.

12. Adam M. Brandenburger and Barry J. Nalebuff, *Co-opetition* (New York: Currency, 1996), 120–22.

27. Great (Growth) Expectations

1. Warren Buffett and Charlie Munger, "It's Stupid the Way People Extrapolate the Past—and Not *Slightly* Stupid, But *Massively* Stupid," *Outstanding Investor Digest*, December 24, 2001.

2. Chris Zook with James Allen, *Profit from the Core* (Boston: Harvard Business School Press, 2001), 11–13.

3. I mention this because voluminous evidence suggests that mergers and acquisitions are a value negative or, at best, a value neutral activity. So growth via acquisition is often not value creating.

4. Firm sizes and cities follow a Zipf distribution. See Robert L. Axtell, "Zipf Distribution of U.S. Firm Sizes," *Science* 293 (September 2001): 1818–1820.

5. This is an inappropriate use of the term "law of large numbers." For a further explanation, see Peter L. Bernstein, *Against the Gods: The Remarkable Story of Risk* (New York: John Wiley & Sons, 1996), 122–23.

6. Jeremy J. Siegel, *Stocks for the Long Run*, 3rd ed. (New York: McGraw Hill, 2002), 150–56.

7. Joseph Fuller and Michael C. Jensen, "Dare to Keep Your Stock Price Low," *The Wall Street Journal*, December 31, 2001.

8. Alfred Rappaport, "The Economics of Short-Term Performance Obsession," *Financial Analysts Journal* 61, no. 3 (May–June 2005): 65–79.

28. Diversify Your Mind

1. See Norman L. Johnson, "What a Developmental View Can Do for You (or the Fall of the House of Experts)," talk at CSFB Thought Leader Forum, September 2000, Santa Fe, N.M., http://www.capatcolumbia.com/ CSFB%20TLF/2000/ johnson00_sidecolumn.pdf.

2. Michael J. Mauboussin, "Revisiting Market Efficiency: The Stock Market as a Complex Adaptive System" *Journal of Applied Corporate Finance* 14, no. 4 (Winter 2002): 47–55.

3. Norman L. Johnson, "Diversity in Decentralized Systems: Enabling Self-Organizing Solutions," *LANL*, LA-UR-99-6281, 1999. For more on this, see http://ishi.lanl.gov.

4. James Kennedy and Russell C. Eberhart, *Swarm Intelligence* (San Francisco: Morgan Kaufmann, 2001), 105.

5. William H. Calvin, "The Emergence of Intelligence," *Scientific American Presents* 9, no. 4 (November 1998): 44–51.

6. Gary Klein, *Sources of Power: How People Make Decisions* (Cambridge, Mass.: MIT Press, 1998).

7. Michael T. Kaufman, *Soros: The Life and Times of a Messianic Billionaire* (New York: Knopf, 2002), 141.

8. See "Informal Learning in the Workplace," http://www.learning-org.com/98.01/0331.html.

9. Arthur Zeikel, "Organizing for Creativity," *Financial Analyst Journal* 39 (November–December 1983): 25–29.

29. From Honey to Money

1. Thomas D. Seeley, *The Wisdom of the Hive: The Social Physiology of Honey Bee Colonies* (Cambridge, Mass.: Harvard University Press, 1995), 259. Also, see http://www.pbs.org/wgbh/nova/bees.

2. Cited in Steven Johnson, *Emergence: The Connected Lives of Ants, Brains, Cities, and Software* (New York: Scribner, 2001), 33.

3. Seeley, *The Wisdom of the Hive*, 240–62; also see http://www.nbb.cornell.edu/neurobio/department/Faculty/seeley/seeley.html.

4. Eric Bonabeau, Marco Dorigo, and Guy Theraulaz, *Swarm Intelligence: From Natural to Artificial Systems* (New York: Oxford University Press, 1999), 39–55. Also see Edmund Burke and Graham Kendall, "Applying Ant Algorithms and the No Fit Polygon to the Nesting Problem," *University of Nottingham Working Paper*, 1999, http://www.asap.cs.nott.ac.uk/publications/pdf/gk_ai99.pdf.

5. See Iowa Electronic Markets Web site, http://www.biz.uiowa.edu/iem.

6. James Surowiecki, "Decisions, Decisions," *The New Yorker*, March 28, 2003, available from http://www.newyorker.com/archive/2003/03/24/030324ta_talk_surowiecki.

7. See Hollywood Stock Exchange Web site, http://www.hsx.com.

8. See Betfair Web site, http://www.betfair.com.

9. Alfred Rappaport and Michael J. Mauboussin, *Expectations Investing* (Boston: Harvard Business School Press, 2001), 132–34.

10. Howard Rheingold, *Smart Mobs: The Next Social Revolution* (New York: Perseus, 2002).

11. Ken Brown, "Stocks March to the Beat of War, Weak Economy," *Wall Street Journal*, March 31, 2003.

30. Vox Populi

1. Michael Idinopulos and Lee Kempler, "Do You Know Who Your Experts Are?" *The McKinsey Quarterly* 4 (2003): 60–69; see http://www.mckinseyquarterly.com/article_abstract.asp?ar=1358&L2=18&L3=31&srid=6&gp=1.

2. Nancy Weil, "Innocentive Pairs R&D Challenges with Researchers," *Bio-IT World*, May 29, 2003.

3. Some companies are trying to create an internal mechanism to match questions with answers. For example, Hewlett-Packard has a system called SHOCK (Social Harvesting of Community Knowledge); see http://www.hpl.hp.com/research/idl/projects/shock.

4. Francis Galton, "Vox Populi," *Nature* 75 (March 7, 1907): 450–451; reprint, 1949. Also, James Surowiecki, *The Wisdom of Crowds: Why the Many Are Smarter Than the Few and How Collective Wisdom Shapes Business, Economies, Societies and Nations* (New York: Random House, 2004).

5. Norman L. Johnson, "Collective Problem Solving: Functionality beyond the Individual," *LA-UR-98–2227* (1998); Jack L. Treynor, "Market Efficiency and the Bean Jar Experiment," *Financial Analysts Journal* (May–June 1987): –53; Sherry Sontag and Christopher Drew, *Blind Man's Bluff: The Untold Story of American Submarine Espionage* (New York: Perseus Books, 1998), 58–59.

6. Kay-Yut Chen, Leslie R. Fine, and Bernardo A. Huberman, "Predicting the Future," *Information Systems Frontiers* 5, no. 1 (2003): 47–61, http://www.hpl. hp.com/shl/papers/future/future.pdf.

31. A Tail of Two Worlds

1. This process is know as Brownian motion. Albert Einstein pointed out that this motion is caused by random bombardment of heat-excited water molecules on the pollen.

2. See GloriaMundi, "Introduction to VaR," http://www.gloriamundi.org/ introduction.asp.

3. Edgar E. Peters, *Fractal Market Analysis* (New York: John Wiley & Sons, 1994), 21–27.

4. Roger Lowenstein, *When Genius Failed: The Rise and Fall of Long-Term Capital Management* (New York: Random House, 2000), 72. Lowenstein is quoting Jens Carsten Jackwerth and Mark Rubinstein, "Recovering Probability Distributions from Option Prices," *Journal of Finance* 51, no. 5 (December 1996): 1612. Jackwerth and Rubinstein note that assuming annualized volatility of 20 percent for the market and a lognormal distribution, the 29 percent drop in the S&P 500 futures was a twenty-seven-standard-deviation event, with a probability of 10^{-160}.

5. Per Bak, *How Nature Works* (New York: Springer-Verlag, 1996).

6. See chapter 22.

7. Sushil Bikhchandani and Sunil Sharma, "Herd Behavior in Financial Markets," *IMF Staff Papers* 47, no. 3 (September 2001); see http://www.imf. org/External/Pubs/FT/staffp/2001/01/pdf/Bikhchan.pdf.

8. Michael S. Gibson, "Incorporating Event Risk into Value-at-Risk," *The Federal Reserve Board Finance and Economics Discussion Series*, 2001–17 (February 2001); see http://www.federalreserve.gov/pubs/feds/2001/200117/ 200117abs.html.

32. Integrating the Outliers

1. Daniel Bernoulli, "Exposition of a New Theory on the Measurement of Risk," *Econometrica*, 22 (January 1954): 23–36. Originally published in 1738. Daniel's cousin, Nicolaus, initially proposed the game.

2. See *The Stanford Encyclopedia of Philosophy*, s.v. "St. Petersburg Paradox," http://plato.stanford.edu/entries/paradox-stpetersburg.

3. Much of this section relies on Larry S. Liebovitch and Daniela Scheurle, "Two Lessons from Fractals and Chaos," *Complexity*, Vol. 5, 4, 2000, 34–43. See http://www.ccs.fau.edu/˜liebovitch/complexity-20.html.

4. See chapter 29.

5. Benoit B. Mandelbrot, "A Multifractal Walk down Wall Street," *Scientific American*, February 1999, 70–73. Also see, Benoit B. Mandelbrot, *Fractals and Scaling in Finance: Discontinuity, Concentration, Risk* (New York: Springer Verlag, 1997).

6. If you assume that you flipped a coin nonstop sixteen hours a day (estimating eight hours of sleep), and if each coin flip takes three seconds, it would take 14.3 years to complete 100 million coin tosses.

7. Didier Sornette, *Why Stock Markets Crash: Critical Events in Complex Financial Systems* (Princeton, N.J.: Princeton University Press, 2003); also see Sornette's Web site, http://www.ess.ucla.edu/faculty/sornette/.

8. See another classic article: Peter L. Bernstein, "Growth Companies Vs. Growth Stocks," *Harvard Business Review* (September–October 1956): 87–98.

9. Peter L. Bernstein, *Against the Gods: The Remarkable Story of Risk* (New York: Wiley, 1996), 107–109.

10. David Durand, "Growth Stocks and the Petersburg Paradox," *Journal of Finance* 12 (September 1957): 348–63.

11. Stephen R. Waite, *Quantum Investing* (New York: Texere, 2003), 129.

12. Michael J. Mauboussin, Bob Hiler, and Patrick J. McCarthy, "The (Fat) Tail that Wags the Dog," *Credit Suisse First Boston Equity Research*, February 4, 1999.

33. The Janitor's Dream

1. Quoted in Sandra Blakeslee, "Scientist at Work: John Henry Holland; Searching for Simple Rules of Complexity," *New York Times*, December 26, 1995.

2. William H. Calvin, *How Brains Think: Evolving Intelligence, Then and Now* (New York: Basic Books, 1996).

3. John H. Holland, *Hidden Order: How Adaptation Builds Complexity* (Reading, Mass.: Helix Books, 1995), 10–37.

4. See chapter 11.

5. Michael J. Mauboussin, "Revisiting Market Efficiency: The Stock Market as a Complex Adaptive System," *Journal of Applied Corporate Finance* 14, no. 4 (Winter 2002): 47–55.

6. Norman L. Johnson, "Diversity in Decentralized Systems: Enabling Self-Organizing Solutions," LANL, LA-UR-99–6281, 1999.

7. Max Bazerman, *Judgment in Managerial Decision Making*, 4th ed. (New York: Wiley, 1998), 6–17.

34. Chasing Laplace's Demon

1. See Michael Gazzaniga, "Whole Brain Interpreter," http://pegasus.cc.ucf.edu/~fle/gazzaniga.html.

2. Joseph LeDoux, *The Emotional Brain: The Mysterious Underpinnings of Emotional Life* (New York: Touchstone, 1996), 32–33.

3. As per Wolpert's Faraday lecture at the Royal Society, 2001. Also see Lewis Wolpert, *Six Impossible Things Before Breakfast: The Evolutionary Origins of Belief* (New York: W. W. Norton, 2007); Gilles Fauconnier and Mark Turner, *The Way We Think: Conceptual Blending and the Mind's Hidden Complexities* (New York: Basic Books, 2002), 76; and Paul R. Ehrlich, *Human Natures: Genes, Cultures, and the Human Prospect* (Washington, D.C.: Island Press, 2000), 132.

4. Michael J. Mauboussin, "Revisiting Market Efficiency: The Stock Market as a Complex Adaptive System," *The Journal of Applied Corporate Finance* 14, no. 4 (Winter 2002): 47–55.

5. Duncan J. Watts, *Six Degrees: The Science of a Connected Age* (New York: W. W. Norton, 2003), 204–7.

6. David M. Cutler, James M. Poterba, and Lawrence H. Summers, "What Moves Stock Prices?" *The Journal of Portfolio Management* (Spring 1989): 4–12.

7. Peter Coy, "He Who Mines the Data May Strike Fool's Gold," *Business-Week*, June 16, 1997.

8. Gary Belsky and Thomas Gilovich, *Why Smart People Make Big Money Mistakes—and How to Correct Them: Lessons From the New Science of Behavioral Economics* (New York: Simon and Schuster, 1999), 137–38.

35. More Power to You

1. George Kingsley Zipf, *National Unity and Disunity: The Nation as a Bio-Social Organism* (Bloomington, Ind.: Principia Press, 1941), 398–99.

2. For example, in log 10 the scale would be 10^1 (= 10), 10^2 (= 100), and 10^3 (= 1,000) versus the more familiar 10, 11, 12.

3. Richard Koch, *The 80/20 Principle: The Secret to Success by Achieving More with Less* (New York: Currency, 1998).

4. Rob Axtell, "Zipf's Law of City Sizes: A Microeconomic Explanation Far from Equilibrium," presentation at a RAND workshop, Complex Systems and Policy Analysis: New Tools for a New Millennium, September 27–28, 2000, Arlington, Va.

5. These modifications are lucidly explained in Murray Gell-Mann, *The Quark and the Jaguar: Adventures in the Simple and the Complex* (New York: W. H. Freeman, 1994), 92–100.

6. Robert L. Axtell, "Zipf Distribution of U.S. Firm Sizes," *Science* 293 (September 7, 2001): 1818–20; see http://www.sciencemag.org/content/vol293/issue5536/index.shtml.

7. These include self-organized criticality, highly optimized tolerance (HOT), and the Gibrat process. Not all of these processes are mutually exclusive.

8. Per Bak, *How Nature Works: The Science of Self-Organized Criticality* (New York: Springer-Verlag, 1996), 1–3.

9. Robert Axtell, "The Emergence of Firms in a Population of Agents: Local Increasing Returns, Unstable Nash Equilibria, and Power Law Size Distributions," *Brookings Institution, Center on Social and Economics Working Paper* 3, June 1999. Also see Robert L. Axtell and Richard Florida, "Emergent Cities: A Microeconomic Explanation of Zipf's Law," *Brookings Institution and Carnegie Mellon University Working Paper*, September 2000.

10. Michael Batty, "Rank Clocks," *Nature*, vol. 444, November 30, 2006, 592–596.

11. Albert-László Barabási, *Linked: The New Science of Networks* (Cambridge, Mass.: Perseus, 2002), 69–72; Bernardo A. Huberman, *The Laws of the Web: Patterns in the Ecology of Information* (Cambridge, Mass.: MIT Press, 2001), 25–31; Lada A. Adamic, "Zipf, Power-laws, and Pareto—a Ranking Tutorial," Information Dynamics Lab, HP Labs, Working Paper, http://ginger.hpl.hp.com/shl/papers/ranking/ranking.html.

36. The Pyramid of Numbers

1. See chapter 35.

2. Paul Colinvaux, *Why Big Fierce Animals Are Rare* (Princeton, N.J.: Princeton University Press, 1978), 10–31.

3. James H. Brown and Geoffrey B. West, eds., *Scaling in Biology* (Oxford: Oxford University Press, 2000).

4. Robert L. Axtell, "Zipf Distribution of U.S. Firm Sizes," *Science* 293 (September 7, 2001): 1818–20.

5. Eugene Stanley et al., "Scaling Behavior in Economics: I. Empirical Results for Company Growth," *Journal de Physique* (April 1997): 621–33.

6. Axtell, "Zipf Distribution."

7. Corporate Strategy Board, "Stall Points: Barriers to Growth for the Large Corporate Enterprise," *Corporate Strategy Board* (March 1998).

8. Steven Klepper, "Entry, Exit, Growth, and Innovation Over the Product Life Cycle," *American Economic Review* 86, no. 3 (1996): 562–83. Also see Bartley J. Madden, *CFROI Valuation: A Total System Approach to Valuing the Firm* (Oxford: Butterworth-Heinemann, 1999), 18–21.

9. Louis K. C. Chan, Jason Karceski, and Josef Lakonishok, "The Level and Persistence of Growth Rates," *The Journal of Finance* 58, no. 2 (April 2003): 671.

10. At the time this essay was written, the upcoming year (T + 1), embedded-asset growth is 8.8 percent for the fifty largest market-capitalization companies versus 5.6 percent for the S&P 500, and CFROI is 8.8 percent against 7.6 percent. For 2008 (T + 5), the large companies reflect asset growth and CFROI of 8.9 percent and 10.9 percent, respectively. For the S&P 500, the corresponding numbers are 7.2 percent and 9.0 percent.

11. Financial services stands out as a sector that has increased significantly as a percentage of S&P 500 earnings (about 30 percent, excluding finance arms) and as a percentage of the GDP (roughly 21 percent versus 15 percent in 1980). Historically, sectors that have risen to such levels (energy and technology) have seen their importance wane. For more on this, see Paddy Jilek, Bradford Neuman, and Arbin Sherchan, "U.S. Investment Digest: Five Tidbits," *Credit Suisse First Boston Equity Research*, September 5, 2003.

37. Turn Tale

1. Malcolm Gladwell, *The Tipping Point: How Little Things Can Make a Big Difference* (Boston, Mass.: Little, Brown and Company, 2000), 3–4.

2. Michael J. Mauboussin, Alexander Schay, and Stephen G. Kawaja, "Network to Net Worth: Exploring Network Dynamics," *Credit Suisse First Boston Equity Research*, May 11, 2000.

3. Benjamin Graham, "Stock Market Warning: Danger Ahead!" *California Management Review* 11, no. 3 (Spring 1960): 34.

4. Duncan J. Watts, *Small Worlds* (Princeton, N.J.: Princeton University Press, 1999).

5. Christopher D. Carroll, "The Epidemiology of Macroeconomic Expectations," Johns Hopkins Working Paper, July 9, 2002, http://www.econ.jhu.edu/people/ccarroll/EpidemiologySFI.pdf. Also, Michael J. Mauboussin, "Revisiting Market Efficiency: The Stock Market as a Complex Adaptive System," *Journal of Applied Corporate Finance* 14, no. 4 (Winter 2002): 47–55.

6. See Joseph de la Vega's *Confusion de Confusiones* (1688), Charles MacKay's *Extraordinary Delusions and the Madness of Crowds* (1841), and Edwin Lefevre's *Reminiscences of a Stock Operator* (1923).

7. Warren E. Buffett, Berkshire Hathaway Annual Letter to Shareholders, 1987, http://berkshirehathaway.com/letters/1987.html.

8. Benjamin Graham and David L. Dodd, *Security Analysis* (New York: McGraw Hill, 1934), 11.

9. Irving Lester Janis, *Groupthink: Psychological Studies of Policy Decisions and Fiascoes* (New York: Houghton Mifflin, 1982).

38. Stairway to Shareholder Heaven

1. Jennifer Quellette, "Jackson Pollock—Mathematician," *The Fine Arts Magazine*, January 25, 2002.

2. One example is the children's book character, Olivia. See Ian Falconer, *Olivia* (New York: Atheneum Books for Young Readers, 2000).

3. Benoit B. Mandelbrot, "A Multifractal Walk Down Wall Street," *Scientific American* (February 1999): 71.

4. Richard P. Taylor, B. Spehar, C.W.G. Clifford, and B.R. Newell, "The Visual Complexity of Pollock's Dripped Fractals," *Proceedings of the International Conference of Complex Systems,* 2002, http://materialscience.uoregon.edu/taylor/art/TaylorICCS2002.pdf.

5. Richard P. Taylor, "Order in Pollock's Chaos," *Scientific American,* December 2002, http://materialscience.uoregon.edu/taylor/art/scientificamerican.pdf.

6. Robert L. Axtell, "Zipf Distribution of US Firm Sizes," *Science* 293 (September 2001): 1818–1820; Youngki Lee, Luís A. Nunes Amaral, David Canning, Martin Meyer, and H. Eugene Stanley, "Universal Features in the Growth Dynamics of Complex Organizations," *Physical Review Letters* 81, no. 15 (October 1998): 3275–3278, http://polymer.bu.edu/hes/articles/lacms98.pdf.

7. Mandelbrot, "A Multifractal Walk Down Wall Street." Stock price changes are more accurately described as multifractal. Multifractals accommodate some adjustments to get to statistical similarity on various levels. For example, for asset prices, time (the horizontal axis) is lengthened or shortened to show level similarity.

8. Bartley J. Madden, Michael J. Mauboussin, John D. Lagerman, and Samuel T. Eddins, "Business Strategy/Life Cycle Framework: Positioning Firm Strategy as the Primary Cause of Long-Term CFROIs and Asset Growth Rates," *Credit Suisse First Boston Equity Research*, April 22, 2003.

9. Alfred Rappaport and Michael J. Mauboussin, *Expectations Investing* (Boston: Harvard Business School Press, 2001).

10. Michael J. Mauboussin, Alexander Schay, and Patrick McCarthy, "Competitive Advantage Period: At the Intersection of Finance and Competitive Strategy," *Credit Suisse First Boston Equity Research*, October 4, 2001.

11. Michael J. Mauboussin and Kristen Bartholdson, "Measuring the Moat: Assessing the Magnitude and Sustainability of Value Creation," *Credit Suisse First Boston Equity Research*, December 16, 2002.

Conclusion: The Future of Consilience in Investing

1. J. Doyne Farmer and Fabrizio Lillo, "On the Origin of Power Law Tails in Price Fluctuations," *Quantitative Finance* 4, no. 1 (2004): 7–11.

2. Duncan J. Watts, *Small Worlds: The Dynamics of Networks Between Order and Randomness* (Princeton, N.J.: Princeton University Press, 1999).

3. James H. Brown and Geoffrey B. West, eds., *Scaling in Biology* (Oxford: Oxford University Press, 2000).

References

Adamic, Lada A. "Zipf, Power-Laws, and Pareto—a Ranking Tutorial." Information Dynamics Lab, HP Labs, Working Paper. http://ginger.hpl.hp.com/shl/papers/ranking/ranking.html.

Alvarez, A. *Poker: Bets, Bluffs, and Bad Beats.* San Francisco: Chronicle Books, 2001.

Anderson, Carl, and John J. Bartholdi III. "Centralized Versus Decentralized Control in Manufacturing: Lessons from Social Insects." In *Complexity and Complex Systems in Industry*, ed. Ian P. McCarthy and Thierry Rakotobe-Joel, 92–105. Warwick: University of Warwick, 2000.

Armstrong, J. Scott. "The Seer-Sucker Theory: The Value of Experts in Forecasting." *Technology Review* 83 (June–July 1980): 16–24.

Arthur, W. Brian. "Increasing Returns and the New World of Business." *Harvard Business Review* (July–August 1996): 101–9.

——. "Inductive Reasoning and Bounded Rationality: The El Farol Problem." Paper given at the American Economic Association Annual Meetings, 1994. Published in *American Economic Review* (Papers and Proceedings) 84 (1994): 406–11. http://www.santafe.edu/arthur/Papers/El_Farol.html.

Asch, Solomon E. "Effects of Group Pressure Upon the Modification and Distortion of Judgment." In *Groups, Leadership, and Men*, ed. Harold Guetzkow, 177–90. Pittsburgh: Carnegie Press, 1951.

Aunger, Robert. *The Electric Meme: A New Theory of How We Think.* New York: Free Press, 2002.

Axelrod, Robert. *The Complexity of Cooperation: Agent-Based Models of Competition and Collaboration.* Princeton, N.J.: Princeton University Press, 1997.

——. *The Evolution of Cooperation.* New York: Basic Books, 1984.

Axelrod, Robert, and Michael D. Cohen. *Harnessing Complexity.* New York: Free Press, 1999.

Axtell, Robert. "The Emergence of Firms in a Population of Agents: Local Increasing Returns, Unstable Nash Equilibria, and Power Law Size Distributions."

Brookings Institution, Center on Social and Economics Working Paper, June 3, 1999.

——. "Zipf Distribution of U.S. Firm Sizes." *Science* 293 (September 2001): 1818–20. http://www.sciencemag.org/content/vol293/issue5536/index.shtml.

——. "Zipf's Law of City Sizes: A Microeconomic Explanation Far from Equilibrium." Presentation at a RAND workshop, Complex Systems and Policy Analysis: New Tools for a New Millennium, September 27–28, 2000, Arlington, Va.

Axtell, Robert L., and Richard Florida. "Emergent Cities: A Microeconomic Explanation of Zipf's Law." *Brookings Institution and Carnegie Mellon University Working Paper*, September 2000.

Baer, Gregory, and Gary Gensler. *The Great Mutual Fund Trap*. New York: Broadway Books, 2002.

Bak, Per. *How Nature Works: The Science of Self-Organized Criticality*. New York: Springer-Verlag, 1996.

Barabási, Albert-László. *Linked: The New Science of Networks*. Cambridge, Mass.: Perseus, 2002.

Barberis, Nicholas, and Ming Huang. "Mental Accounting, Loss Aversion, and Individual Stock Returns." *Journal of Finance* 56, no. 4 (August 2001): 1247–92.

Batten, David F. *Discovering Artificial Economics: How Agents Learn and Economies Evolve*. New York: Westview Press, 2000.

Batty, Michael. "Rank Clocks." *Nature* 444 (November 2006): 592–96.

Bazerman, Max. *Judgment in Managerial Decision Making*. 4th ed. New York: Wiley, 1998.

Bechara, Antoine, Hanna Damasio, Daniel Tranel, and Antonio R. Damasio. "Deciding Advantageously Before Knowing the Advantageous Strategy." *Science* 275 (February 1997): 1293–95.

Beinhocker, Eric D. "Robust Adaptive Strategies." *Sloan Management Review* 40, no. 3 (Spring 1999): 95–106.

Belsky, Gary, and Thomas Gilovich. *Why Smart People Make Big Money Mistakes—and How to Correct Them: Lessons from the New Science of Behavioral Economics*. New York: Simon and Schuster, 1999.

Benartzi, Shlomo, and Richard H. Thaler. "Myopic Loss Aversion and the Equity Premium Puzzle." *The Quarterly Journal of Economics* (February 1995): 73–92. http://gsbwww.uchicago.edu/fac/richard.thaler/research/myopic.pdf.

Bennis, Warren. "Will the Legacy Live On?" *Harvard Business Review* (February 2002): 95–99.

Berkshire Hathaway. Annual Shareholder Letters. http://www.berkshirehathaway. com/letters/letters.html.

Bernoulli, Daniel. "Exposition of a New Theory on the Measurement of Risk." *Econometrica* 22 (January 1954): 23–36.

Bernstein, Peter L. *Capital Ideas: The Improbable Origins of Modern Wall Street.* New York: The Free Press, 1992.

———. *Against the Gods: The Remarkable Story of Risk.* New York: Wiley, 1996.

———. "Growth Companies vs. Growth Stocks." *Harvard Business Review* (September–October 1956): 87–98.

Bernstein, William J. "Of Risk and Myopia." *Efficientfrontier.com* (2002). http:// www.efficientfrontier.com/ef/102/taleb.htm.

Besanko, David, David Dranove, and Mark Shanley. *Economics of Strategy.* 2nd ed. New York: John Wiley & Sons, 2000.

Betfair Web site. http://www.betfair.com.

Beyer, Andrew, et al. *Bet with the Best: All New Strategies from America's Leading Handicappers.* New York: Daily Racing Form Press, 2001.

Bibliography of Zipf's Law. http://www.nslij-genetics.org/wli/zipf.

Bikhchandani, Sushil, David Hirshleifer, and Ivo Welch. "Informational Cascades and Rational Herding: An Annotated Bibliography." *Working Paper: UCLA/Anderson and Michigan/GSB* (June 1996).

Bikhchandani, Sushil, and Sunil Sharma. "Herd Behavior in Financial Markets." *IMF Staff Papers* 47, no. 3 (September 2001). http://www.imf.org/External/ Pubs/FT/staffp/2001/01/pdf/bikhchan.pdf.

"Binary: It's Digitalicious." Binary code translation Web site. http://nickciske. com/tools/binary.php.

Bischoff, R. "Informal Learning in the Workplace." January 26, 1998. http:// www.tlrp.org/dspace/retrieve/226/Informal+Learning+in+the+workplace1. doc.

Blakeslee, Sandra. "Scientist at Work: John Henry Holland; Searching for Simple Rules of Complexity." *New York Times*, December 26, 1995.

Bogle, John C. "The Emperor's New Mutual Funds." *The Wall Street Journal*, July 8, 2003.

———. "Mutual Fund Directors: The Dog That Didn't Bark." January 28, 2001. http://www.vanguard.com/bogle_site/sp20010128.html.

———. "The Mutual Fund Industry in 2003: Back to the Future." Remarks before the Harvard Club of Boston, January 14, 2003. http://www.vanguard.com/ bogle_site/sp20030114.html.

———. "The Mutual Fund Industry Sixty Years Later: For Better or Worse?" *Financial Analysts Journal* 61, no. 1 (January–February 2005): 15–24.

Bonabeau, Eric, Marco Dorigo, and Guy Theraulaz. *Swarm Intelligence: From Natural to Artificial Systems.* New York: Oxford University Press, 1999.

Bosch-Domènech, Antoni, and Shyam Sunder. "Tracking the Invisible Hand: Convergence of Double Auctions to Competitive Equilibrium." *Computational Economics* 16, no. 3 (December 2000): 257–84.

Brandenburger, Adam M., and Barry J. Nalebuff. *Co-opetition.* New York: Currency, 1996

Britton, B.C., ed. *Executive Control Processes.* Hillsdale, N.J.: Lawrence Erlbaum Associates, 1987.

Brown, James H., and Geoffrey B. West, eds. *Scaling in Biology.* Oxford: Oxford University Press, 2000.

Brown, Ken. "Stocks March to the Beat of War, Weak Economy." *The Wall Street Journal*, March 31, 2003.

Brown, Shona L., and Kathleen M. Eisenhardt. *Competing on the Edge: Strategy as Structured Chaos.* Boston: Harvard Business School Press, 1998.

Buffett, Warren, and Charlie Munger. "It's Stupid the Way People Extrapolate the Past—and Not *Slightly* Stupid, But *Massively* Stupid." *Outstanding Investor Digest*, December 24, 2001.

Bullard, Mercer. "Despite SEC Efforts, Accuracy in Fund Names Still Elusive." *The Street.com*, January 30, 2001. http://www.thestreet.com/funds/mercerbullard/1282823.html.

Burke, Edmund, and Graham Kendall. "Applying Ant Algorithms and the No Fit Polygon to the Nesting Problem." *University of Nottingham Working Paper*, 1999. http://www.asap.cs.nott.ac.uk/publications/pdf/gk_ai99.pdf.

Bygrave, William D., Julian E. Lange, J. R. Roedel and Gary Wu. "Capital Market Excesses and Competitive Strength: The Case of the Hard Drive Industry, 1984–2000." *Journal of Applied Corporate Finance* 13, no. 3 (Fall 2000): 8–19.

Calvin, William H. "The Emergence of Intelligence." *Scientific American Presents* 9, no. 4 (November 1998): 44–51.

———. *How Brains Think: Evolving Intelligence, Then and Now.* New York: Basic Books, 1996.

Campbell, John Y., Martin Lettau, Burton Malkiel, and Yexiao Xu. "Have Individual Stocks Become More Volatile? An Empirical Exploration of Idiosyncratic Risk." *Journal of Finance* 54 (February 2001): 1–43.

Carlile, Paul R., and Clayton M. Christensen. "The Cycles of Theory Building in Management Research." Working Paper, January 6, 2005. http://www.
innosight.com/documents/Theory%20Building.pdf.

Carroll, Christopher D. "The Epidemiology of Macroeconomic Expectations."
Johns Hopkins Working Paper, July 9, 2002. http://www.econ.jhu.edu/people/
ccarroll/EpidemiologySFI.pdf.

Chan, Louis K. C., Jason J. Karceski, and Josef Lakonishok. "The Level and
Persistence of Growth Rates." *The Journal of Finance* 58, no. 2 (April 2003):
644–84.

Chen, Kay-Yut, Leslie R. Fine, and Bernardo A. Huberman. "Predicting the
Future." *Information Systems Frontiers* 5, no. 1 (2003): 47–61. http://www.
hpl.hp.com/shl/papers/future/future.pdf.

Chordia, Tarun, Richard Roll, and Avanidhar Subrahmanyam. "Evidence on the
Speed of Convergence to Market Efficiency." Working Paper, April 29, 2002.
http://www.anderson.ucla.edu/acad_unit/finance/wp/2001/11-01.pdf.

Christensen, Clayton M. *The Innovator's Dilemma: When New Technologies Cause
Great Companies to Fail.* Boston: Harvard Business School Press, 1997.

——. "The Past and Future of Competitive Advantage." *MIT Sloan Management Review* (Winter 2001): 105–9.

Christensen, Clayton M., and Michael E. Raynor. *The Innovator's Solution: Creating
and Sustaining Successful Growth.* Boston: Harvard Business School Press, 2003.

Christensen, Clayton M., Paul Carlile, and David Sundahl. "The Process of
Theory-Building." *Working Paper, 02–016.* For an updated version of this
paper, see http://www.innosight.com/documents/Theory%20Building.pdf.

Churchill, Winston S. Speech. "The Price of Greatness is Responsibility." 1943.
http://www.winstonchurchill.org/i4a/pages/index.cfm?pageid5424.

Cialdini, Robert B. *Influence: The Psychology of Persuasion.* New York: William
Morrow, 1993.

——. "The Science of Persuasion." *Scientific American*, February 2001, 76–81.

Clancy, Barbara, and Barbara Finley. "Neural Correlates of Early Language Learning." In *Language Development: The Essential Readings*, ed. Michael Tomasello
and Elizabeth Bates, 307–30. Oxford: Blackwell, 2001. An earlier version
is available from http://crl.ucsd.edu/courses/commdis/pdf/neuralcorrelates
chapter-nofigures.pdf.

Coen, Corinne, and Rick Riolo. "El Farol Revisited: How People in Large Groups
Learn to Coordinate Through Complementary Scripts." *Organizational*

Learning and Knowledge Management conference proceedings, 4th International Conference, June 2001, London, Ont.

Colinvaux, Paul. *Why Big Fierce Animals Are Rare*. Princeton, N.J.: Princeton University Press, 1978.

Collins, Jim. *Good to Great*. New York: HarperBusiness, 2001.

Cornell, Bradford. *The Equity Risk Premium: The Long-Run Future of the Stock Market*. New York: Wiley, 1999.

Corporate Strategy Board. "Stall Points: Barriers to Growth for the Large Corporate Enterprise." *Corporate Strategy Board* (March 1998).

Coy, Peter. "He Who Mines the Data May Strike Fool's Gold." *BusinessWeek*, June 16, 1997.

Crist, Steven. *Betting on Myself: Adventures of a Horseplayer and Publisher*. New York: Daily Racing Form Press, 2003.

Cutler, David M., James M. Poterba, and Lawrence H. Summers. "What Moves Stock Prices?" *Journal of Portfolio Management* (Spring 1989): 4–12.

Damasio, Antonio R. *Descartes' Error: Emotion, Reason, and the Human Brain*. New York: Avon Books, 1994.

——. *The Feeling of What Happens: Body and Emotion in the Making of Consciousness*. New York: Harcourt Brace & Company, 1999.

Darwin, Charles. *The Origin of Species*. London: John Murray, 1859.

Davis, Bob, and Susan Warren. "How Fears of Impending War Already Take Economic Toll." *The Wall Street Journal*, January 29, 2003.

DeBondt, Werner, and Richard Thaler. "Does the Stock Market Overreact?" *Journal of Finance* 40 (1985): 793–805.

DellaVigna, Stefano, and Joshua Pollet. "Attention, Demographics, and the Stock Market." Working Paper, November 23, 2003. http://fisher.osu.edu/fin/dice/seminars/pollet.pdf.

DeLong, J. Bradford, Andrei Shleifer, Lawrence H. Summers, and Robert J. Waldmann. "Positive Feedback Investment Strategies and Destabilizing Rational Speculation." *Journal of Finance* 45, no. 2 (June 1990): 379–95.

DeLong, J. Bradford, and Lawrence H. Summers. "The 'New Economy': Background, Historical Perspective, Questions, and Speculations." *Federal Reserve Bank of Kansas City Economic Review* (Fourth Quarter 2001).

Dembo, Ron S., and Andrew Freeman. *Seeing Tomorrow: Rewriting the Rules of Risk*. New York: Wiley, 1998.

Dickinson, Rod. "The Milgram Reenactment." http://www.milgramreenactment.org/pages/section.xml?location51.

Dimson, Elroy, Paul Marsh, and Mike Staunton. "Global Evidence on the Equity Risk Premium." *Journal of Applied Corporate Finance* 15, no. 4 (Fall 2003): 27–38.

Dugatkin, Lee Alan. *The Imitation Factor: Evolution Beyond the Gene.* New York: Free Press, 2000.

Dugatkin, Lee Alan, and Jean-Guy J. Godin. "How Females Choose Their Mates." *Scientific American* (April 1998): 56–61.

Durand, David. "Growth Stocks and the Petersburg Paradox." *Journal of Finance* 12 (September 1957): 348–63.

The Economist. "Other People's Money: A Survey of Asset Management." July 5, 2003.

———. "Survey of the 'New Economy.'" September 21, 2000.

Eguiluz, Victor M., and Martin G. Zimmerman. "Transmission of Information and Herd Behavior: An Application to Financial Markets." *Physical Review Letters* 85, no. 26 (December 2000): 5659–62.

Ehrlich, Paul R. *Human Natures: Genes, Cultures, and the Human Prospect.* Washington, D.C.: Island Press, 2000.

Eisenhardt, Kathleen M., and Donald N. Sull. "Strategy as Simple Rules." *Harvard Business Review* (January 2001): 107–16.

Ellis, Charles D. "Will Business Success Spoil the Investment Management Profession?" *The Journal of Portfolio Management* (Spring 2001): 11–15.

Elton, Charles S. *Animal Ecology.* Chicago: The University of Chicago Press, 2001.

Enriquez, Juan, *As the Future Catches You.* New York: Crown Business, 2000.

Epstein, Richard A. *The Theory of Gambling and Statistical Logic.* London: The Academic Press, 1977.

Epstein, Seymour. "Cognitive-Experiential Self-Theory: An Integrative Theory of Personality." In *The Relational Self: Theoretical Convergences in Psychoanalysis and Social Psychology,* ed. R. C. Curtis, 111–37. New York: Guilford Press, 1991.

———. "Integration of the Cognitive and the Psychodynamic Unconscious." *American Psychologist* 49, no. 8 (August 1994): 709–24.

Erickson, Todd, Carin Cooney, and Craig Sterling. "US Technology Sector: Mean Reversion Analysis." *CSFB HOLT Research*, February 2, 2004.

Falconer, Ian. *Olivia.* New York: Atheneum Books for Young Readers, 2000.

Fama, Eugene F., Lawrence Fisher, Michael C. Jensen, and Richard Roll. "The Adjustment of Stock Prices to New Information." *International Economic Review* 10, no. 1 (February 1969).

Fama, Eugene F., and Kenneth R. French. "Disappearing Dividends: Changing Firm Characteristics or Lower Propensity to Pay?" *CRSP Working Paper 509.* June 2000. http://papers.ssrn.com/sol3/papers.cfm?abstract_id=203092.

———. "The Equity Premium." *Journal of Finance* 57 (2002): 637–59.

Farmer, J. Doyne, and Fabrizio Lillo. "On the Origin of Power Law Tails in Price Fluctuations." *Quantitative Finance* 4, no. 1 (2004): 7–11.

Fauconnier, Gilles, and Mark Turner. *The Way We Think: Conceptual Blending and the Mind's Hidden Complexities.* New York: Basic Books, 2002.

Fehr, Ernst. "The Economics of Impatience." *Nature*, January 17, 2002, 269–70.

Feltovich, Paul J., Kenneth M. Ford, and Robert Hoffman, eds. *Expertise in Context: Human and Machine.* Menlo Park, Cal.: AAAI Press and Cambridge, Mass.: MIT Press, 1997.

Fine, Charles H. *Clockspeed: Winning Industry Control in the Age of Temporary Advantage.* Reading, Mass.: Perseus Books, 1998.

Fisher, Kenneth L., and Meir Statman. "Cognitive Biases in Market Forecasts." *Journal of Portfolio Management* 27, no. 1 (Fall 2000): 72–81.

Fisher, Lawrence, and James H. Lorie. "Rates of Return on Investments in Common Stocks." *Journal of Business* 37, no. 1 (January 1964): 1–24.

Foderaro, Lisa W. "If June Cleaver Joined 'Sex and the City': Tupperware Parties for the Cosmo Set." *New York Times*, February 1, 2003.

Foster, Richard, and Sarah Kaplan. *Creative Destruction: Why Companies that Are Built to Last Underperform the Market—and How to Successfully Transform Them.* New York: Doubleday, 2001.

Fuller, Joseph, and Michael C. Jensen. "Dare to Keep Your Stock Price Low." *The Wall Street Journal*, December 31, 2001.

Galton, Francis. "Vox Populi." *Nature* 75 (March 1907): 450–451. Reprint, 1949.

Gawande, Atul, *Complications: A Surgeon's Notes on an Imperfect Science.* New York: Picador, 2002.

Gazzaniga, Michael. "The Whole-Brain Interpreter." http://pegasus.cc.ucf.edu/~fle/gazzaniga.html.

Gell-Mann, Murray. *The Quark and the Jaguar: Adventures in the Simple and the Complex.* New York: W. H. Freeman, 1994.

Gibson, Michael S. "Incorporating Event Risk into Value-at-Risk." *The Federal Reserve Board Finance and Economics Discussion Series, 2001–17*, February 2001. http://www.federalreserve.gov/pubs/feds/2001/200117/200117abs.html.

Gigerenzer, Gerd. *Calculated Risks.* New York: Simon & Schuster, 2002.

Gillon, S. *The Story of the 29th Division.* London: Nelson & Sons, n.d.

Gilovich, Thomas, Dale Griffin, and Daniel Kahneman, eds. *Heuristics and Biases: The Psychology of Intuitive Judgment*. Cambridge: Cambridge University Press, 2002.

Gilovich, Thomas, Robert Valone, and Amos Tversky. "The Hot Hand in Basketball: On the Misperception of Random Sequences." *Cognitive Psychology* 17 (1985): 295–314.

Gladwell, Malcolm. *The Tipping Point: How Little Things Can Make a Big Difference*. Boston, Mass.: Little, Brown and Company, 2000.

Glassman, James K., and Kevin A. Hassett. *Dow 36,000: The New Strategy for Profiting from the Coming Rise in the Stock Market*. New York: Times Books, 1999.

GloriaMundi. "Introduction to VaR." http://www.gloriamundi.org/introduction.asp.

Goodgame, Dan. "The Game of Risk: How the Best Golfer in the World Got Even Better." *Time*, August 14, 2000.

Gopnik, Alison, Andrew Meltzoff, and Patricia Kuhl. *The Scientist in the Crib: What Early Learning Tells Us About the Mind*. New York: First Perennial, 2001.

Gould, Stephen Jay. "The Streak of Streaks." *New York Review of Books*, August 18, 1988. http://www.nybooks.com/articles/4337.

——. *Triumph and Tragedy in Mudville*. New York: W. W. Norton, 2003.

Graham, Benjamin. "Stock Market Warning: Danger Ahead!" *California Management Review* 11, no. 3 (Spring 1960).:34.

Graham, Benjamin, and David L. Dodd. *Security Analysis*. New York: McGraw Hill, 1934.

Greenspan, Alan. "The Structure of the International Financial System." Remarks at the Securities Industry Association Annual Meeting. 5 November 1998. http://www.federalreserve.gov/boarddocs/speeches/1998/19981105.htm.

Greenwald, John. "Doom Stalks the Dotcoms." *Time*, April 17, 2000.

Griffin, Dale, and Amos Tversky. "The Weighing of Evidence and the Determinants of Confidence." In *Heuristics and Biases: The Psychology of Intuitive Judgment*, ed. Thomas Gilovich, Dale Griffin, and Daniel Kahneman, 230–49. Cambridge: Cambridge University Press, 2002.

Grossman, Sanford J., and Joseph E. Stiglitz. "On the Impossibility of Informationally Efficient Markets." *American Economic Review* 70 (1980): 393–408.

Haffner, Katie. "In an Ancient Game, Computing's Future." *New York Times*, August 1, 2002.

Hanson, Robin D. "Decision Markets." *IEEE Intelligent Systems* (May–June 1999): 16–19. http://hanson.gmu.edu/decisionmarkets.pdf.

Hargadon, Andrew. *How Breakthroughs Happen*. Boston: Harvard Business School Press, 2003.

Hayek, Freidrich. "The Use of Knowledge in Society." *American Economic Review* 35, no. 4 (September 1945): 519–30. http://www.virtualschool.edu/mon/ Economics/HayekUseOfKnowledge.html.

Holland, John H. *Hidden Order: How Adaptation Builds Complexity*. Reading, Mass.: Helix Books, 1995.

Hollywood Stock Exchange. Web site. http://www.hsx.com.

Huberman, Bernardo A. *The Laws of the Web: Patterns in the Ecology of Information*. Cambridge, Mass.: MIT Press, 2001.

Hulbert, Mark. "The Five-Year Forecast Looks Great, or Does It?" *New York Times*, January 25, 2004.

IBM Research. "Deep Blue: FAQ." http://www.research.ibm.com/deepblue/ meet/html/d.3.3.html.

Idinopulos, Michael, and Lee Kempler. "Do You Know Who Your Experts Are?" *The McKinsey Quarterly* 4 (2003): 60–69.

Ijiri, Yuji, and Herbert A. Simon. *Skew Distributions and the Sizes of Firms*. New York: North-Holland, 1977.

Innocentive. Web site. http://www.innocentive.com.

Iowa Electronic Markets. Web site. http://www.biz.uiowa.edu/iem.

Janis, Irving Lester. *Groupthink: Psychological Studies of Policy Decisions and Fiascoes*. New York: Houghton Mifflin, 1982.

Jensen, Michael C. "The Performance of Mutual Funds in the Period 1945–1964." *Journal of Finance* 23 (1968): 389–416.

Jilek, Paddy, Bradford Neuman, and Arbin Sherchan. "U.S. Investment Digest: Five Tidbits." *Credit Suisse First Boston Equity Research*, September 5, 2003.

Johnson, Norman L. "Biography." http://ishi.lanl.gov.

——. "Collective Problem Solving: Functionality Beyond the Individual." LA-UR-98-2227, 1998.

——. "Diversity in Decentralized Systems: Enabling Self-Organizing Solutions." LA-UR-99-6281, 1999.

——. "What a Developmental View Can Do for You (or the Fall of the House of Experts)." Talk at CSFB Thought Leader Forum, September 2000, Santa Fe, N.M. http://www.capatcolumbia.com/CSFB%20TLF/2000/johnson00_ sidecolum.pdf.

Johnson, Steven. *Emergence: The Connected Lives of Ants, Brains, Cities, and Software*. New York: Scribner, 2001.

Joseph de la Vega. *Confusion de Confusiones*. 1688.

Kahneman, Daniel. "Maps of Bounded Rationality: A Perspective on Intuitive Judgment and Choice." Nobel Prize Lecture. 8 December 2002. http://www.nobel.se/economics/laureates/2002/kahnemann-lecture.pdf.

Kahneman, Daniel, and Amos Tversky. "Prospect Theory: An Analysis of Decision Under Risk." *Econometrica* 47 (1979): 263–91.

Kahneman, Daniel, Paul Slovic, and Amos Tversky, eds. *Judgment Under Uncertainty: Heuristics and Biases.* Cambridge: Cambridge University Press, 1982.

Kauffman, Stuart. *At Home in the Universe.* Oxford: Oxford University Press, 1996.

Kaufman, Michael T. *Soros: The Life and Times of a Messianic Billionaire.* New York: Knopf, 2002.

Kaufman, Peter D., ed. *Poor Charlie's Almanack.* Virginia Beach, Va.: The Donning Company Publishers, 2005.

Kennedy, James, and Russell C. Eberhart. *Swarm Intelligence.* San Francisco: Morgan Kaufmann, 2001.

Keynes, John Maynard. *The General Theory of Employment.* New York: Harcourt, Brace and Company, 1936.

Klein, Gary. *Sources of Power: How People Make Decisions.* Cambridge, Mass.: MIT Press, 1998.

Klepper, Steven. "Entry, Exit, Growth, and Innovation Over the Product Life Cycle." *American Economic Review* 86, no. 3 (1996): 562–83.

Knight, Frank H. *Risk, Uncertainty, and Profit.* Boston: Houghton and Mifflin, 1921. http://www.econlib.org/library/Knight/knRUP.html.

Koch, Richard. *The 80/20 Principle: The Secret to Success by Achieving More with Less.* New York: Currency, 1998.

Kranhold, Kathryn. "Florida Might Sue Alliance Capital Over Pension Fund's Enron Losses." *The Wall Street Journal,* April 23, 2002.

Krugman, Paul. *The Self-Organizing Economy.* Oxford: Blackwell Publishers, 1996.

Laing, Jonathan R. "A Truly Amazing Run: But, with Dangers Ahead, Can Bill Gross Keep Outracing the Market?" *Barron's,* March 17, 2003.

Lakoff, George, and Mark Johnson. *Metaphors We Live By.* Chicago: The University of Chicago Press, 1980.

Lakonishok, Josef, Andrei Shleifer, and Robert W. Vishny. "Contrarian Investment, Extrapolation, and Risk." *Journal of Finance* 49, no. 5 (December 1994): 1541–78.

Laplace, Pierre Simon. *A Philosophical Essay on Probabilities.* Minneola, N.Y.: Dover Publications, 1996.

LeDoux, Joseph. *The Emotional Brain: The Mysterious Underpinnings of Emotional Life*. New York: Touchstone, 1996.

———. *Synaptic Self: How Our Brains Become Who We Are*. New York: Viking, 2002.

Lee, Youngki, Luís A. Nunes Amaral, David Canning, Martin Meyer, and H. Eugene Stanley. "Universal Features in the Growth Dynamics of Complex Organizations." *Physical Review Letters* 81, no. 15 (October 1998): 3275–3278. http://polymer.bu.edu/hes/articles/lacms98.pdf.

Lefevre, Edwin. *Reminiscences of a Stock Operator*. 1923.

Lessand, Donald. "The Soft Revolution: Achieving Growth By Managing Intangibles." *The Journal of Applied Corporate Finance* 11, no. 2 (Summer 1998): 8–27.

Lev, Baruch. *Intangibles: Management, Measurement, and Reporting*. Washington, D.C.: Brookings Institution Press, 2001.

Lewellen, Jonathan. "Predicting Returns with Financial Ratios." *MIT Sloan Working Paper 4374-02*, February 2002.

Lichenstein, Sarah, Baruch Fischhoff, and Lawrence D. Phillips. "Calibration of Probabilities." In *Judgment Under Uncertainty: Heuristics and Biases*, ed. Daniel Kahneman, Paul Slovic, and Amos Tversky, 306–34. Cambridge: Cambridge University Press, 1982.

Liebovitch, Larry S., and Daniela Scheurle. "Two Lessons from Fractals and Chaos." *Complexity* 5, no. 4 (2000): 34–43.

Lipshitz, Raanan, Gary Klein, Judith Orasanu, and Eduardo Salas. "Taking Stock of Naturalistic Decision Making." Working Paper, July 15, 2000.

Loest, Robert. "Fitness Landscapes and Investment Strategies, Parts 1 and 2." *Portfolio Manager Commentary—IPS Funds* (July–August 1998).

Lowenstein, Alice. "The Low Turnover Advantage." *Morningstar Research*. September 12, 1997. http://news.morningstar.com/news/ms/FundFocus/lowturnover1.html.

Lowenstein, Roger. *When Genius Failed: The Rise and Fall of Long-Term Capital Management*. New York: Random House, 2000.

Lyman, Peter, and Hal R. Varian. "How Much Information? 2003." http://www.sims.berkeley.edu/research/projects/how-much-info-2003.

MacGregor, Donald G. "Imagery and Financial Judgment." *Journal of Psychology and Financial Markets* 3, no. 1 (2002): 15–22.

MacKay, Charles. *Extraordinary Popular Delusions and the Madness of Crowds*. New York: Three Rivers Press, 1995.

Madden, Bartley J. *CFROI Valuation: A Total System Approach to Valuing the Firm.* Oxford: Butterworth-Heinemann, 1999.

Madden, Bartley J., Michael J. Mauboussin, John D. Lagerman, and Samuel T. Eddins. "Business Strategy/Life Cycle Framework: Positioning Firm Strategy as the Primary Cause of Long-Term CFROIs and Asset Growth Rates." *Credit Suisse First Boston Equity Research*, April 22, 2003.

Maguire, Steve. "Strategy Is Design: A Fitness Landscape Framework." In *Managing Complexity in Organizations: A View in Many Directions*, ed. M. Lissack and H. Gunz, 67–104. Westport, Conn.: Quorum Books, 1999.

Major League Baseball Historical Player Stats. http://mlb.mlb.com/NASApp/mlb/stats/historical/individual_stats_player.jsp?c_id5mlb&playerID5113376.

Malkiel, Burton G. "The Efficient Market Hypothesis and Its Critics." *Journal of Economic Perspectives* 17, no. 1 (Winter 2003): 78.

——. Interview on ABC's *20/20*. November 27, 1992. http://www.ifa.tv/Library/Support/Articles/Popular/NewsShowTranscript.htm.

——. *A Random Walk Down Wall Street.* New York: W. W. Norton, 2003.

——. "Returns from Investing in Equity Mutual Funds, 1971–1991." *Journal of Finance* 50, no. 2 (June 1995): 549–72.

Mandelbrot, Benoit B. *Fractals and Scaling in Finance: Discontinuity, Concentration, Risk.* New York: Springer Verlag, 1997.

——. "A Multifractal Walk Down Wall Street." *Scientific American* (February 1999): 70–73.

Manning, Gerard. "A Quick and Simple Introduction to *Drosophila melanogaster*." http://www.ceolas.org/fly/intro.html.

Marquet, Pablo A., et al. "Lifespan, Reproduction, and Ecology: Scaling and Power-Laws in Ecological Systems." *Journal of Experimental Biology* 208 (April 2005): 1749–69.

Mauboussin, Michael J. "Get Real." *Credit Suisse First Boston Equity Research*, June 23, 1999.

——. "Long Strange Trip: Thoughts on Stock Market Returns." *Credit Suisse First Boston Equity Research*, January 9, 2003.

——. "Measuring the Moat: Assessing the Magnitude and Sustainability of Value Creation." *Credit Suisse First Boston Equity Research*, December 16, 2002.

——. "Puggy Pearson's Prescription." *The Consilient Observer* 1, no. 11 (June 2002).

——. "Revisiting Market Efficiency: The Stock Market as a Complex Adaptive System." *Journal of Applied Corporate Finance* 14, no. 4 (Winter 2002): 47–55.

———. "Whither Enron: Or—Why Enron Withered." *The Consilient Observer* 1, no. 1 (January 2002).

Mauboussin, Michael J., and Alexander Schay. "Fill and Kill: Succeeding with Survivors Is Nothing New." *Credit Suisse First Boston Equity Research*, April 5, 2001.

———. "Innovation and Markets: How Innovation Affects the Investing Process." *Credit Suisse First Boston Equity Research*, December 12, 2000.

Mauboussin, Michael J., Alexander Schay, and Stephen G. Kawaja. "Network to Net Worth: Exploring Network Dynamics." *Credit Suisse First Boston Equity Research*, May 11, 2000.

Mauboussin, Michael J., Alexander Schay, and Patrick McCarthy. "Competitive Advantage Period: At the Intersection of Finance and Competitive Strategy." *Credit Suisse First Boston Equity Research*, October 4, 2001.

Mauboussin, Michael J., Bob Hiler, and Patrick J. McCarthy. "The (Fat) Tail that Wags the Dog." *Credit Suisse First Boston Equity Research*, February 4, 1999.

McLean, Bethany, and Peter Elkind. *The Smartest Guys in the Room.* New York: Penguin Group, 2003, 132.

Moore, Geoffrey A., Paul Johnson, and Tom Kippola. *The Gorilla Game: Picking Winners in High Technology.* New York: HarperBusiness, 1999.

Munger, Charlie. "A Lesson on Elementary, Worldly Wisdom as It Relates to Investment Management and Business." *Outstanding Investor Digest*, May 5, 1995.

Muoio, Anna. "All the Right Moves." *Fast Company*, May 1999. http://www.fastcompany.com/online/24/chess.html.

Nelson, Richard R., and Sidney G. Winter. *An Evolutionary Theory of Economic Change.* Cambridge, Mass.: Harvard University Press/Belknap Press, 1982.

Neyer, Rob. ESPN Baseball Archives, January 2002. http://espn.go.com/mlb/s/2002/0107/1307254.html.

Niederhoffer, Victor. *The Education of a Speculator.* New York: Wiley, 1997.

Nocera, Joe, "On Oil Supply, Opinions Aren't Scarce." *The New York Times*, September 10, 2005.

NOVA. "Tales from the Hive." http://www.pbs.org/wgbh/nova/bees.

Olsen, Robert A., "Professional Investors as Naturalistic Decision Makers: Evidence and Market Implications." *The Journal of Psychology and Financial Markets* 3, no. 3 (2002): 161–67.

Page, Scott E., *The Difference: How the Power of Diversity Creates Better Groups, Firms, Schools, and Societies.* Princeton, N.J.: Princeton University Press, 2007.

Peters, Edgar E. *Fractal Market Analysis*. New York: Wiley, 1994.

Pinker, Steven. *The Language Instinct: How the Mind Creates Language*. New York: HarperCollins, 1994.

Poundstone, William. *Prisoner's Dilemma*. New York: Anchor Books, 1992.

Pringle, David, and Raju Narisetti. "Nokia's Chief Guides Company Amid Technology's Rough Seas." *The Wall Street Journal*, November 24, 2003.

Quellette, Jennifer. "Jackson Pollock—Mathematician." *The Fine Arts Magazine*, January 25, 2002.

Rappaport, Alfred. "How to Avoid the P/E Trap." *The Wall Street Journal*, March 10, 2003.

———. "The Economics of Short-Term Performance Obsession." *Financial Analysts Journal* 61, no. 3 (May–June 2005): 65–79.

Rappaport, Alfred, and Michael J. Mauboussin. *Expectations Investing: Reading Stock Prices for Better Returns*. Boston: Harvard Business School Press, 2001.

———. "Exploiting Expectations." *Fortune*, January 21, 2002, 113–15.

———. "Pitfalls to Avoid." http://www.expectationsinvesting.com/pdf/pitfalls.pdf.

Raup, David M. *Extinction: Bad Genes or Bad Luck?* New York: W. W. Norton, 1991.

Rennie, John. "Editor's Commentary: The Cold Odds Against Columbia." *Scientific American*, February 7, 2003.

Resnick, Mitchel. *Turtles, Termites, and Traffic Jams*. Cambridge, Mass.: MIT Press, 1994.

Rheingold, Howard. *Smart Mobs: The Next Social Revolution*. New York: Perseus, 2002.

Rifkin, Glenn. "GM's Internet Overhaul." *Technology Review* (October 2002): 62–67.

Rogers, Everett. *Diffusion of Innovations*. New York: Free Press, 1995.

Roll, Richard. "A Critique of the Asset Pricing Theory's Tests: Part 1: On Past and Potential Testability of the Theory." *Journal of Financial Economics* 4 (1977): 129–76.

———. "Rational Infinitely-Lived Asset Prices Must be Non-Stationary." Working Paper, November 1, 2000.

Rosenzweig, Phil, *The Halo Effect: … and Eight Other Business Delusions that Deceive Managers*. New York: Free Press, 2006.

Rottenstreich, Yuval, and Christopher K. Hsee. "Money, Kisses, and Electric Shocks." *Psychological Science* 12, no. 3 (May 2001), 185–90.

Rubin, Robert. Commencement Day Address. Harvard University, 7 June 2001. http://www.commencement.harvard.edu/2001/rubin.html.

———. Commencement Address. University of Pennsylvania, 1999. http://www.upenn.edu/almanac/v45/n33/speeches99.html.

Rubin, Robert E., and Jacob Weisberg. *In an Uncertain World.* New York: Random House, 2003.

Russo, J. Edward, and Paul J. H. Schoemaker. *Winning Decisions: Getting It Right the First Time.* New York: Doubleday, 2002.

Samuelson, Paul A. "Risk and Uncertainty: A Fallacy of Large Numbers." *Scientia* 98 (1963): 108–13.

Sapolsky, Robert M. *A Primate's Memoir.* New York: Scribner, 2001.

———. *Why Zebras Don't Get Ulcers: An Updated Guide to Stress, Stress-Related Disease, and Coping.* New York: W. H. Freeman and Company, 1994.

Schlender, Brent. "The Bill and Warren Show." *Fortune,* July 20, 1998, 48–64.

Schwartz, Peter. *Inevitable Surprises: Thinking Ahead in a Time of Turbulence.* New York: Gotham Books, 2003.

Seeley, Thomas D. Biography. http://www.nbb.cornell.edu/neurobio/department/Faculty/seeley/seeley.html.

———. *The Wisdom of the Hive: The Social Physiology of Honey Bee Colonies.* Cambridge, Mass.: Harvard University Press, 1995.

Seuss, Dr. *I Can Read with My Eyes Shut!* New York: Random House, 1978.

Shefrin, Hersh, *Beyond Greed and Fear: Understanding Behavioral Finance and the Psychology of Investing.* Boston: Harvard Business School Press, 2000.

Shiller, Robert. Web site. http://www.econ.yale.edu/~shiller/.

Shleifer, Andrei. *Inefficient Markets: An Introduction to Behavioral Finance.* Oxford: Oxford University Press, 2000.

Siegel, Jeremy J. *Stocks for the Long Run.* 3rd ed. New York: McGraw Hill, 2002.

Sklansky, David. *The Theory of Poker.* 4th ed. Henderson, Nev.: Two Plus Two Publishing, 1999.

Slovic, Paul, Melissa L. Finucane, Ellen Peters, and Donald G. MacGregor. "Risk as Analysis and Risk as Feelings." Paper presented at the Annual Meeting of the Society for Risk Analysis, New Orleans, Louisiana, December 10, 2002. http://www.decisionresearch.org/pdf/dr502.pdf.

Smith, Vernon L. "An Experimental Study of Competitive Market Behavior." *Journal of Political Economy* 70, no. 3 (June 1962): 111–37.

Social Security. "FAQ." http://www.socialsecurity.gov/history/hfaq.html.

Sontag, Sherry, and Christopher Drew. *Blind Man's Bluff: The Untold Story of American Submarine Espionage*. New York: Perseus Books, 1998.

Sornette, Didier. Biography. http://www.ess.ucla.edu/faculty/sornette.

——. *Why Stock Markets Crash: Critical Events in Complex Financial Systems*. Princeton, N.J.: Princeton University Press, 2003.

Soros, George. *Soros on Soros*. New York: Wiley, 1995.

Spanier, David. *Easy Money: Inside the Gambler's Mind*. New York: Penguin, 1987.

Spence, John. "Bogle Calls for a Federation of Long-Term Investors." Index Funds, Inc. http://www.indexfunds.com/articles/20020221_boglespeech_com_gen_JS.htm.

Stalin, Josef. Speech. February 9, 1946. http://www.marx2mao.com/Stalin/SS46.html.

Stanley, Eugene, et al. "Scaling Behavior in Economics: I. Empirical Results for Company Growth." *Journal de Physique* (April 1997): 621–33.

Steinhardt, Michael. *No Bull: My Life In and Out of Markets*. New York: John Wiley & Sons, 2001.

"Stern Stewart EVA Roundtable." *Journal of Applied Corporate Finance* 7, no. 2 (Summer 1994): 46–70.

Stewart, Thomas A. "How to Think with Your Gut." *Business 2.0*, November 2002.

Strogatz, Steven. *Sync: The Emerging Science of Spontaneous Order*. New York: Hyperion Books, 2003.

Surowiecki, James. "Damn the Slam PAM Plan!" *Slate*, July 30, 2003.

——. "Decisions, Decisions." *New Yorker*, March 28, 2003. http://www.newyorker.com/archive/2003/03/24/030324ta_talk_surowiecki.

——. *The Wisdom of Crowds: Why the Many Are Smarter Than the Few and How Collective Wisdom Shapes Business, Economies, Societies and Nations*. New York: Random House, 2004.

Taleb, Nassim Nicholas. *Fooled By Randomness: The Hidden Role of Chance in Markets and in Life*. New York: Texere, 2001.

——. *The Black Swan: The Impact of the Highly Improbable*. New York: Random House, 2007.

Tallis, Frank. *Hidden Minds: A History of the Unconscious*. New York: Arcade Publishing, 2002.

Taylor, Richard P. "Order in Pollock's Chaos." *Scientific American* (December 2002). http://materialscience.uoregon.edu/taylor/art/scientificamerican.pdf.

Taylor, Richard P., B. Spehar, C.W.G. Clifford, and B.R. Newell, "The Visual Complexity of Pollock's Dripped Fractals," *Proceedings of the International Conference of Complex Systems,* 2002, http://materialscience.uoregon.edu/taylor/art/TaylorICCS2002.pdf.

Tetlock, Philip E. *Expert Political Judgment: How Good Is It? How Can We Know?* Princeton, N.J.: Princeton University Press, 2005.

Thaler, Richard H. *The Winner's Curse: Paradoxes and Anomalies of Economic Life.* Princeton, N.J.: Princeton University Press, 1994.

Thaler, Richard H., Amos Tversky, Daniel Kahneman, and Alan Schwartz. "The Effect of Myopia and Loss Aversion on Risk Taking: An Experimental Test." *The Quarterly Journal of Economics* (May 1997): 647–61.

Thorp, Edward O. *Beat the Dealer.* New York: Vintage Books, 1966.

Tilson, Whitney. "Charlie Munger Speaks." Fool.com. May 15, 2000. http://www.fool.com/boringport/2000/boringport00051500.htm.

Treynor, Jack L. "Market Efficiency and the Bean Jar Experiment." *Financial Analysts Journal* (May–June 1987): 50–53.

Tversky, Amos, and Daniel Kahneman. "Belief in the Law of Small Numbers." *Psychological Bulletin* 76 (1971): 105–10.

———. "Extensional Versus Intuitive Reasoning: The Conjunction Fallacy in Probability Judgment." In *Heuristics and Biases: The Psychology of Intuitive Judgment,* ed. Thomas Gilovich, Dale Griffin, and Daniel Kahneman, 19–48. Cambridge: Cambridge University Press, 2002.

USA Networks. *SEC Filing,* October 24, 2001.

Utterback, James M. *Mastering the Dynamics of Innovation.* Boston: Harvard Business School Press, 1994.

van Marrewijk, Charles. *International Trade and the World Economy.* Oxford: Oxford University Press, 2002. http://www.oup.com/uk/orc/bin/9780199250042/.

Waite, Stephen R. *Quantum Investing.* New York: Texere, 2002.

Waldrop, Mitchell M. *Complexity: The Emerging Science at the Edge of Order and Chaos.* New York: Simon & Schuster, 1992.

Wärneryd, Karl-Erik. *Stock-Market Psychology.* Cheltenham, UK: Edward Elgar, 2001.

Watts, Duncan J. "A Simple Model of Global Cascades on Random Networks." *Proceedings of the National Academy of Sciences* 99, no. 9 (April 2002): 5766–71.

———. *Six Degrees: The Science of a Connected Age.* New York: W. W. Norton, 2003.

REFERENCES AND FURTHER READING 309

——. *Small Worlds: The Dynamics of Networks Between Order and Randomness.* Princeton, N.J.: Princeton University Press, 1999.

Weil, Nancy. "Innocentive Pairs R&D Challenges with Researchers." *Bio-IT World*, May 29, 2003.

Welch, Ivo. "Herding Among Security Analysts." *Journal of Financial Economics* 58, no. 3 (December 2000): 369–96.

Wermers, Russ. "Mutual Fund Herding and the Impact on Stock Prices." *Journal of Finance* 54, no. 2 (April 1999): 581–622.

——. "Mutual Fund Performance: An Empirical Decomposition into Stock-Picking Talent, Style, Transaction Costs, and Expenses." *Journal of Finance* 55, no. 4 (August 2000): 1655–703.

Wetzel, Chris. Web site. http://www.rhodes.edu/psych/faculty/wetzel/courses/ wetzelsyllabus223.htm.

Wiggins, Robert R., and Timothy W. Ruefli. "Hypercompetitive Performance: Are the Best of Times Getting Shorter?" Paper presented at the Academy of Management Annual Meeting 2001, Business Policy and Strategy (BPS) Division, March 31, 2001, Washington, D.C.. http://www.wiggo.com/Academic/ WigginsHypercompetition.pdf.

——. "Sustained Competitive Advantage: Temporal Dynamics and the Incidence and Persistence of Superior Economic Performance." *Organizational Science* 13, no. 1 (January–February 2002): 82–105.

Wilson, Edward O. *Consilience: The Unity of Knowledge.* New York: Alfred A. Knopf, 1998.

Wolfram, Stephen. *A New Kind of Science.* Champaign, Ill.: Wolfram Media, 2002.

Wolpert, Lewis. *Six Impossible Things Before Breakfast: The Evolutionary Origins of Belief.* New York: W. W. Norton, 2007.

Zajonc, Robert B. "Feeling and Thinking: Preferences Need No Inferences." *American Psychologist* 35 (1980): 151–75.

Zeikel, Arthur. "Organizing for Creativity." *Financial Analysts Journal* 39 (November–December 1983): 25–29.

Zipf, George Kingsley. *Human Behavior and the Principle of Least Effort.* Cambridge, Mass.: Addison-Wesley Press, 1949.

——. *National Unity and Disunity: The Nation as a Bio-Social Organism.* Bloomington, Ind.: Principia Press, 1941.

Zook, Chris, with James Allen. *Profit from the Core*. Boston: Harvard Business School Press, 2001.

Zovko, Ilija I., and J. Doyne Farmer. "The Power of Patience: A Behavioral Regularity in Limit Order Placement." *Santa Fe Institute Working Paper No. 02–06–027*, June 2002.

Zuckerman, Gregory. "Stars of the '90s Aren't Likely to Lead the Next Rally." *The Wall Street Journal*, December 17, 2001.

Further Reading

INVESTMENT PHILOSOPHY

Fisher, Philip A. *Common Stocks and Uncommon Profits*. New York: Wiley, 1996.

Graham, Benjamin. *The Intelligent Investor: A Book of Practical Counsel*. New York: McGraw Hill, 1985.

Lewis, Michael. *Moneyball: The Art of Winning an Unfair Game*. New York: W. W. Norton, 2003.

Poundstone, William. *Fortune's Formula: The Untold Story of the Scientific System That Beat the Casinos and Wall Street*. New York: Hill and Wang, 2005.

Rappaport, Alfred. "The Economics of Short-Term Performance Obsession." *Financial Analysts Journal* 61, no. 3 (May/June 2005): 65–79.

Rubin, Robert E., and Jacob Weisberg. *In an Uncertain World: Tough Choices from Wall Street to Washington*. New York: Random House, 2003.

Sklansky, David. *Getting the Best of It*. 2nd ed. Henderson, Nev.: Two Plus Two Publishing, 1997.

Szenberg, Michael, ed. *Eminent Economists: Their Life and Philosophies*. Cambridge: Cambridge University Press, 1992.

PSYCHOLOGY OF INVESTING

Chancellor, Edward. *Devil Take the Hindmost: A History of Financial Speculation*. New York: Farrar, Strauss & Giroux, 1999.

Csikszentmihalyi, Mihaly. *Creativity: Flow and the Psychology of Discovery and Invention*. New York: HarperCollins, 1996.

Gilbert, Daniel. *Stumbling on Happiness*. New York: Alfred A. Knopf, 2006.

Gladwell, Malcolm. *Blink: The Power of Thinking Without Thinking.* New York: Little, Brown, 2005.

Heuer, Richards J., Jr. *Psychology of Intelligence Analysis.* Washington, D.C: U.S. Government Printing Office, 1999.

Munger, Charlie. "The Psychology of Human Misjudgments." Speech at Harvard Law School, circa June 1995.

Nofsinger, John R. *Investment Madness.* New York: Prentice Hall, 2001.

Pinker, Steven. *How the Mind Works.* New York: W. W. Norton, 1997.

Schelling, Thomas C. *Micromotives and Macrobehavior.* New York: W. W. Norton, 1978.

Thaler, Richard H. *Advances in Behavioral Finance.* New York: Russel Sage Foundation, 1993.

——. *The Winner's Curse.* Princeton, N.J.: Princeton University Press, 1994.

INNOVATION AND COMPETITIVE STRATEGY

Axelrod, Robert. *The Evolution of Cooperation.* New York: Basic Books, 1984.

Besanko, David, David Dranove, and Mark Shanley. *Economics of Strategy.* 3rd ed. New York: Wiley, 2004.

Christensen, Clayton M., Erik A. Roth, and Scott D. Anthony. *Seeing What's Next: Using Theories of Innovation to Predict Industry Change.* Boston, Mass.: Harvard Business School Press, 2004.

Evans, Philip, and Thomas S. Wurster. *Blown to Bits: How the New Economics of Information Transforms Strategy.* Boston, Mass.: Harvard Business School Press, 1999.

Ghemawat, Pankaj. *Strategy and The Business Landscape.* 2nd ed. Upper Saddle River, N.J.: Pearson Prentice Hall, 2006.

McTaggart, James, Peter Kontes, and Michael Mankins. *The Value Imperative: Managing for Superior Shareholder Returns.* New York: The Free Press, 1994.

Porter, Michael E. *Competitive Advantage: Creating and Sustaining Superior Performance.* New York: Simon & Schuster, 1985.

——. *Competitive Strategy: Techniques for Analyzing Industries and Competitors.* New York: The Free Press, 1980.

Reichfield, Frederick F. *The Loyalty Effect.* Boston, Mass.: Harvard Business School Press, 1996.

Shaprio, Carl, and Hal R. Varian. *Information Rules: A Strategic Guide to the Network Economy.* Boston, Mass.: Harvard Business School Press, 1999.

Warsh, David. *Knowledge and the Wealth of Nations: A Story of Economic Discovery.* New York: W. W. Norton, 2006.

SCIENCE AND COMPLEXITY THEORY

Arthur, W. Brian, Steven N. Durlauf, and David A. Lane, eds. *The Economy as an Evolving Complex System II.* Reading, Mass.: Addison-Wesley, 1997.

Ball, Philip, *Critical Mass: How One Thing Leads to Another.* New York: Farrar, Straus and Giroux, 2004.

Beinhocker, Eric D. *The Origin of Wealth: Evolution, Complexity, and the Radical Remaking of Economics.* Boston: Harvard Business School Press, 2006.

Camacho, Juan, and Ricard V. Solé. "Scaling and Zipf's Law in Ecological Size Spectra." *Santa Fe Institute Working Paper 99–12–076,* 1999.

Dawkins, Richard. *The Blind Watchmaker: Why the Evidence of Evolution Reveals a Universe Without Design.* New York: W.W. Norton, 1996.

Dennett, Daniel C. *Darwin's Dangerous Idea: Evolution and the Meanings of Life.* New York: Simon & Schuster, 1995.

Diamond, Jared. *Guns, Germs, and Steel: The Fates of Human Society.* New York: W. W. Norton, 1997.

Gladwell, Malcolm. *The Tipping Point: How Little Things Can Make a Big Difference.* New York: Little, Brown, 2000.

Hagstrom, Robert G. *Investing: The Last Liberal Art.* New York: Texere, 2002.

LeBaron, Blake. "Financial Market Efficiency in a Coevolutionary Environment." *Proceedings of the Workshop on Simulation of Social Agents: Architectures and Institutions, Argonne National Laboratory and University of Chicago,* October 2000, Argonne 2001, 33–51.

Mandelbrot, Benoit, and Richard L. Hudson. *The (Mis)Behavior of Markets: A Fractal View of Risk, Ruin, and Reward.* New York: Basic Books, 2004.

Rothschild, Michael. *Bionomics.* New York: Henry Holt and Company, 1990.

Schroeder, Manfred. *Fractals, Chaos, and Power Laws: Minutes from an Infinite Paradise.* New York: W. H. Freeman, 1991.

Seeley, Thomas A., P. Kirk Visscher, and Kevin M. Passino. "Group Decision Making in Honey Bee Swarms." *American Scientist* 94 (May–June 2006): 200–229.

Simon, Herbert A. *The Sciences of the Artificial.* Cambridge, Mass.: The MIT Press, 1996.

Whitfield, John. *In the Beat of a Heart: Life, Energy, and the Unity of Nature.* New York: Joseph Henry Press, 2006.

FURTHER ACKNOWLEDGMENTS

Sente. www.senteco.com.

CFROI® is a registered trademark in the United States and other countries (excluding the United Kingdom) of Credit Suisse or its affiliates.

Page locators in italics indicate exhibits.